The Natural History of Insects

Anonymons

BIBLIOLIFE

Harper's Stereotype Edition.

THE

NATURAL HISTORY

OF

INSECTS.

ILLUSTRATED BY NUMEROUS ENGRAVINGS.

FIRST SERIES.

NEW-YORK:

PRINTED AND PUBLISHED BY J. & J. HARPER,
NO. 82 CLIFF-STREET.
AND SOLD BY THE PRINCIPAL BOOKSELLERS THROUGHOUT
THE UNITED STATES.

1832.

CONTENTS.

CHAPTER I.—THE HIVE BEE.

Page

QUEEN BEE—Her Treatment by her Subjects.............. 25

CHAPTER II.—THE HIVE BEE.

Mode of Communication among Bees—Antipathy between rival
Queens—Their Combats—Helplessness when mutilated—Senses
of Bees—Manner of discovering Bees' Nests practised by American Honey-hunters 37

CHAPTER III—THE HIVE BEE.

Interior Arrangements of a Bee-hive—Structure of a Comb—Form
of the Cells—Worker-Bees—Collection of Honey—Elaboration
of Wax—Bee-bread—Cleanliness of Bees 46

CHAPTER IV.—THE HIVE BEE

Fertility of Queen Bee—Swarming—Ventilation of the Hive—
Irascibility—Duels—Robberies—Defences of Bees 68

CHAPTER V—THE HUMBLE BEE

Builds her own Habitation—Curious Division of Labour—Remarkable for Good-nature and Affection for her Young—Ingenuity in
overcoming Difficulties—The Carpenter-Bee—The Mason-Bee—
—The Upholsterer-Bee 82

CHAPTER VI—THE COMMON WASP.

The Nest—Construction and Materials—Form of the Combs—
Affection for its Young—Manner of feeding them—Solitary
Wasps—Hornets 100

CHAPTER VII.—ANTS

Page

Their Industry—Affection for their Young—Courage—Their Anger
—Unite in Myriads for War and Extermination—The Fallow
Ants—The Sanguine Ants—The Legionary Ants—Attack other
Ants, and reduce them to Slavery 118

CHAPTER VIII.—TERMITES, or WHITE ANTS

Their Destructiveness—Clear the Ground of all dead vegetable
Matter—Societies composed of four sorts of Individuals—Eaten
as Food by the Indians—Appear in countless Myriads at the end
of the Rainy Season—Prodigious Fertility of the Queen—Size,
Form, and interior Arrangements of their Hills—Marching Ants   145

CHAPTER IX.—PARASITICAL INSECTS.

Gall Insect—Cochineal Insect—The Scarlet Colour used in Dyeing 161

CHAPTER X.—APHIS, or PLANT-LOUSE.

Every Tree, every part of a Tree, has its peculiar Species—Suck
vegetable Juices—Shelter themselves from bad Weather in the
concave parts of Leaves 176

CHAPTER XI

Gnat—Bug—Flea—Chigoe—Louse—Mites and Ticks—Gad-fly.... 190

CHAPTER XII

Ichneumon-Fly—Its Eggs deposited in the Bodies of other Living
Insects—Deposites thirty or forty in the Body of a Caterpillar—
Dragon-Fly—Its Voracity—Ferocity. 208

CHAPTER XIII.—THE ANT-LION.

Forms a funnel-shaped Excavation in the Sand—Uses its Leg like
a Shovel to remove the Sand—Secures its Prey by Stratagem—
Its Ingenuity and Perseverance in getting rid of Impediments—
Spins a Cocoon, and is Transformed into a Beautiful Fly—The
Lion-Worm 21

CHAPTER XIV.—THE SPIDER

Its Spinning Apparatus—Its Web—The Hawk-Spider—The Gar
den-Spider—The Water-Spider—The Hunting-Spider—Gossamer-Spider—Pen-Spider—Attachment of the Spider to its Young 225

CHAPTER XV—CATERPILLARS

Page

Their Singular Habits—The Grub of the domestic Moth—Fabricates a Mantle—Habits of the Field-Moth—Caddis-Worm 250

CHAPTER XVI—SOCIAL CATERPILLARS

Move in regular Files—Form Nests lined with Silk—The "Processionary"—The Leaf-rolling—The Leaf-bending—Leaf-mining Caterpillar 266

CHAPTER XVII—CHRYSALIS, or AURELIA.

Caterpillar, when about to Change into a Chrysalis, fastens itself to a Leaf or Stem—Spins a little Web—Gets rid of its old Case—Suspends itself by a Girth or Belt formed of Silk 285

I.—B

INTRODUCTION.

ALL that is cognizable to sense is reducible to two classes of existences—the one passive, inert, and governed by the general laws of nature ; the other active, combating and modifying these laws. The first class comprehends inorganic or inanimate existence ; the second, animate or organic existence. Animate beings are composed of organs which, though varying in number, figure, and function, in the infinite varieties of living creatures, may, nevertheless, be classed under two heads : 1st. Organs destined to preserve the individual. 2d. Organs appropriated to the perpetuation of the species. To the first class belong the organs of nutrition, locomotion, and sensation ; to the second, the organs of generation. A scale or gradation of animated beings may therefore be established, on the ground of their possessing more or fewer of these organs.

The simplest animal with which we are acquainted is to be found in water either in a stagnant state or impregnated with decayed vegetable matter : it is of microscopic minuteness, a single living point, without any organ whatever, and called *Monas.* A drop of putrid water contains myriads of these in motion. One degree higher in the scale of existence are the Polypi—creatures possessing the form of a vegetable, with the consistence of a jelly. Their internal organization consists only of a sac, the first indication of a stomach. They have no head, nor organs of sense, muscles, nor vessels. Like plants, they perpetuate their species by buds. They live in water.

The next class of animals, also aquatic, are of a star-like form. Besides the mouth and stomach common to them with the polypi, slight indications of a nervous and respiratory system are discoverable in their organization. None of their movements seem connected with muscular action, though their substance in many instances is capable of contraction and dilatation. They are multiplied, not only by buds or gemmæ, but also by eggs, where the new individual, separating from the parent, is thrown off by the mouth : they live in the ocean.

Worms have the organs of locomotion more fully developed, the body of the animal being divided into rings,—a faint approach to the articulation of the limbs in more perfect creatures. The long intestinal canal is widened at one part, so as to give a notion of the division into stomach and intestine. They possess a circulatory system of vein and artery, but no heart. Their respiratory organs are of the simplest kind. They are furnished with a long nervous cord, running from one extremity of the body to the other, in the course of which nodules of nervous matter are placed, from which little nerves are radiated to the neighbouring parts. The sexes are in some united in the same individual, in others separate. They multiply by eggs.

The Molluscæ have the organs of digestion and circulation well developed ; a liver, stomach, intestines, a heart with two chambers, arteries and veins circulating cold blood ; a nodulated nervous system, organs of touch, rudiments of a tongue, and something like an organ of hearing, and a respiratory system. The organs of locomotion are not much developed.

The Crustacea, or such animals as resemble the lobster, possess lateral appendages fixed to the trunk, which assist them to move : their structure is similar to that of the molluscæ ; but they have, in addition, a more perfect apparatus of the senses.

Ascending in the scale of beings, we next come to

INSECTS.

The English word insect is derived from the Latin word insectum, which is probably a corruption or contraction of intersectum, " cut between ;" and the name as applied to a class of animals, is doubtlessly suggested by the bodies of these animals being so made up of distinct parts as to give the appearance of their being notched or intersected.

Insects have organs of nutrition, locomotion, generation, and sensation. Their organization is defective principally in the circulating and respiratory systems. They inhabit the earth, the air, or the water, and move with rapidity in all situations. They possess the five senses, and are endowed with wonderful instincts. The organs of nutrition and generation are as perfect as those of more elevated orders.

Insects have been called hexapodes, from their having six feet. Their body is for the most part composed of various joinings or articulations. These joinings are comprehended in the head, thorax or chest, abdomen or belly.

The head has a moveable junction or articulation with the second division or thorax, in the greater number of insects. The mouth, antennæ, and eyes are parts of the head.

Mouth.—All insects either divide their food or suck it. In all, therefore, the mouth is modelled to answer one or other of these purposes.

In those which divide their food, the parts of the mouth are, an upper lip, and an under lip fixed to a piece called the chin; between these two there are four lateral pieces, two on each side; the two upper are called mandibles, the two lower maxillæ or jaws. To the two lower are attached one or more moveable adjuncts called palpi. The under lip has also two appendices, called labial palpi.

With the palpi the insect seems to judge of the quality of its food; which it touches and examines with these organs. The mandibles or upper jaws cut the food. The lower jaws or maxillæ divide and masticate it. The motion of these parts is horizontal and not vertical, as with us : the upper and under lips move forwards, backwards, and vertically, and their office appears to be to prevent the egress of the food.

The mouth of those insects which suck is elongated into a beak or tongue, or proboscis.

This is a tube attached to the head of the insect. In some, the bee for instance, it is composed of two pieces connected by a joint, for if it were constantly extended, it would be too much exposed to accidental injuries : therefore, in its indolent state, it is doubled up by means of the joint ; and in that position lies secure under a scaly pent-house. In many species of the butterfly, the proboscis, when not in use, is coiled up like a watch spring. In some insects, the proboscis, or tongue, or trunk, is shut up in a sharp-pointed sheath ; which sheath being of a much firmer texture than the proboscis itself, as well as sharpened at the point, pierces the substance which contains the food, and then opens within the wound to allow the enclosed tube, through which the juice is extracted, to perform its office.

Antennæ.—Almost all insects have two of these organs. Their functions are not distinctly known : in some insects they are organs of sense, in others they exist, but are so imperfect as to raise doubts as to their utility ; nature, however, often repeats the shape of a part without repeating its function ; thus the mammæ are allotted to males as well as females : hence the non-existence of the function in some animals cannot be taken as a positive ground for denying the existence of that function in similar organs in other animals.

Eyes.—These organs are constantly found in the head of insects. Their usual number is two, placed laterally ; their surface is cut into so many facets that Leeuwenhoek has counted seventeen thousand two hundred and thirty-five in the cornea of a butterfly ; each facet may be considered as a crystalline lens, concave within and convex without: they have no lids. In some orders of insects, besides these two lateral eyes, there are, for the most part, three others placed between the antennæ ; their surface is smooth, they are called stemmata, their use is unknown, although it is supposed they assist in vision, since the eyes of spiders are nearly of the same form, and in them these are the sole organs of that faculty.

The Thorax.—The next division of the body of the insect, placed immediately behind the head, is the thorax ; this supports the members, namely the wings and legs. The wings are composed of two membranes, an upper one, in which nervures or cords are traced ; a lower one, separable from the upper. These nervures or cords contain a spiral vessel ; " whence they appear," says Kirby, " to be air vessels communicating with the trachea in the trunk. The expansion of the wing at the will of the insect is a problem that can only be solved, by supposing that a subtle fluid is introduced into these vessels, which seems perfectly analogous to those in the wings of birds ; and that thus an impulse is communicated to every part of the organ sufficient to keep it in proper tension:

we see by this, that a wing is supported in its flight like a sail by its cordage."

The Abdomen.—This is, the third division of the insect; it is composed of rings, which vary in number from one to fifteen: most of these rings have an open pore placed laterally; these are the breathing holes through which the fluids of the animal become aërated; they are termed stigmata. In some, the last ring contains the anus, or vent, and the organs of generation; in some, it includes either the means of defence of the insect, such as a sting, or instruments which are subservient to its instincts, as saws, ovipositors, pincers, &c.

The Organs of Digestion.—These consist of a gullet, one or more stomachs, and an intestinal canal, into which numerous fine vessels secrete a fluid analogous to saliva and to bile.

In the higher animals, the steps by which the raw food is assimilated to the body can be made out. We know that the secretions result from glands and minute arteries, and that absorbents take up that which is prepared in the great reservoirs of life, the stomach and intestines, to pour it into the veins, and thence into the heart. The circle is clearly traceable by reasoning and by sense; but insects have no true circulating nor absorbent system; and yet they secrete fluids which not only serve for digestion, but for defence. The ant disgorges an acid; the bee elaborates a poison; the glow-worm an unctuous fluid, which, becoming

luminous, attracts the male. What then are the
instruments by which food is assimilated in the
insect? Cuvier supposes that it is taken up by the
pores of the body as water by a sponge, by imbi-
bition.

The muscles of insects are disposed in bundles,
the fibres of which are not connected together by a
cellular membrane ; they are fixed to the hard
parts, which are to be moved by horny tendons.
The body of the insect being symmetrical, the
arrangement of muscles is simple. The segments
of the abdomen have similar muscles, and one side
corresponds to the other.

The thorax contains the muscles which move
the head up or down ; those which move the wings
and the feet, and some others of which the uses
are only guessed at. The muscles of a species
of caterpillar, the *cossus ligniperda,* have been
reckoned, by Lyonnet, to amount to four thousand
—this makes them nine times more than those of
man. The prodigious power of some of these
living atoms is scarcely imaginable. The flea,
called by the Arabians "the father of leapers,"
and the locust, jump two hundred times their own
length. Supposing the same relative force to be
infused into the body of a man six feet high, he
would be enabled to leap three times the height of
St. Paul's. Insects walk, run, leap, fly, glide, and
swim ; thus combining all the movements of all
animated beings.

All insects have a knotted nervous system. The
knot nearest the head is composed of two lobes,

from which nerves pass to the eyes, the antennæ, and the mouth.

The situation of the organs of smell and hearing has not been determined; that they possess this sense is a matter of inference from the various facts offered in the study of their habits.

The most remarkable circumstance in the history of insects is their metamorphosis. The changes which they undergo fixed the attention of the earliest observers: they exist in four progressive forms :—1. The egg; 2. Larva, grub, worm, or caterpillar; 3. Chrysalis, aurelia, nymph, or pupa; 4. Imago, or perfect state.

The eggs vary in colour, shape, consistence, and the covering with which many are clothed. Some insects deposite them in places where the natural food of the tribe is most abundant; and without ever having seen their parent, the instincts of the young teach them to act as they had been acted by; others protect the egg till the larva is produced. In the flesh-fly the first stage of the metamorphosis passes within the body of the parent, and the larva, or worm, is brought forth alive. In some insects the parent retains the young within the body, some time after it has been evolved from the egg, and then gives birth to the pupa. Other insects produce their young in a perfect state, so as to require no farther changes.

In the larva state the insect appears to attain its greatest weight. In this it moults, or changes its skins several times, and the same colours are not always reproduced : in this state the insect is incapable of producing its kind.

In the state of pupa, nymph, or chrysalis, the insect is ordinarily incapable of taking food, and contains within itself a sketch of its ultimate form.

Naturalists have described various states of metamorphosis; all these, however, may be reduced to two : 1. Partial metamorphosis, in which the insect does not vary in its form in such a way as not to be recognised in all its states as the same individual. 2. Complete metamorphosis; in which the pupæ take no food, are incapable of motion, and the change is such, that nothing but the evidence of sense could convince us of the identity of the insect in its first and its last state.

INSECTS.

CHAPTER I.

THE HIVE BEE.

Queen Bee—Her Treatment by her Subjects

THE scene presented by the interior of a bee-hive
has seldom failed to interest even the most incurious
observer, while it fills with astonishment the mind
of the enlightened and profound philosopher. When
the day is fine and the sun shining brightly, the habitation of these marvellous little creatures exhibits the aspect of a populous and busy city. The
gates are crowded with hundreds of industrious
workers—some on the wing in search of sustenance ; others returning from the fields laden with
food—some earnestly engaged in building—some
in tending the young—others employed in cleansing
their habitation—while four or five may be seen
dragging out the corpse of a companion, and, as it
would appear, scrupulously paying the last honours
to the dead. At one moment the entrances of the
little city are comparatively free ; at another,
crowds of its inhabitants may be seen struggling at
the gates, making the best of their way to escape
from the rain, which, by some peculiar sensation,
they have discovered to be at hand. It can therefore excite no wonder that the habits of these interesting insects should have attracted the attention
of some of the best observers of ancient and of

C

modern times. History does not inform us who first drew these creatures from the wilderness, and rendered their industry subservient to the purposes of man—purposes for which the cultivation of the sugar-cane now partially provides. According to Cicero and Pliny, the philosopher Hyliscus quitted human society, and retired to the desert in order to contemplate the more peaceful industry of the bee. The thousand moral qualities which have been gravely attributed to them will probably excite a smile. They who wished to observe their habits and proceedings, were admonished first to examine their consciences—for it is said that these beings could not endure the presence of the adulterer, and gave no quarter to the thief. But putting aside fables, emanating from the imagination of the ancients, the real history of the bee is abundantly interesting.

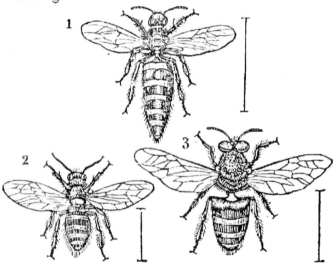

A community or swarm of bees consists, first, of workers (fig. 2); these are of no sex; amount generally to many thousands in number, and are easily recognised by their industry, and by the smallness of their size : 2dly, of males (fig. 3); of which several hundreds belong to each community; these are larger than the working bee, and live idly : over all presides a queen, the most important member of the whole of this little commonwealth (fig. 1). A person may keep hives for years, and never see this insect, about which more extraordinary things have been seen and written, than the reader would be disposed to believe. Aristotle and the more ancient naturalists have given very marvellous accounts of the perfect despotism and strict discipline established among these insects, as well as of the consummate wisdom with which every thing is ordered for the common good.

Reaumur and Huber have fully determined the influence which the presence of the queen has upon her subjects. The former divided a swarm, and placed them in two glass hives, one of which, therefore, had a queen ; the other being without one. The account which he gives of the conduct of these two sets of insects is too curious to be omitted.

" After the tumult, excited by their removal into a little glass hive, was calmed, and I had looked at it for ten minutes, for the first time of my life, I succeeded in seeing a queen bee, which was walking at the bottom of the case. I was recompensed in this instance, for my disappointments in the various attempts that I had previously made—for now I could view her as often as I wished. Indeed, I had it in my power to point her out to a large party who were at my house, not one of whom but evinced the greatest curiosity to see this renowned sovereign.

" For the first few minutes, in which I followed her with my eyes, I was tempted to believe that the stories of the respect paid her by the other bees, the train by which she was attended, were imagi-

nary fables rather than real facts. She was alone,
and walking perhaps at a slower pace than the rest.
The friends who were with me were pleased to discover in her gait something of gravity and majesty.
She advanced, unattended, to one of the squares of
the hive, up which she mounted to join a group of
her subjects perched at the top. In a little time
she reappeared at the bottom, but still sadly neglected. She ascended a second time, and I lost
sight of her for a few instants—she then appeared
for the third time at the bottom of the hive. Now,
however, twelve or fifteen bees were ranged around
her, and seemed to form her train. In the first
moments of trouble and confusion we think only
of ourselves. If we were in a large saloon, and
it had suddenly broken down, in the confusion we
should forget that others dearer than ourselves
were in the room. Thus it was with these bees,
for being huddled into the little glass hive, turned
topsy-turvy, the first impulse of each seemed self-
preservation, and it was only when they had reco-
vered their composure, that they began to recollect
the mother which in their fright they had forgotten
and neglected.

" In spite of my inclination to believe that the first
train which I had perceived was the effect of chance
—in spite of my disposition to think that a big bee
would be followed precisely because it was big—I
was forced to acknowledge that there was some
other foundation for the homage, the cares, and attentions which the rest paid to her who was destined to be the mother of a numerous progeny. The
queen, with her little suite, disappeared for a moment among a cluster of bees. In a short time she
reappeared at the bottom of the hive, when a dozen
others hastened to join the train. A row flanked
her on each side as she walked, others met her before, and made way as she advanced ; and, in a very
short time, she was surrounded by a circle of up-

wards of thirty bees. Some of these, approaching nearer than others, licked her with their trunks; others extended this organ filled with honey for her to sip; sometimes I saw her stop to partake of the food; at other times she sucked while in motion.

"For several hours, consecutively, I observed this insect, and always saw her surrounded by bees who appeared anxious to render her good offices."

The farther detail of the "History of the Divided Swarm" is equally instructive. It should be observed, that the little glass hive in which was placed the mother, or queen, contained only about a fifth part of the original swarm, which had been divided on a Saturday. On the Sunday, the bees seemed discouraged, went out into the fields, and came back, bringing with them very little material. On the Monday, they laboured rather more assiduously, as, in six hours, they had formed a little comb containing sixteen or eighteen cells; but at two o'clock of the same day they quitted the hive. Reaumur, however, once more enclosed them in it. On the Tuesday, they remained profoundly still; and although the sun was warm, and the time of the day (about eleven) that at which the hive presents the busiest scene, they were resting in groups. All this seemed to prove that they were not content with their lodging. They had a queen, and the materials for building, and yet not a cell was constructed. In a few moments, while Reaumur was pondering on the motives of these insects, or rather on the obstacles which contravened their instincts—the queen was seen on the floor of the hive; a dozen common bees instantly came buzzing around her, the hum increased, and the whole hive appeared shortly in a state of great agitation. Little divisions were formed, one or two workers going out, were followed by the queen, and then the whole left the glass hive for the second time.

According to their usual custom, they flew round

and round in circles, and at last settled in a solid mass on one of the branches of a neighbouring tree. As soon as Reaumur saw this, he ran to discover the queen, and found her, not in this mass, but quietly seated on a leaf, and at a little distance from it, "apparently," says he, "as if aware that it would be inconvenient to bear the whole weight of her subjects." It would seem that she had but to indicate the spot near which the bees were to settle, by hovering round it, in order to bring them thither. As soon as the cluster which had settled on the branch had become of considerable size, she quitted the leaf on which she had settled, and joined them. This was sufficient to attract the others, which were still circling about in the air, and she was soon covered and concealed by them.

"These bees," says Reaumur, "seemed to have good reasons for quitting the hive. Instinct, no doubt, taught them that their present habitation was too small to accommodate the numerous progeny of the queen, and afford room for the necessary cells."

Thinking that the disproportion between the number of the bees and the size of the hive might have been the cause of their disgust, Reaumur this time contrived to enclose only four or five hundred along with the queen. But this step proved unfortunate. The little colony remained in the greatest agitation, and altogether neglected the queen, who wandered up and down quite unattended and in the most desolate condition. The rest, however, who had not been enclosed with the queen, did not imitate the example of her fellow-captives, but soon found her out; and, not being able to obtain admission, covered the hive in a mass. Having got rid of these, he was desirous of trying whether those bees which, three days before, on the original division of the swarm, had been separated from the queen, would recognise her after this lapse of time. Having placed the little glass hive near the box in which these had been enclosed, in less than a quarter of an hour they seemed to have discovered that a queen was in captivity, and scarcely a single bee remained in the box, but all came and covered the glass hive. At first Reaumur attributed this effect to the attraction of the constant noise kept up by the agitation of the bees within the glass hive; but when this hive was placed, under the same circumstances, near another which possessed a queen, very few of the workers of the latter hive seemed disposed to quit their own habitation and sovereign in order to attend the stranger, however hard her lot. It would appear, then, that the bees who were without a queen knew where there was one, but those who possessed one paid no regard to another. Having kept the queen and her five hundred subjects prisoners, Reaumur opened the entrances of the glass hive; upon which most of them went into the fields, but returned, bringing with them some of the other bees which had been excluded when the five hundred were enclosed with the queen. How these creatures had found out their queen excited Reaumur's wonder. Observing his glass hive becoming too full, he contrived to make the mass of supernumeraries join another set.

On the Wednesday, however, the bees left the glass hive for the third time, but after a short space returned; which encouraged him to hope that they would permanently adhere to it. The next day the workers laboured in good earnest, brought home good loads of materials on their thighs, and constructed cells. But the situation of the hive being too hot, they quitted it for the fourth time, fled to a large hive in the neighbourhood, and were massacred by its inhabitants.

Such was the end of this division of the original swarm. That of the other was not less tragical. It has been already observed, that when Reaumur divided the swarm, the largest portion was without a queen—these he placed in a flat and commodious habitation, giving them the means of free egress and ingress. The number of those who went into the fields was very limited, and these returned unladen with any of the fruits of their labour.

Although the days were fine, the number of the workers very great, the hive such as they liked, for they evinced no symptom of a wish to quit it, still not a cell was made, while, during the same space of time, the bees of the little glass hive, although they had but a slender portion of labourers, contrived to make two little combs. Thus it would appear that all their instincts hinge on the love of offspring. Those bees which possessed a queen, capable of giving birth to thousands of young, prepared cells for their dwelling, and honey for their food; and this they effected under every disadvantage. Those, on the contrary, which were without a mother-bee, and, therefore, without the hope of a numerous progeny, were content to live from day to day. They went into the fields for their repast, but did not bring back materials which would construct a single cell. It seemed as if they were content with feeding themselves, and had lost all motive to lay up a store of provisions for future purposes. In a word, it was evident that it was not for themselves that they gathered or laboured.

Wishing to stimulate them to exertion, Reaumur gave them another hive, but they were as tranquil in their new as they had been in their old habitation.

Their number daily diminished, so that at the end of three weeks scarcely a thousand remained, and the whole of these were one morning found dead at the bottom of the hive.

This was not a solitary experiment. Reaumur and others have repeated it too often to require farther proof—that the loss of the mother-bee destroys all motive to exertion, so that she may truly be called the soul of the hive.

"We are only sure of one principle of action," says Reaumur, " among bees—the love for their queen, or rather the numerous posterity to which she is to give birth. Each bee seems to be actuated either by a sensation which has in view the welfare of all, or by the love of posterity. Whether they construct cells or most carefully polish them, or labour to gather a harvest of honey, it is never directly for themselves. This may appear somewhat paradoxical to those who have remarked that, at the end of winter, the bees consume the honey they had stored up in spring and summer. But the experiments just detailed show, that the moment they lose the hope of a numerous progeny, they cease to gather the food which is necessary for their own preservation; life seems to them of no value when unsupported by this hope, and so they choose to die. The love of offspring appears, therefore, to be the all-moving principle." Swammerdam was of this opinion; and all who study the habits of the bee attentively must coincide with him.

From what has been detailed, little doubt can be entertained that, be the moving spring what it may, the conduct of bees to the mother is tender, true, and full of devotion. To ascertain whether this feeling of attachment and devotion was confined to the particular queen which gave them birth, Reaumur made an experiment.

He shut up a queen taken from one hive, with some workers taken from another, so that both were strangers to each other. "I was curious," he says, "to note how she would be received, and I saw she was received like 'a queen.' Bees to the number of a dozen or more surrounded her, and treated her with great honour. It happened that the box in which she had been enclosed was filled with dust, in consequence of which, when introduced among the

workers, she was literally gray with that which stuck
about her.   The first care of the bees was to unpow-
der and clean their future sovereign.   For more than
two hours she remained at the bottom of the hive,
surrounded and sometimes covered by them, while
they licked her on all sides.   It seemed as if they
were anxious to warm her, and in truth she required it, as she was benumbed by the coldness of
the night, and had only been revived by me in the
morning with artificial heat.   I could not help ad-
miring the anxiety and assiduity of their attentions.
They relieved each other in the task of cleaning her.
They removed her to another spot more than an inch
distant; some were upon, some under her. For
more than two hours I witnessed this interesting
scene."

For a day or two, Reaumur kept them close prisoners; but subsequently placed them near the very
spot from which they had been taken, and gave them
the liberty of egress.   He found, however, that,
though they went out, they returned to their new
habitation and new queen, and constructed cells for
her accommodation.

This fact removed Reaumur's doubt.   These bees
had been taken from a populous hive well stored,
and yet they completely forgot their old companions
and their birth-place, put up with all the inconveniences of a small hive, and undertook to labour for
a stranger.

But although thus prodigal of their affections to
any mother, still a certain number of hours must
elapse before they will adopt a stranger; and then the
lives of a thousand of their fellow-labourers are nothing to them in comparison with that of the elected
queen.

Reaumur found a queen and some workers appa-
parently dead from cold.   Some of the latter he had
resuscitated, so that, though feeble, yet they could
walk.   The others with the queen were still motion-

less. Putting them all into a box, he gradually warmed it in the hope of reviving the whole.

As soon as some of the workers came to life, they ranged themselves round the dead mother as if compassionating her situation. With their trunks they licked her breast, head, and body, but took not the slightest notice of the other bees, although as dead as this sole object of their care.

Reaumur watched with anxiety for the signs of returning life in the queen. "At first," says he, "one limb quivered, and after a short interval, the motion was reiterated. No sooner was this evidence of life given, than a humming was instantly heard in the box where previously all had been silence. Many persons who were with me, and who watched the revival of the queen, were struck with the sound as being more acute than usual, and all named it the song of rejoicing."*

It appears, however, that the workers do not at all times pay the same attention to their queen; while she continues in a state of infecundity, she seems for the most part an object of indifference to them; but as soon as this event has taken place, she is treated with the honour due to the future mother of a populous colony.

"I have," says Huber, "seen workers bestow every attention on a queen, though sterile; and after her death treat the dead body as they had treated herself when alive, and long prefer it, though inanimate, to the most prolific queens I offered them."

---

* When Schirach had once smoked a hive to oblige the bees to retire to the top of it, the queen with some of the rest flew away. Upon this, those that remained in the hive sent forth a most plaintive sound, as if they were deploring their loss: when their sovereign was restored, their lugubrious sounds were succeeded by an agreeable humming, which announced their joy at the event. Huber says, that once when all the worker brood was removed from the hive, and only male brood left, the bees appeared in a state of extreme despondency. Assembled in clusters on the combs, they lost all their activity. The queen dropped her eggs at random, and instead of the usual active hum, a dead silence reigned in the hive.

It would perhaps be incorrect to ascribe this conduct to motives similar to those which influence human agents. And yet it is difficult, if not impossible, to resist the impression, that although not exactly similar, they are at least analogous. These humble creatures cherish their queen, feed her, and provide for her wants. They live only in her life, and die when she is taken away. Her absence deprives them of no organ, paralyzes no limb, yet in every case they neglect all their duties for twenty-four hours. They receive no stranger queen before the expiration of that time ; and if deprived of the cherished object altogether, they refuse food, and quickly perish. What, it may be asked, is the physical cause of such devotion ? What are the bonds that chain the little creature to its cell, and force it to prefer death, to the flowers and the sunshine that invite it to come forth and live ? This is not a solitary instance in which the Almighty has made virtues apparently almost unattainable by us, natural to animals ! For while man has marked, with that praise which great and rare good actions merit, those few instances in which one human being has given up his own life for another—the dog, who daily sacrifices himself for his master, has scarcely found an historian to record his common virtue.

CHAPTER II.

THE HIVE BEE.

Mode of Communication among Bees—Antipathy between rival Queens—Their Combats—Helplessness when mutilated—Senses of Bees—Manner of discovering Bees' Nests practised by American Honey-hunters

LIKE every other animal living in society, bees have a medium of communication. The effects produced upon them by the loss of their queen will furnish proof of this fact. In a well-peopled and thriving hive, each bee is employed in its appropriate avocation, some in attending the young, some in making cells. At first, when the queen has been abstracted, every thing goes on well for about an hour; after this space of time, some few of the workers appear in a state of great agitation; they forsake the young, relinquish their labour, and begin to traverse the hive in a furious manner. In their progress, wherever they meet a companion, they mutually cross their antennæ,* and the one which seems to have first discovered the national loss, communicates the sad news to its neighbour, by giving it a gentle tap with these organs. This one in its turn becomes agitated, runs over the cells, crossing and striking others. Thus in a short time the whole hive is thrown into confusion, every thing is neglected, and the humming may be heard at a distance. This agitation lasts from four to five hours, after which the bees are calmed, and begin to adopt the measures which are necessary to repair their loss.

That the agitation of the bees arises from the loss of the queen scarcely admits of a doubt.

" I cannot doubt," says Huber, " that the agitation

* Feelers

I.—D

arises from the workers having lost their queen;
for on restoring her, tranquillity is instantly re-esta-
blished among them, and, what is very singular, they
recognise her. This expression must be interpreted
literally—for the substitution of another queen is not
attended with the same effect, if she be introduced
into the hive within the first twenty-four hours after
removal of the reigning one. Here the agitation
continues, and the bees treat the stranger just as they
do when the presence of their own queen leaves
them nothing to desire. But if twenty-four hours
have elapsed before substituting the stranger queen,
she will be well received, and reign from the moment
of her introduction into the hive."

Huber introduced a fertile queen, eleven months
old, into a hive which had lost its own twenty-four
hours before. Immediately on placing this female
stranger on the comb, the workers which were near
the spot touched her with their antennæ, and passing their trunks over every part of her body, gave
her honey. Then these gave place to others, which
treated her exactly in the same manner. Vibrating
their wings at once, they all ranged themselves in a
circle around their adopted sovereign; hence resulted
a kind of agitation, which was gradually communicated to other workers situated on the same surface
of the comb, and induced them to come and reconnoitre, in their turn, what was going on. These arriving, and breaking through the circle formed by
the foremost ranks, approached the queen, touched
her with their antennæ, and gave her honey. After
this little ceremony, they retired, and placing themselves behind the others, enlarged the circle, where
they vibrated their wings without tumult or disorder.
When she began to move, they were so far from op-
posing her progress, that they opened the circle at
that part towards which she turned, followed her,
and surrounded her with a guard.

The treatment which they bestow upon a stranger

queen, while their own is still in the hive, deserves
to be mentioned. The entrance of their habitation
is carefully guarded, and sentinels are placed, so
that nothing, not even one of their own companions,
can move either by day or by night, without first
undergoing a strict scrutiny. As soon as a stranger
queen enters the hive, a circle of bees imprison the
intruder so closely, that not only is it impossible for
her to move, but she is often suffocated. One
queen, it would seem, is alone required for a hive;
nature, therefore, among other curious knowledge,
has not failed to impart this to the bees. As soon
as the stranger is imprisoned, another set of workers
go and confine the original queen; and for what
reason?—to force the two to fight for the throne.
This fact is corroborated by repeated experiments.
If there be the least disposition on the part of either
to move towards the other, the workers make way
and allow them to approach: if, on the contrary,
they attempt to flee, the workers return and pinion
them closely. But it is seldom necessary to stimulate queen bees to combat; for nature has taken care
to secure her own ends, by inspiring them with the
most determined antipathy towards those of their
own sex and grade. Huber repeatedly introduced
stranger queens into the hive already supplied with
a sovereign, and in every instance a mortal combat
ensued.

The intervals between the rings of the belly are
the vulnerable points, the rest of the body being
encased in armour impervious to the sting. As
soon as they come within view of each other, they
rush impetuously to the fight, endeavour to hit each
other at an advantage, dart out the sting furiously,
and the weapon may be seen to glance off the
corslet and scales; at last the strongest or the
most fortunate contrives to mount upon her enemy,
or fix her by the wing against a comb, and curving
her body under her antagonist's belly, inflicts a

wound which for the most part proves instantane-
ously mortal. In these combats, it sometimes happens that the position of both is such, that each can
pierce its antagonist: when their situation is thus
critical, both become panic-struck, instantly disengage themselves, and retreat. This happened so
invariably, that Huber looks on it as a special instinct causing their separation, since by the death
of both the colony would be ruined.

Whatever may be the number of queens introduced into a hive, one only is allowed to survive.
It was suspected that the workers themselves despatched them, but in no instance does this appear
to be the case. On one occasion, Huber wished to
release a queen which was kept in close confine-
ment. Upon this the workers became so enraged,
that they stung indiscriminately, and thus the queen
perished; but as a proof that this was accidental,
he states, that many of the workers themselves
were killed. That this antipathy of queens is natural, is proved by the fact, that it holds good even
against the almost universal instinct of maternal
feeling. The queen bee at certain seasons, as shall
be hereafter explained, lays eggs, which in due
time are destined to bring forth other queens. It
might be supposed that, in this case, the feelings of
a mother would have their full sway—not so. As
soon as her young are about to assume a shape
like her own, even when they are as yet in their
cradle, and incapable of self-defence, she is stimulated to the utmost fury by their presence; she
tears open the cells which contain them, and, in-
serting the end of her body in the breach she has
made, inflicts a mortal wound on her own offspring.
Whatever may be the motive to such an action, we
must regard it as intended to answer other purposes
than gratifying the revenge of a poor insect. It
forms a part of the economy of nature. It is evidently the intention of the Author of nature that

this should take place, for an especial provision appears to be made for such an attack on the young queens. The cocoon* which the royal grubs spin differs from that spun by the workers' grubs. The latter are closed in every direction, so that the silk coating would ward off the sting. The former, on the contrary, are left open and uncovered on the only part of the body which is vulnerable—the lower rings of the belly.

Hence it appears that bees remember, recognise, and distinguish—that they act differently towards different queens; that they take measures to reduce their hives to the simplest economy, by getting rid of supernumeraries; that in order to effect this they do not trust to that instinctive antipathy of queens to each other, but seem to take precautions that it should be forced into action: for it has been observed, that they confine both queens as soon as it is known that a stranger is in the hive. If they did not, it is very possible that a long period might elapse before the rivals should meet, and it is certain that, if fecundated, the prodigious fertility of one of these creatures would be wasted, since one hive of workers is not more than adequate to provide for the progeny of one queen.

Observing the effect of the antennæ in agitating bees, Huber contrived a beautiful series of experiments to ascertain their uses. He divided a hive into two portions by the sudden introduction of a grating, through which a bee might hear, see, and smell, but not touch its queen. In the course of an hour one of these divisions was agitated, and the bees were seen scampering over their cells, neglecting their labours, and crossing their antennæ. In the other, they were quietly at work. It was easy, therefore, to infer in which half the queen had been included. In the division which was destitute of a queen, the workers, after waiting the usual time,

---

* The ball made by an insect while in its grub-state is a cocoon.

began to construct royal cells for the purpose of replacing their lost sovereign.

Seeing, then, that it was not by means of the
sense of sight, hearing, smelling, or of any other
unknown sense which acted at a distance, that the
agitation of bees was excited, Huber so contrived
the grating, that the interstices were just large
enough to admit the antennæ, but not the head of
the bee to pass through them. On one side of this
grating, a queen bee was placed with a few workers,
who immediately paid her the usual homage, by
forming a circle with their heads turned towards
her, offering her honey, and other marks of attention. On the other side were the rest of the swarm.
In this experiment the bees seemed perfectly aware
that the queen was not lost; there was no neglect
of labour, no hurry, but every thing went on in a
very orderly manner.

"The means of communicating with this queen,"
says the same observer, "were very singular. An
infinite number of antennæ thrust though the grating, and turned in all directions, plainly indicated
that the bees were occupied in searching for her.
She gave decisive proof that she was aware of the
interest which was taken in her existence, by always
remaining fixed on the grating, and crossing her
antennæ with those so evidently employed in ascertaining her presence. The bees attempted to pull
her through to themselves, for her legs were seized,
and firmly held by the antennæ which were passed
to the other side. Their trunks were likewise observed to be introduced to the queen's division; and,
while a captive, she was fed by her subjects from
within the hive."

To make out the use of the antennæ, Huber amputated them altogether; this experiment produced
some remarkable results. The queen, when thus
mutilated, ran about the combs, dropped her eggs
any where but in the cells; could not direct her

proboscis aright, for if she required honey, she stretched it out at random, and by chance only, to the mouths of the workers. The antennæ of a second queen having been amputated, she was put into the same hive as the first, and acted in the same manner; she, too, ran about in a delirium, retired to the corners of the hive, and strove to get out. Two remarkable things occurred in these experiments:—1st, the workers, though they knew they were queens, for they paid them the honours of a sovereign, did not know one queen from another; for, as it has been already stated, they imprison a strange queen when she enters a hive already provided with one. In this case both queens had their respective courts. 2dly, The dreadful anti pathy of queens to each other was annihilated by the removal of the antennæ; for the two rivals often met, but never took the least notice of each other.

When Huber put in a third queen, whose antennæ were entire, the bees treated her immediately as a stranger, and instantly imprisoned her.

These experiments throw some light on the mode in which communication takes place between bees. In the first place, it is not improbable that of themselves they distinguish between a queen and a worker, since they pay homage to the queen. We may then conjecture, that in order to distinguish one queen from another, some communication must be made by the individual queen to her subjects that she is their sovereign, since where the antennæ were amputated in two queens, both were equally well treated, while a third, who had the antennæ entire, was instantly recognised as a stranger.

One of the mutilated queens strove to get out of the hive, and not the slightest attempt was made by the other bees to accompany her. Now, where the antennæ have not been amputated, the queen communicates some sensation to the workers, which, as Huber conjectures, agitates them so much, that the heat of the hive becomes so intolerable as to force them to quit it. The mutilation of workers by amputation of the antennæ produces similar effects; it causes them to neglect their labours, run into corners, or to some sunny spot, and ultimately quit the hive never to return. Hence, it would seem that the antennæ are the organs of communication. As a farther proof of it, the sentinels, in a moonlight night, may be seen patrolling round their habitation with these feelers stuck out. If some unhappy moth, slyly endeavouring to steal into the habitation, happen to come in contact with them, the signal is made, and a body of guards soon rush out to chastise the interloper.

The senses of smell, taste, feeling, vision, are attributed to bees; Huber doubts that they possess the sense of hearing; their sense of sight is certainly acute in an extraordinary degree. If a dozen hives be placed together, the bee, though at a great distance, first rises in the air, and then, with almost the swiftness of a bullet, proceeds in a straight line to the entrance of its own habitation. If the eyes be varnished over, they rise up in the air, or fly at random.

This capacity of the bee to make its way directly to its nest has been made use of as a guide. In New-England, the honey-hunters set a plate of honey or sugar upon the ground; and in a short time this is discovered by the wild bees. Having caught two or three of those that have taken their fill, the hunter first releases one, which, rising into the air, flies straight to the nest. He now walks at right angles to the course of the bee for a few hundred yards, and then lets another go, which also, after rising, flies to the nest. Observing, with his pocket compass, the angle where the two lines formed by the two courses of the bees meet, there he knows will be the spot at which the nest is placed.

The honey-rattel, a quadruped, is equally sagacious with this biped honey-seeker.   Near sunset,
the rattel will sit and hold one of his paws over his
eyes to get a distinct view of the bees which, at this
hour, he knows are bound to their nest, and thither
he follows.

The antennæ are supposed to be the organ of
touch.   Certain it is that these organs alone enable
the bee to work in the darkness of the hive.

The sense of taste is, according to Huber, not
very refined, for it matters little to what neighbourhood the bee goes to gather honey, or from what
flower.   Hence the quality of honey varies in different hives, and in some it is said even to be poisonous.

The sense of smell, no doubt, is also acute.   Some
honey being placed behind a shutter by Huber,
so that it could not be seen, in a quarter of an hour
four bees, a butterfly, and some house-flies, discovered it.   Huber placed honey in boxes with
small cord valves; and put them two hundred yards
from the apiary.   In a quarter of an hour, some
bees had pushed against the valves, and entered.
Here the emanation from the honey was almost pent
up within the boxes, and the sense of sight could
not have assisted them.

Huber thinks that the sense of hearing is very
obtuse in bees.   He says, that thunder, or the report
of a gun, has little or no effect upon them.   It
would, therefore, seem that the popular notion, that
they are affected by the sound of a tin kettle, is not
well founded; however, it cannot be denied that
sounds are made by the flapping of the wings and
other movements of the body which are distinctly
heard and understood by bees.

Instances have been stated in which bees *recollected* their queen.   Another may be adduced which
appears to prove that the faculty of recollection embraced a considerable lapse of time.   " In autumn,"

says Huber, "honey had been placed in a window, where the bees resorted to it in multitudes. It was removed, and the shutters closed during winter; but when opened again on the return of spring, the bees came back, though no honey remained: undoubtedly they remembered it; therefore, an interval of several weeks did not obliterate the impression they had received."

CHAPTER III.

THE HIVE BEE.

Interior Arrangements of a Bee-hive—Structure of a Comb—Form of the Cells—Worker-Bees—Collection of Honey—Elaboration of Wax—Bee-bread—Cleanliness of Bees

The reader must now be introduced to the interior of the hive, and made acquainted with the architecture of these insects. In order to observe the habits of this insect-world, the best plan is either to have several glass hives, or overturn some common ones, that a comparative view may be taken of the works carrying on in the interior.

"It is absolutely necessary," says Reaumur, "that more than one hive should be thus exposed; for then we shall see the disposition of the combs to be various in the different ones. They are not restricted to a uniform mode of constructing their cells, but accommodate the structure to circumstances."

The combs do not touch each other, but are separated by intervals sufficiently wide to permit the bees to work at the surface of each contiguous comb, and approach any cell without quite touching each other—besides these highways, the little city

contains also narrower passages, by which the communication between one cake and another is mate-
rially shortened. The honey-comb is placed vertically in the hive. Each comb is composed of two
layers of six-sided cells, united by their bases.

If the bee formed its comb like the wasp, having
the opening of the cells towards one of its faces,
and the base towards the other, it is evident that
the number of cells placed in one comb would have
formed two combs—and two combs, each containing a single set of cells, would of course take up
more room than a single comb, in which the two
rows of cells are united base to base.

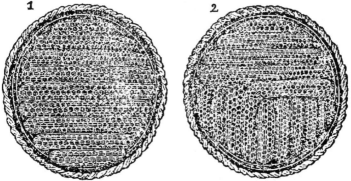

The cells are usually placed in a horizontal position, so that their mouths open towards the sides
of the hive. The bottom of the cells, instead of
forming one flat square, is composed of three
lozenge-shaped pieces, so united as to make the
cell end in a point;—consequently, the whole is
a hexagonal tube, terminating in a pyramidal cavity.

If the two cells had been a single hexagonal tube,
intersected in the middle by a flat instead of a pyramidal division, not only the shape would not have
answered the purpose of the bees, but more wax
would have been expended in its construction.

Hence it appears that both the body and the base of the tube are the best fitted for their purposes; that the greatest strength and the greatest capacity are obtained with the least expenditure of wax, in an hexagonal tube with a pyramidal base.

As the bottom of each cell is formed of three lozenge-shaped pieces, it is obvious that their junction might have been formed at any imaginable angle. Like the slated roofs of our houses, it might have been of any inclination. Reaumur suspected that, as the bottom of the cells had a uniform inclination, this particular direction was the one which caused the least expenditure of wax. He therefore asked Kœnig, an able analyst, to solve the following question —among all the hexagonal tubes with pyramidal bases, composed of three similar and equal rhombs, to determine that which can be constructed with the least possible quantity of matter? Kœnig, not at all aware of the object which Reaumur had in view when he proposed this problem, worked it out, and found,—that if three rhombs or lozenges were so inclined to each other, that the great angles measured 109° 26′, and the little angles 70° 34′, this construction would require the least quantity of matter. Maraldi measured the angles formed at the bottom of a cell, and found that the great angles gave 109° 28′, the little one 70° 32′!— Such an agreement between the solution and the actual measurement is, it must be acknowledged, sufficiently surprising. It is impossible to look at a cell without fancying that some profound geometrician had not only furnished the general plan, but also assisted in its execution. The bees appear, says Reaumur, to have had a problem to solve, which would puzzle many a mathematician. "A quantity of matter being given, it is required to form out of it cells which shall be equal and similar, and of a determinate size, but the largest possible with relation to the quantity of matter employed, while they shall occupy the least possible space." By making the form of the cell hexagonal, the bee has fully answered all the conditions of the problem: this form occupies the least possible space, while its construction consumes the least possible quantity of material.

It has been stated, that the combs are composed of two sets of cells, united by their bases. Now, if each set were first thoroughly formed, and then the two cemented together, it is evident that there would be a great waste of wax, since each of the cells would have a distinct pyramidal base. Instead, however, of proceeding thus, the bees take the bases of one set of cells as bases for those which they build on the opposite surface (see fig. 1). If three pins be passed through the middle of each of the rhombs composing the pyramidal base of a cell, they will pierce three cells of the opposite surface; consequently, in each comb, the base of each cell is composed of three rhombs, furnished by three different cells of the other layer of the comb.

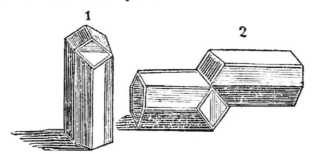

It has been already stated that the community of bees is divided into three classes—workers, males, and a female. Huber has found that there is a division of labour among the workers; one set of workers are finished architects, who plan and build the edifice—they at the same time are the nurses of the young; while the other are mere bricklayers and

plasterers, who only bring the raw material, but do
not give it shape. The former he calls the nurse-
bees; the latter, wax-workers.

Wax is not, like honey, a simple substance extracted by bees from the flower. On the contrary,
it is a secretion found in the form of scales under
their belly. The wax-workers, having gorged themselves with the nectar of flowers, hang motionless
in festoons in the hive; and in the course of twenty-
four hours scales of a white matter like talc are
formed under the rings of the abdomen. The nurse-
bees secrete wax too, but in very inconsiderable
quantities. Huber having provided a hive with honey and water, it was resorted to in crowds by bees,
which, having satisfied their appetite, returned to the
hive. They then formed festoons, remained motionless for twenty-four hours, and after a time scales
of wax appeared. An adequate supply of wax for
the construction of a comb having been elaborated,
one of the bees disengaged itself from the centre of
the group, and clearing a space about an inch in dia
meter, at the top of the hive, applied the pincers of
one of its legs to its side, detached a scale of wax,
and immediately began to mince it with the tongue.
During the operation, this organ was made to assume every variety of shape; sometimes it appeared
like a trowel, then flattened like a spatula, and at
other times like a pencil ending in a point. The
scale, moistened with a frothy liquid, became glutinous, and was drawn out like a riband. This bee,
which Huber has immortalized by the epithet of
"founder," then attached all the wax it could con-
coct to the vault of the hive, and went its way; a
second now succeeded, and did the like; a third followed, but, owing to some blunder, did not put the
wax in the same line with that placed by its prede-
cessor; upon which, says Huber, "another bee, apparently sensible of the defect, removed the displaced wax, and carrying it to the former heap, de-

posited it there exactly in the order and direction
pointed out."

The result of this series of operations was a little
block of wax, fixed to the vault of the hive, running
in a straight line, rugged in surface, but circular in
its edges, half an inch long, one-sixth of an inch high,
and about the twenty-fourth part of an inch thick.
The wax-workers, or common labourers, having de-

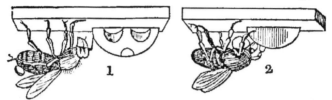

posited the requisite stock of materials, an architect,
or nurse-bee, quitted the cluster, inspected both sides
of the block, felt here and there with its antennæ,

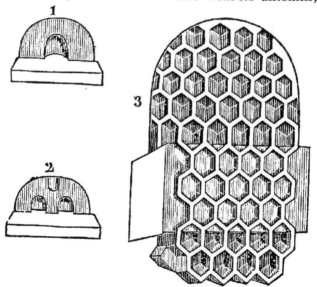

Fig. 1 and 2, represent the mode of making the first cells
Fig. 3.   The hexagonal shape of the perfect cell.

and then, like a skilful mason, proceeded to excavate exactly in the centre, as much of the block as
equalled the diameter of a common cell; and after
kneading the material which it had removed, the insect placed it carefully at the sides of the excavation. Having performed its task, it was succeeded
by a second bee; and in this manner upwards of
twenty workers succeeded each other, each one taking care to push forwards the material excavated so
as to extend the walls of the cell. When the cell
had risen and been extended on one side, a bee quitted the swarm, and after encircling the block, began
on the side opposite to that of the first cell, and, assisted by another, sketched out two, which were
so situated, that the partition between them was
precisely opposite the first cell, on the reverse side.
Those who wish for a more minute detail of this
operation may consult Huber's account. They never at first begin two masses for combs at the same
time, but scarcely are some rows of cells constructed
in the first comb, before two other masses, one on
each side of it, are established at equal distances
from it, and then again two more exterior to these.

As the stock of raw material is gradually exhausted
during the progress of these operations, the wax
workers continue adding to it a fresh supply. The
expedition with which they effect their various objects
is very great. When settled for the first time in a new
hive, they will sometimes construct a comb twenty-
seven inches long, by seven or eight inches wide, in
the space of twenty-four hours; and in the course
of five or six days they will half-fill the hive: hence
it appears, that, in the first fifteen days after they take
possession of a new habitation, there is as much wax
made as they elaborate during the remainder of the
year.

There are three sorts of cells; the first are for the
larvæ of workers; the second for those of the males
or drones, which are larger than the former, and are

usually situated in the middle of the comb; the third are the royal cells. An inattentive observer might perhaps be led to infer, that the various cells composing a cake are little habitations in which the workers might repose themselves after the labours of the day, each in its own house. This, however, is not the fact: for some of these are filled with honey, and others closed up. On a more careful inspection, it will be seen that most of the cells contain a little worm: the young of the bee—an object evidently of the most anxious care and attention to those appointed to watch and feed them. But although indefatigably industrious, even these insects, when tired with labour, require repose, and cease to work when the ordinary motive for exertion is withdrawn. It is curious to observe their mode of rest; four or five cling to a part of the hive, and extend their hind legs, whence others suspend themselves by their fore feet. These do the same neighbourly turn for another line, and thus at all times either bunches (fig. 1) or festoons (fig. 2) of bees may be

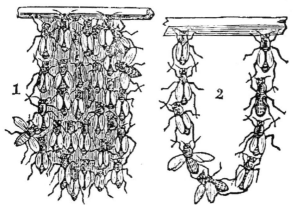

seen reposing. Huber, however, has seen the workers retiring sometimes to a cell, and remaining motionless for twenty minutes.

The length of the period which elapses before they assume their ultimate form, varies in the three kinds of bees, and is thus stated by Huber. "The worm of the worker takes twenty days, the male twenty-four, the queen sixteen days, in arriving at maturity. The worker remains three days in the egg; five in the grub state, when the bees close up its cell with a waxen covering; it is thirty-six hours in spinning its cocoon; in three days it changes to a nymph, passes six in that form, and then comes forth a perfect bee.

"The male passes three days in the egg; six and a half as a worm, and on the twenty-fourth makes its appearance as a winged animal.

"The royal insect passes three days in the egg; is five a worm, when the bees close its cell, and it immediately begins its cocoon, which is finished in twenty-four hours. During eleven days, and even sixteen hours of the twelfth, it remains in a state of complete repose. Its transformation into a nymph then takes place, in which state four days and a part of a fifth are passed."

On the fifth day after her appearance, the queen quits the hive for the purpose of fecundation: forty-six hours afterward she begins to lay eggs, and a hive will often consist of forty thousand inhabitants, the most of them her own offspring. The first eggs of the queen always give birth to workers. In spring she lays about two thousand eggs of males, resumes it again in August, but during the rest of the intervals she exclusively lays workers' eggs. It is curious that oviposition is retarded by cold; during winter it does not take place. Huber relates an instance where a queen, instead of laying her eggs forty-six hours after fecundation, did not do so for several months, owing to her impregnation having taken place just before winter.

The queen must be at least eleven months old, before she begins to lay the eggs of males. The bees, both workers and queen, know the period of oviposition proper for each kind of egg, and take care to provide suitable cells at a proper period.

Huber removed all the worker-cells from a hive, and left nothing but male cells; the bees, instead of repairing the damage done to the hive, by uniting the fragments of comb, seemed quite disheartened, went into the fields, but returned unladen. The queen, too, hesitated about laying her worker-eggs in the large male cells, and at last they were seen to drop from her at random. However, six eggs were deposited regularly; but the workers did not treat them very carefully. They were removed next day, and the cells left empty. In order to re-animate them, he gave the bees a piece of comb, composed of worker-cells, but which were filled with male instead of worker-eggs. For twelve days the bees obstinately abstained from working in wax, but at last they positively removed the whole of the male brood, and cleaned the cells, just as if they had been aware that the eggs which were to come from the queen required worker-cells. As soon as this was done, the queen no longer dropped her eggs at random, but deposited them in the cells. The male cells were then taken away, and the worker-cells restored; upon which the ordinary labours of the hive were resumed. If the workers reasoned and felt, here is a fact which would at once attest their foresight, and their affection for their queen; they knew she required worker-cells, and accordingly, to accommodate her, they pulled out the male brood, which, under other circumstances, they would have fondly nourished.

Hence it is reasonable to infer that the ovaries of the queen contain a regular succession of eggs, and that the bees know this as well as herself, at least they act as if they knew it. There is, however, a curious effect produced by retarding the fecundation of the queen. Huber found, that if fecundation

took place in the first fifteen days of a queen's life,
the regular series of eggs was deposited; but if delayed beyond the twenty-second day, the queen laid
only the eggs of males for the rest of her life. Now,
it must be remembered that, in the natural state,
she must have been at least eleven months old before male eggs could be laid, and yet it appears that,
simply by retarding fecundation twenty-two days,
she begins immediately to bring forth male eggs;
of this extraordinary fact no satisfactory explanation has been hitherto given. The instinct of the
queen seems affected by the delay; for although,
when fecundation has not been retarded, she never
fails to deposite the different sorts of eggs in their
proper cells; when it has, she lays them indiscriminately in any cells. The workers too are puzzled;
for in the natural state they can accurately distinguish between the different kinds of eggs, and they
never fail to give a peculiar covering to the male
cells; but when the impregnation of the queen happens to have been retarded, they feed the worms
of drones, deposited in a royal cell, as if they were
royal worms.

The royal cells differ essentially from the others,
both in form and position; they are not placed horizontally like the other cells, but vertically, and resemble a pear with the small end downwards. When
the queen lays in them, they are like the cup
of an acorn; after this they are modelled to the py-
riform shape, and quite closed up. In the construction of these cells, the bees seem to lose sight of
their customary habits of economy; no expenditure
of materials is considered too great; no space necessary for the accommodation of the future queen
is grudged. More wax is expended in constructing
the cradle of the infant queen, than would suffice to
build one hundred or one hundred and fifty ordinary
cells; and no labour is spared in rendering it compact and solid.

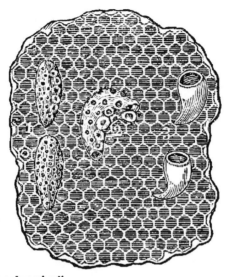

Fig. 1. Closed royal cell.
   2. Another varied in shape.
   3. Two cells just commenced; their apertures are here drawn looking upwards, to show their cavity. This position is the reverse of the natural one.

One of the most astonishing facts connected with the economy of bees, is the manner in which, when deprived of their queen, they proceed to repair their loss: for this purpose they construct several of these royal cells, and taking a common worker-worm out of the ordinary cells, they put it into a royal one, feed the insect with royal food, which is more pungent than that destined for worker grubs, and in a few days, instead of a worker, they have a queen. This extraordinary discovery, made by Schirach, has been confirmed by Huber, and is now admitted by all naturalists. In many parts of Germany, and more especially in Lusatia and Saxony, the peasants, availing themselves of this discovery, are enabled to multiply their swarms of bees at pleasure; they shut up a few hundred working bees

with a piece of honey-comb containing common
grubs three or four days old. the worker bees immediately set about destroying some of the common
cells; construct royal cells in their stead; deposite
the grubs in these cells, and administer to them food
proper for grubs destined to become queens. This
experiment is constantly repeated, and never found
to fail. In the proper time a number of young
queens is produced, the supernumeraries are destroyed; and at length only one survives to govern
the hive. Thus wonderfully does nature provide
for the preservation of the species—the life of thousands of these insects depending on that of a queen.
In order to guard against the possibility of extermination, she has taught the bee the miracle of converting the whole of the instincts and organization
of one kind into those of another, by the simple
means of providing a different and a more pungent
kind of food for the subject of its marvellous experiment. There seems, however, to be a natural
provision for this change; for it is found that all the
workers are imperfect females, whose organs are
not developed· the food simply farthers this developement. But whether we look to the design or
the means used, or the circumstances under which
it is effected, it is one of the most striking facts in
the whole range of natural history.

As soon as the queen bee has laid her eggs in the
various cells, the nurses are incessantly occupied in
watching over the brood. For this purpose, they
now forego every other employment. There is
usually but one egg deposited in each cell; but
when the fecundity of the queen happens to exceed
the number of cells already prepared, three or four
eggs may be found crowded together in the same
repository. But this is an inconvenience which
the working bees will not permit to continue; they
seem to be aware that two young ones placed in
the same cell, when they grow larger, would first

embarrass, and then destroy each other. Hence, they take care that no cell shall contain more than one egg; all the rest they remove or destroy.

The single egg which is left remaining is glued by its smaller end to the bottom of the cell, which it touches only in a single point. A day or two after the egg has been thus deposited, the worm is excluded from the shell; presenting the appearance of a maggot rolled up in a ring, and reposing softly in a bed of whitish-coloured jelly, upon which the little animal soon begins to feed. The instant the little worm appears, the working bees attend it with the most anxious tenderness; watching the cell with unremitting care, they furnish the infant insect with a constant supply of the whitish substance, on which it both feeds and lies. These nurses evince for the offspring of another greater affection than many parents show towards their own children. They regularly visit each cell at very short intervals, in order to see that nothing be wanting; and they are constantly engaged in preparing the white mixture on which the insect feeds.

Thus attended and plentifully fed, the worm, in less than ten days' time, acquires its full growth, and ceases to take its usual food. Perceiving that it has no occasion for a farther supply, they perform the last office of tenderness, and shut the little animal up in its cell; they close the mouth of the aperture with a waxen lid; and the worm, thus effectually secured against every external injury, is left to itself.

The worm is no sooner shut up, than it throws off its inactivity and begins to labour; alternately elongating and contracting its body, it contrives to line the sides of its apartment with a soft material, which it spins after the manner of other caterpillars, before they undergo their last transformation. The cell having been thus prepared, the animal passes into the aurelia state; when, although in a state of perfect inactivity, it exhibits not only the legs but the wings of the future bee. Thus, in about twenty or one-and-twenty days, the bee acquires its perfect form, and becomes in every respect fitted for its future labours. When all its parts have acquired their proper strength and consistence, the young insect pierces with its teeth the waxen door of the prison in which it is confined.

The different transformations will be best understood by the subjoined cut. the first represents the egg stuck to the bottom of the cell by a glutinous matter; its form is oblong. The next gives a view of a cell with the worm hatched and coiled up. The third shows the worm changed into a nymph.

When quite freed from its cell, it is as yet moist and encumbered with the spoils of its former situation, but the officious bees soon come to its relief; one party is seen to flock around it, and lick it clean on all sides with their trunks, while another band may be observed equally assiduous in feeding it with honey; others immediately begin to cleanse the cell which the young insect has just quitted, and fit it for the accommodation of a new inhabitant. The young bee soon repays their care by its industry; for the moment its external parts become dry, it discovers its natural appetites for labour. Freed from the cell and properly equipped for duty, it at once issues from the hive, and, instructed only by its natural instinct, . proceeds in quest of flowers, selects only those which contain a supply of honey; rejects such as are barren, or have been already drained by other adventurers; and when loaded, is never at a loss for its way back to the common habitation. After this first

sally, it unremittingly pursues, throughout the whole
course of its future existence, the task which its instinct thus impels it to begin.

There are three substances for which bees forage
during their excursions from the hive : honey, or a
saccharine matter extracted from the nectary of
flowers—the pollen or fertilizing dust of the anthers
—and an odoriferous resin called propolis.

Honey is extracted from that part of the flower
called the nectarium. For the purpose of collecting
this fluid substance, the insect is furnished with a
trunk or tongue, which it is capable of doubling up
or elongating at pleasure. This is not formed in
the manner of a tube, by which the fluid is to be
sucked up, but like a tongue, to lick away the honeyed
juice which nature has secreted in the little glands
which were always known to the bee, although they
had, until a very recent period, completely eluded
the researches of the most skilful botanists. From
the tongue this sweet juice is conveyed to the mouth :
it then passes through the gullet into the first stomach or honey-bag, which, when filled, appears like
an oblong bladder, and as transparent as crystal (*see
fig. p.* 62). Children in country places are well
acquainted with this bladder, and destroy many bees
in order to get at their store of honey. When the
bee has sufficiently filled this bag, it returns to the
hive, and, reserving only a small part of its load for
its own use, disgorges the remainder into one of the
cells. Sometimes the insect may be seen delivering
its surplus store to another bee, which appears ready
to receive it at the entrance of the hive ; when it flies
off for a fresh supply. Some honeycombs are always
left open for the common use of the workers engaged
in the hive ; but the greater number of the cells filled
during the course of the summer are carefully
stopped up until the internal supply of honey begins
to fail, and it becomes necessary to have recourse to
their contents. When the harvest of honey is so

I.—F

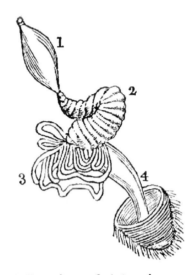

1. Honey-bag, or first stomach.
2. Second stomach.
3. Biliary and salivary ducts.
4. Large intestines.

plentiful that the bees have not sufficient room for it, they either lengthen their cells or build new ones.

The pollen or yellow dust, which loosely adheres to the central parts of flowers, is another substance eagerly sought after by the industrious bee. The breast, legs, and many other parts of the body are covered with a fine down or hair. The insect enters the cup of a flower charged with this yellow farina, rolls itself round, and soon becomes quite covered with this vegetable dust. Nature has provided the bee with means admirably adapted to secure the treasure thus collected on its body; the last joint but one of each leg being formed exactly like a brush. These natural brushes are passed one after another over the various parts of its body, and by that means the pollen is collected into two little heaps. The thighs of the last pair of the insect's legs are furnished with two cavities fringed with hair: these form a convenient little basket for the use of the bee. The dust collected from a thousand flowers is kneaded into diminutive pellets and stuck into these cavities; and when these balls have been increased to the size of a grain of pepper, away flies the insect to deposite its store in the hive.

But this meal or dust is not always to be obtained in sufficient quantities: early in the season, before the flowers upon which the bee feeds are generally blown, this pollen is contained in a capsule from which, in its then immature state, it is not easily dislodged. The bee, however, well knows where the object of its search lies concealed—it examines and feels these repositories: having discovered one sufficiently advanced towards maturity to answer its purpose, it pinches the capsule with its teeth, and then takes possession of the hidden treasure.

When a bee, charged with a load of this vegetable dust, reaches the hive, it enters one of the cells head foremost. The pellets are then detached from the hollow cavities in which they have been carried, and being moistened and mixed with a small portion of honey, they are kneaded into a substance called by the country people bee-bread. An adequate supply of this food is indispensable for the health and strength of bees during the winter season. Bees may be robbed of their honey, and will thrive if fed during the winter with treacle; but no proper substitute has yet been found for this bee-bread. When deprived of this necessary of life, they become consumptive and die.

The gathering of the pollen affords a striking illustration of the means indirectly employed by nature to second her purposes. The pollen is the fertilizing dust of flowers; it is necessary for some of it to fall on a particular part of the pistil, in order that the flower shall give place to fruit, enclosing the seed of a future plant. Now, it has been remarked by a great number of naturalists, that the bee, when it collects the pollen from one plant, does not go to a different sort of plant for more, but, labouring to collect the same kind of fertilizing dust, it seeks only the same kinds of flowers. Since the fecundation of the vegetable kingdom is effected in no small degree through the medium of insects, which, while searching for their own food, unconsciously sprinkle the fertilizing pollen on the reproductive organs of plants, it follows, that had the bee gone from one kind of flower to another, this would have given rise to hybrid plants, and thus have counteracted the purposes of nature.

"I have frequently," says Dobs, "followed a bee loading the farina bee-bread or crude wax on its legs, through part of a great field in flower, and on whatever flower it first alighted and gathered the farina, it continued gathering from that kind of flower, and passed over many other species, though very numerous in the field, without alighting on or loading from them—though the flower it chose was much scarcer than the others. so that if it began to load from a daisy, it continued loading from the same, neglecting clover, honeysuckles, and the violet. What farther confirms my observation is, that each load on the legs of a bee is of one uniform colour.

Besides honey and pollen, there is a third substance which bees collect as essential for their purposes This is a resinous gum, differing from wax in tenacity as well as in various other qualities, it is an exuding substance found in certain trees, such as the birch, the willow, and the poplar. To the ancients it was known under the name of propolis. Near the outlet of one of his hives, Huber placed some branches of the poplar tree, which exudes a transparent juice of the colour of garnet. Several worker-bees were soon seen perching upon these branches; having detached some of this resinous gum, they formed it into pellets, and deposited them in the baskets of their thighs; thus loaded, they flew to the hive where some of their fellow-labourers instantly came to assist them in detaching this viscid substance from their baskets. These pellets were laid in a little heap as near as possible to the place in which it was afterward used. In the instance observed by Huber, the propolis was attached to the roof the hive, exactly in the centre between two of the combs, so that it lay in a situation equally convenient with respect to the cells of either. A bee then drew out a thread from the viscid mass; it then cut it off with its teeth, and laid hold of it with the claw of one of its feet. Thus equipped, the insect was seen to enter one of the cells which had been but just formed. The object of this manœuvre was soon apparent; when the insect came out, one of the angles formed by the junction of two of the six sides forming the cell, was found lined and soldered with propolis. The process was regularly repeated, until all the angles had been lined and secured in a similar manner; not indeed by the same bee, but by others which shared in this labour. Having finished one cell, they proceeded to another, until all the cells destined for the young had been thus soldered and strengthened.

Propolis is the substance used in all cases in which strength and solidity are required. It is well known that the habitation of bees ought to be very close; if it contained any cracks or unstopped crevices, other insects might enter the hive, or the rain might penetrate into the interior, which would be attended with fatal consequences. Any deficiencies in these respects, which may arise either from the unskilfulness or negligence of man, the insects supply by their own industry; so that when they take possession of a new habitation, their first and principal care is to close up all crannies with propolis. When the bees begin to work with this substance it is soft, but every day it acquires a firmer consistence; until at length it assumes a brown colour, and becomes much harder than wax.

When the foundations of the combs are laid, the first row of cells differs from the succeeding ones in that it is composed of five instead of six sides: the fifth or broadest being the side or base by which the comb was suspended from the roof of the hive. As long as the cells are but few in number, and not overloaded with honey, this pentagonal row is sufficiently strong to support the comb; but when the wants of the hive render it necessary to construct more cells and increase the stock of honey, their instinct informs the bees, that the foundations of the comb are not sufficiently strong to support the increased weight. Accordingly, they are seen, in a sort of fury, to fall upon and destroy the pentagonal cells, and for the wax with which they were originally constructed, to substitute a composition of propolis and wax. This substance was, by the ancients, termed *pissoceros.* The tenacity and strength of this material render the foundations of the combs perfectly secure, and relieve the bees from all subsequent anxiety on that account. The ingenuity evinced by the bees in the performance of this task is no less worthy of admiration than the sagacity which enables them to find out its necessity. It is evident that, if the first row of cells were removed at once, the comb itself would fall; since it is attached to the roof of the hive by means of this row. In order to guard against this danger, the bees work at alternate sides of the comb; they remove first one portion of the old comb, substituting for the brittle wax the strong and tenacious cement called pissoceros, before they touch the other.

Among other virtues possessed by bees, cleanliness is one of the most marked; they will not suffer the least filth in their abode. It sometimes happens that an ill-advised slug or ignorant snail chooses to enter the hive, and has even the audacity to walk over the comb; the presumptuous and foul intruder is quickly killed, but its gigantic carcase is not so speedily removed.   Unable to transport the corpse out of their dwelling, and fearing "the noxious smells" arising from corruption, the bees adopt an efficacious mode of protecting themselves; they embalm their offensive enemy, by covering him over with propolis; both Maraldi and Reaumur have seen this.   The latter observed that a snail had entered a hive, and fixed itself to the glass side, just as it does against walls, until the rain shall invite it to thrust out its head beyond its shell.   The bees, it seemed, did not like the interloper, and not being able to penetrate the shell with their sting, took a hint from the snail itself, and instead of covering it all over with propolis, the cunning economists fixed it immoveably, by cementing merely the edge of the orifice of the shell to the glass with this resin, and thus it became a prisoner for life, for rain cannot dissolve this cement, as it does that which the insect itself uses.*

* When they expel their excrements, they go apart that they may not defile their companions, and in winter when prevented by extreme cold, or the injudicious practice of wholly closing the hive, from going out for this purpose, their bodies sometimes become so swelled from the accumulation of fœces, that when at last able to go out, they cannot fly, and falling on the ground in the attempt, they perish with cold, the sacrifice of personal neatness —Kirby, vol ii p 200.

CHAPTER IV.

THE HIVE BEE.

Fertility of Queen Bee—Swarming—Ventilation of the Hive—Irascibility—Duels—Robberies—Defences of Bees.

As spring advances, the losses which the hive has sustained in the autumn and winter are repaired. The fertility of the queen-mother is prodigious. Schirach says, that in the course of one season, a single female will lay from 70,000 to 100,000 eggs. Huber and Reaumur's estimate is not so high; but the lowest is very considerable: hence the habitation is soon overpeopled, and it becomes necessary, therefore, that thousands should quit their homes, and lay the foundation of another kingdom. This expatriation is not confined to the young brood, who have not as yet laboured, but the old; they who with infinite travail had already constructed one city, voluntarily leave all they have done, to begin life again.

About the time when the queen lays royal eggs, the workers make preparation for the male insects; consequently, males and females appear about the same period, when Providence has covered the surface of the earth with the flowers from which the young bee may collect its food. The same kind hand has appointed the autumn, when the fruit is ripe, for the birth-time of the young wasp.

Sometimes there are as many as twenty royal cells, each of which contains a queen. The natural hatred subsisting between female bees has been mentioned, but this passion, apparently so vile and injurious, is the means by which the species is saved, and

its instinctive habits perpetuated. While the metamorphosis of the young queens is proceeding, each
cell is sedulously surrounded with a guard.

As soon as the worm is transformed into a nymph,
and not before, the old queen becomes infuriated.
She rushes towards the royal cells, and instantly begins to tear them open. The guards make way for
her, and allow her to do what she pleases. As the
cells, however, are considerably thicker than those
of the common bee, she soon exhausts herself by her
labour, and generally, after she has opened one or
two of them, and most barbarously murdered her
own offspring, she languidly attempts to gnaw at a
third. The sight of these cells agitates her to such
a degree, that she runs about the hive in a state of delirium. This excitement she soon communicates to
the workers by touching their antennæ, and, after
scampering about in all directions, a great portion of
them, accompanied by their old queen, rush out of
the hive to seek another home. In every instance
it is the old queen which leads the first swarm. Ex-
perience enables the apiarists to foretel this event:
for, on the evening previous to swarming, the bees
often suddenly leave off their labours, as if aware of
the approaching change ; while a few scouts are sent
out in search of a spot fit to receive the new colony.
Something very like concerted action and foresight
is evident in these proceedings. But after every
preliminary step for departure has been taken, it frequently happens that a cloud, obscuring the sun, will
put an end to their plan, and cause them to return
peaceably to the hive. Instinct here is so closely
allied to reason, that it is difficult to mark the distinc-
tion. If it were blind impulse that drove them out
of their hive, why do they change their purpose ?
Nay, farther, like *reasoning* beings capable of erring,
they sometimes make a false judgment, and after
hesitating, actually do swarm, and are caught in the
so much dreaded shower.

After the old queen is gone, the bees watch the royal cells; and as soon as the worms are in a state to become nymphs, they close them up.

It is to be remarked that this operation is not done to every cell at once; consequently, the young queens are of various ages: indeed, at least one day intervenes between the laying of one royal egg and another.

By this means, several queens are successively born, and several swarms thrown off. Had, on the contrary, fifteen or sixteen queens appeared at the same time in the same hive, the whole number would have fallen victims to their own passions.

As soon as a young queen is produced, like her mother, she proceeds instantly to attack the other royal cells; but here there is a remarkable difference in the conduct of the workers; for, although they permitted their ancient queen to pursue her sovereign pleasure, they by no means extend the same courtesy to her daughter; but the moment she attempts to approach a cell, the guards surrounding them immediately attack, bite, and drive her off. She then runs to another, and is treated by the guards of that cell in a similar manner; the fury of her passion, constantly excited by the sight of these cells, sends her in a state of fury about the hive; and this, as in the other cases, is communicated to a portion of the workers, and they all quit their native habitation.

In this way several swarms will issue from one hive in the course of one season. This seems to explain the cause of the very undutiful and unusual treatment which the queen experiences from the workers. They know that several queens are necessary, and accordingly guard against the effects of that antipathy which, by destroying the royal brood, would prevent swarming. If it so happen that three or four queens should appear at the same time, or before the redundant population which had left the hive may have been replaced by the birth of additional workers, the bees keep them prisoners by shutting up the cells as fast as the young queens attempt to bite their way out. In this way some of them, when set at liberty, are fit for immediate flight. The royal prisoners, however, are merely detained; for when they pipe for food, and thrust their proboscis through a hole in the cell, made just large enough for that purpose, a nurse-bee standing by instantly supplies them with honey.

In the attack which the young queen makes on the royal cells, irritated by the maltreatment of those who ought to pay her homage, she stands upright, and utters a shrill and clear sound. No sooner is this piping heard, than the bees are immediately paralyzed: they remain motionless, and hang down their heads. Huber and others have remarked this strange effect very often. She then proceeds to tear open the cells, but, in doing so, ceases to pipe, when the bees, recovering from their stupor, drive her away. Again she repeats the cry, and again the same effect is produced. Hence it is evident that, during the swarming season, the instinct of bees undergoes considerable modification: for when they have simply lost their queen, and taken measures to replace her, by building royal cells, and feeding the grubs of common workers, in the manner stated by Schirach, and when several queens make their appearance, they seem to excite them to fight; and the conqueror is chosen their monarch. But in the swarming time, as just detailed, they appear aware that a plurality of queens is necessary to thin the hive, and, in consequence, they forget their habitual respect for the female, treat her roughly, and detain her prisoner, not for any determinate period, but as long as her appearance would be detrimental to their ends. How strangely analogous to human reasoning and calculation is this! What simple sensation can make the bees detain one queen one day, another five days, and let either free just at the very moment her presence becomes essential? Why, too, do they allow the old queen to open the royal cells, and slay as many of the royal nymphs as she has strength to destroy, at the very time that they are wanted, while they bite and drive away a young queen, who might attempt the same thing? One would almost be inclined to think, that the habit of obeying the old queen—that personal attachment, or something not unlike it, for one so long known to them, had some influence upon their proceedings.

The hive is always warm, and the bees lessen the heat by ventilation. This branch of duty devolves on workers alone. They unite their wings by means of their marginal hooks into one piece, and then flap them up and down like a fan. This operation presents something which resembles a designed combination of efforts, for it is not carried on indiscriminately in all parts of the hive. The fanners station themselves, for the most part, at the bottom of the hive, and are usually ranged in files. Some are stationed outside of the hive; these always turn their heads towards the entrance; others are stationed within, and turn theirs in the opposite direction. Their number seldom exceeds twenty at a time; they relieve each other, and the operation is never remitted. If either the hand or wind-gauges be held at the entrance of a bee-hive, a distinct impression of a current of air, now acting, now subsiding, is produced.

After the hive has cast off several swarms, and no more remain than are necessary for the preservation of the city, the bees no longer evince any anxiety about the rest of the royal brood; but allow the royal cells to be torn open by the first-born queen, and either drag out the young themselves, if worms, or permit them to be killed, if nymphs.

Such is a brief account of the phenomena of

swarming. Huber has conjectured that the immediate cause of it lies in the great rise of temperature
occasioned in the hive by the commotion of the
workers. This heat amounts to 104°. It is
usually in spring from 90° to 97°. Perhaps the
conjecture is well-founded; but this agitation occurs,
independently of swarming, from the loss of the
queen, and yet the bees do not think of quitting their
habitation.

So many faculties having been given to bees,
enabling them to provide for their wants, it is not
likely that they should have been left without the
means of defending the possession of whatever is
necessary for them.

The sting by which this little animal defends itself and its property from its natural enemies, is composed of three parts: the sheath and two darts,
which are extremely small and penetrating. Both
the darts are furnished with small points or barbs,
like that of a fish-hook, which, by causing the wound
inflicted by the sting to rankle, renders it more painful. Still the effect of the sting itself would be but
slight, if the insect were not provided with a supply
of poisonous matter, which it injects into the wound.
The sheath, which has a sharp point, makes the
first impression; this is followed by that of the darts,
and then the venomous liquor is poured in. The
sheath sometimes sticks so fast to the wound, that
the insect is obliged to leave it behind; this considerably augments the inflammation of the wound,
and to the bee itself the mutilation proves fatal.
Were it not for the protection of its sting, the bee
would have too many rivals in sharing the produce
of its labours. A hundred lazy animals, fond of
honey and hating labour, would intrude upon the
sweets of the hive; and for want of armed guar-
dians to protect it, this treasure would become the
prey of worthless depredators.

In Mungo Park's last mission to Africa, some of
I.—G

his people, having disturbed a colony of these animals, were so furiously attacked, that both man and beast were put to instant flight. The list of the killed and missing amounted to one horse and six asses—a serious loss to a white man in the midst of inhospitable deserts.

Lesser tells us, that in 1525, during the confusion occasioned by a time of war, a mob of peasants, assembling in Hoherstein, attempted to pillage the house of the minister of Elende, who having in vain employed all his eloquence to dissuade them from their design, ordered his domestics to fetch his beehives, and throw them into the middle of the infuriated multitude. The effect answered his expectations: they were immediately put to flight, and happy were those who escaped unstung.

It sometimes happens that a young swarm choose to enter a hive already occupied; when a most desperate conflict ensues, which will last for hours, and even for days, and the space around will be found covered with the slain. These desperate conflicts not only take place between strangers, but also between inhabitants of the same hive—offspring of the same mother. The causes which bring division into so united a society have not been hitherto ascertained.

On those fine spring days in which the sun is beautiful and warm, duels may often be seen to take place between two inhabitants of the same hive. In some cases, the quarrel appears to have begun within, and the combatants may be seen coming out of the gates eager "for blows." Sometimes a bee peaceably settled on the outside of the hive, or walking about, is rudely jostled by another, and then the attack commences, each endeavouring to obtain the most advantageous position. They turn, pirouette, throttle each other; and such is their bitter earnestness, that Reaumur has been enabled to come near enough to observe them with a lens with-

out causing a separation. After rolling about in
the dust, the victor, watching the time when its
enemy uncovers his body, by elongating it, in the
attempt to sting, thrusts its weapon between the
scales, and the next instant its antagonist stretches
out its quivering wings, and expires. A bee cannot
be killed so suddenly, except by crushing, as by the
sting of another bee. Sometimes the stronger insect produces the death of the vanquished by
squeezing its chest. After this feat has been done,
the victorious bee constantly remains, says Reamur,
near his victim, standing on his four front legs, and
rubbing the two posterior ones together. Sometimes the enemy is killed in the hive; then the victor always carries the corpse out of the city, and
leaves it. These combats are strictly duels, not
more than two being concerned in them; and this
is even the case when armies of bees meet in
combat.

It must also be confessed, that however inclined,
naturally, to industrious habits, the bee will turn
thief, if it cannot obtain food by its own labours.
In hives which are ill managed, and not properly
supplied with food, the bees, instead of continuing
a well-constituted civil society, become a formidably
organized band of robbers, which levy contributions
upon the neighbouring hives. At first, a few enter
the hive by stealth; their numbers are then gradually augmented, and at length grown more bold, an
attack *en masse* is made, and a bloody battle ensues.
When the carnage is ended, and one of the queens
killed, the bees unite under the same sovereign, and
the vacated hive is now ransacked, and its treasures
conveyed to the new city.

A still more extraordinary instance of aggression
sometimes occurs, when this proverbially industrious insect does not disdain to rob on the highway.

Occasionally, one solitary humble bee, which, in
its instincts, compared with the hive bee, is a mere

rustic, may be seen surrounded by four or five of the latter, who waylay it as it returns towards its nest laden with honey. They, however, do not injure it, but just subject it to that degree of restraint and uncomfortable mauling, by pommelling its chest, and pulling its legs, which obliges it to unfold its tongue and disgorge its honey. The robbers, one after another, sip from the honey; and when the insect has been thus eased, it is set at liberty.

Sometimes, a sort of friendly intercourse takes place between two hives. Thus the inhabitants of a hive belonging to Mr. Knight, used to visit that of a cottager, considerably after their working-hours. Each bee, before it entered, seemed to be questioned. On the tenth day, however, these civilities terminated in a battle.

Besides this just exhibition of anger in defence of their lives and property, there are times in which the whole hive becomes infuriated against certain members of their own community. It seems as if the bees are such rigid economists, that whoever is useless must be got rid of. Hence the massacre of drones or male bees; they are born in April and May, and are killed in August. Huber saw them chased from corner to corner of the hive, till at length the whole were huddled together at its bottom, and there massacred.

This murderous work was going on at the very same hour in six different hives, clearly showing that it is not an effect of chance. In one hive, however, in which the fecundation of the queen had been retarded, so that nothing but drones were produced, they were not molested; neither are they touched in hives deprived of the queen. Hence, the fury of the bees against drones is connected with some principle of utility not only drones, but even workers are occasionally slaughtered by their comrades: some conjecture this to take place on account of their old age. A species of workers, differing in colour from the rest, and supposed to be monstrous, have also been observed to be relentlessly massacred.

It is not, however, by force alone that these creatures defend their properties and hives; they possess invention enough to rear regular fortifications for protection. Huber once discovered that great ravages had been committed upon his own hives, and he also learned from all quarters, that a similar calamity had befallen those of his neighbours. At length it was found, that the destruction which had taken place had been caused by that gigantic moth, called the Sphinx Atropos, or Death's Head. How an animal apparently so defenceless should have dared to enter, and then to do what it was found to have done, is still a matter of surprise. It is conjectured by Huber, that the sound which it emits produces effects on the bees similar to that of the queen; and thus disarms them of the power of resisting its depredations. It is clear, however, that in the daylight, which is unnatural to the sphinx, the bees can kill it; at least, they did so in an experiment made by Huber.

As the enterprises of the sphinx became more and more fatal to the bees, Huber determined to construct a grating which should admit a bee, but not the moth. He did so, and the devastation ceased. But what is extraordinary, he found that in other hives, not protected by human ingenuity, the bees had adopted a very similar expedient for their own defence; and to add still more to the wonder, these defences were not alike, but variously constructed in different hives.

" Here, was a single wall whose opening arcades were disposed in its higher parts: there, were several bulwarks behind each other, like the bastions of our citadels, gateways, masked by walls in front, opened on the face of the second row, while they did not correspond with the apertures of the first

Sometimes a series of intersecting arcades permitted free egress to the bees, but refused admit-
tance to their enemies. These fortifications were
massy and their substance firm and compact, being
composed of propolis and wax."

When the entrance of their hives is itself restricted, or care is taken to contract it soon enough
to prevent the devastation of their enemies, bees
dispense with walling themselves in. Here, then,
we have the invention and adaptation of means to
a proposed end.

Nothing is more calculated to convince us that
animals are not mere machines, than seeing them
varying their proceedings according to circumstances. Even their mistakes and irregularities
cause us to doubt the doctrine, that all their actions
are the result of organization. Of this, bees furnish
abundant instances.

"The geometrical regularity with which the
labours of bees are conducted," observes Bonnet,
"has been justly celebrated; it requires, however,
but little observation to perceive much variety in
the construction of the cells—and this is sometimes so remarkable as to strike the most careless
observer. Some of them are circular, and some
elliptical, instead of the usual hexagonal form.
The bottoms of the cells show also considerable
irregularities. It often happens, that instead of
being constructed in the usual manner, of three
lozenge-shaped pieces, they are formed of four, five,
or six pieces, of a shape more or less irregular, but
which approach a quadrilateral form or square, more
nearly than any other figure. The dimensions of
the common cells are still more various than their
opening or their base. The cells are usually about
five lines* in depth; but I have seen some more than
eighteen lines deep. These unusually long cells

* A line is the twelfth part of an inch.

have always one of their sides towards the side of
the hive. They serve only to hold honey wanted
for the daily consumption of the little republic; and
the queen has never been seen laying her eggs in any
cells of this kind. The cells are usually horizontal;
but the long cells just mentioned are frequently inclined towards the horizon."

It has been already stated, that when the grubs
of bees are about to be transformed into nymphs,
the workers carefully close up the cells in which
they are lodged with a lid. This precaution is necessary, in order that their transformation should
be effected in security. The lid used for this purpose is in some degree convex, and never flat like
the lids which shut up the honey-cells; and by this
means the breeding cells may always be distinguished from the honey-cells. When a cell has
been thus closed up, the grub sets about lining the
whole of its walls; this operation requires that it
should move: hence it is necessary that the cell
should be neither too narrow nor too short, to allow
it to move freely. A swarm, which Bonnet had
placed in a very flat glass hive, had constructed a
large comb, running parallel with one of the sides
of the hive; but because the space was narrow, the
bees had not been able to give the cells the usual
depth. These were common cells; nevertheless,
the queen did not omit laying in them; and the
workers fed the grubs which proceeded from these
eggs. Nor did they fail to shut up the cells when
the grubs were on the point of being transformed.

Some days after they had been so shut up, holes
were observed in the lids, more or less in diameter,
through which a part of the body of each worm
had protruded. It appeared that the cells had not
the necessary depth, and that the grubs, finding
themselves too much hampered for room, had
pushed roughly against the lids, from which they
had detached pieces of various sizes. It was in-

teresting to watch what steps the bees would take
in this emergency. Bonnet expected to find that
they would have taken the grubs out of the cells, as
they do when the combs happen to be greatly deranged; but in this he was deceived, and he found
that he had by no means correctly calculated the
resources which instinct placed at their command.
They did not take out a single grub; they left them
all in the cells which they occupied: but because
the cells were not deep enough, they shut them up
with lids somewhat more convex than usual; and
thus found means to add to each cell the depth
which it wanted. In this manner the grubs were
placed at their ease; no openings were afterward
perceived in the lids; only the interval between the
comb and the glass hive was by this means so nar-
rowed that the bees could hardly pass through it.

Some philosophers have maintained that bees and
other social insects act merely from sensation; that
their sensorium is so modelled that they are impelled by a sensation of pleasure alone to the acts
which it is their destiny to perform; that the succession of their different labours is preordained by
the Creator; and a pleasurable sensation attached
to the performance of each task: and that, consequently, when they build cells,—when they sedulously attend to the young brood,—when they collect provisions, these proceedings evince no plan,
no affection, no foresight; but that the enjoyment
of an agreeable sensation is the sole influencing
motive which leads to the performance of each of
these operations. But " surely," observes Kirby
" it would be better to resolve all their proceedings
at once into a direct impulse from the Creator, than
to maintain a theory so contrary to fact, and which
militates against the whole history which M. Huber,
who adopts this theory from Bonnet, has so ably
given of these creatures." That their various employments may afford them agreeable sensations,

is a fact which need not be disputed: but that they act merely from the impulse of these sensations, without any plan previously concerted, seems to be contradictory both to reason and inference. That their proceedings are conducted upon a plan which does not result from mere sensation, is proved by the fact that they vary their proceedings according to circumstances. Their well-known irascibility leaves no room to doubt that they are susceptible of the passion of anger; and that they are liable to be acted on by fear and alarm is universally acknowledged: and, admitting them to be susceptible of anger and fear, it does seem unreasonable to infer that they are, at the same time, incapable of feeling affection. Farther, the precautions which they are known to adopt, to prevent and ward off any evils which seem to threaten them, also prove that they possess a certain degree of foresight. Without rivalling man either in intellect or feeling, they may be endowed with that measure of each which is necessary for their purposes.

After all, the moving principle which impels and regulates the proceedings of the social tribes of insects, is involved in a depth of mystery which, with all our boasted advantages, we in vain attempt to fathom: the motives which urge them to fulfil, in so remarkable, though diversified a way, their different destinies, baffle the researches of human sagacity. But however impenetrable may be the veil which conceals these mysteries from our sight, one thing is clear to demonstration,—that these creatures and their instincts loudly proclaim the power, wisdom, and goodness of the GREAT FATHER of the universe, and prove, beyond all cavil and doubt, the existence of a superintending Providence, which watches with incessant care over the welfare of the meanest of his creatures.

CHAPTER V.

THE HUMBLE BEE.

Builds her own Habitation—Curious Division of Labour—Remarkable for Good-nature and Affection for her Young—Ingenuity in overcoming Difficulties—The Carpenter-Bee—The Mason-Bee—The Upholsterer-Bee

THERE are other sorts of bees, whose history is less imposing perhaps, but not less curious, than that of the species which has been just detailed: some of these live in societies, but their limited number, and the rudeness of their dwellings, when compared with the populousness, the order, and architecture of the hive, make us feel that we are contemplating a village, after having seen a large metropolis. The contrast, however, is interesting; and a true philosopher, after he has marked the manners of a civilized kingdom, always finds his knowledge enlarged by the observation of the simpler habits of the rustic, or even the ruder customs of the savage. The *Humble Bee,* so well known to us, may be truly termed a villager. The community, which numbers from twenty to three hundred, consists of females of two sizes, the very largest, and the small ones; males which are stingless, and neuters. There is a jealousy between the small and large females, but it does not appear that it is of so deadly a nature as that which prevails among the hive bees. Indeed, Reaumur says, that the large ones live peaceably together in the same nest. Like true rustics they are all born to labour. Here there is no queen attended by a numerous guard, enjoying the privilege of doing nothing except laying eggs,—nor idle males, subsisting upon the fruits of the industry of others; but, whether male, female, or neuter, they all share alike the common labour.

It is very probable, that, alone and unattended, the female lays the foundation of the future little village, and that its inhabitants are all her own off-spring. The hive bee must have a ready-made ex-cavation for the reception of its comb—the humble bee raises its dwelling from the foundation. There is nothing imposing in its exterior: on the contrary, a tuft of moss, six or seven inches high, and buried seemingly in a clod, conceals all that is dear to these little creatures. A closer inspection shows, that the mossy filaments are carefully interlaced, and so nicely put together, that not a grain of dirt is inter-mingled with its texture. This light vault, although two or three inches thick, is scarcely capable of sheltering the young from the wind and rain; and to remedy this defect, its inner or concave surface is lined with a species of cement which effectually excludes the wet. If a nest be watched, one of its inhabitants will be soon seen to bury itself in a mossy hole, perhaps a foot from the nest itself. This is the entrance of a covered and secret way, leading to the inside of the habitation. Should the curiosity of the observer overcome his reluctance to destroy the patient labour of the humble bee, he will have an opportunity of observing the mode in which it works. The nest is always placed in the midst of the material from which it is to be constructed, and Reaumur never was able to detect any of its inhabitants bringing moss from a distance: rather than do so, the bee repairs the vault with material taken from the covered way, and even choosing to do without it altogether, rather than forage for moss. In some instances they seem to be led by instinct to vary their proceedings. Thus, Mr. P. Huber, having placed a nest of humble bees under a bell-shaped glass, stuffed the interval between its bottom and the irregular surface on which it rested with a linen cloth: the bees, finding themselves in a situation where no moss was to be obtained, tore this cloth thread by thread, carded it with their feet into a felted mass, and applied it to the same uses as moss, for which it proved an excellent substitute.   Some other humble bees tore the cover of a book with which he had closed the top of a box which contained them, and made use of the detached morsels in covering their nests.

They divide their labour in a curious manner.   A bee settles on a tuft of moss, its head being turned from the nest, and its tail towards it: with its teeth and its first two legs it divides and disentangles the filaments, and transfers them to the two middle legs; the second pair seize and push them to the third pair, and these thrust them as far behind the tail of the bee as they can reach, by which means the moss is advanced towards the place where it is proposed to build the nest, by a space which somewhat exceeds the whole length of the body of one bee; another bee, placed in a line with the first, receives the ball of material with its fore-legs, and like the first, transfers it the whole length of its body; and thus four or five of these insects, stationed in a row, spare time and labour in conveying the material for building, on the same principle that Irish labourers may be seen transferring their wheelbarrows from one to another.

The inside of the nest contains a comb or combs, which show no trace of the geometrical principles recognised in the workmanship of the hive bee. The upper surface of each comb is irregularly convex, its under concave, and it is composed of oval eminences placed against each other (*fig.* 1, *a*).   These

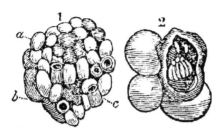

Fig. 1. *a.* Cocoon.
      b. The receptacles for eggs.
      c. Honey pots.

are not cells for the young, as in the comb of the
hive-bee, but cocoons spun by the larva before its
final metamorphosis. By the sides of these oval
bodies, and sometimes covering and concealing them,
are deposited ill-shaped masses (*fig.* 1, *b*), which
constitute the chief object of the labour of these rustics. These are the receptacles for the eggs of the
female, and contain not one egg only, but sometimes
as many as thirty eggs (*fig.* 2). They are filled
with a species of bee-bread, formed of the pollen of
flowers, moistened and prepared by the bee, so that
the young worm, when hatched, is surrounded with
a mass of matter which serves the double purpose of
food and raiment, nourishing and keeping it from external impressions. Besides these receptacles of
eggs, the nest contains also open cylindrical vessels,
which are filled with excellent honey, destined for
the common supply. The humble bee, by-the-way,
has a much finer instinct in discovering the nectar
of flowers than the hive bee; for in many flowers
the nectary is concealed from the hive bee ; the humble bee, however, finds it out, and taps it in the same
manner as a butler gets at the contents of a cask.
In this case, the hive bee, like the cunning inhabitant
of a city, allows the rustic to gather the treasure,
and then waylays and robs it of its load.

I.—H

Huber relates a curious story to illustrate the good-nature and generous disposition of the humble bee. In a time of scarcity, some hive bees, after pillaging the nest of the humble bee, took entire possession of it. one or two, however, of the latter still lingered about their old habitation, and went into the fields to collect honey, which they brought home; the hive bees surrounded, licked them, and presented to them their proboscis, never once showing the sting. By these means, Huber is of opinion, that the humble bee was fairly wheedled out of its stock of honey: these manœuvres lasted three weeks.

Their affection for their young is remarkable. When about to lay her eggs, the female is obliged to watch with the utmost care, and to drive off the workers, who greedily endeavour to devour them. Kirby thinks this instinct is bestowed upon the insect for the purpose of keeping the population within due bounds. For six or eight hours the cell containing her precious charge is anxiously watched by the mother; but, after this period, the desire to devour the egg ceases to animate the workers, and they now appear as assiduous in preserving, as they were before eager to destroy, the young. They know to the hour when the food is consumed by the grub, and introduce a fresh supply through a small hole made in the receptacle, which is then carefully closed. As the grubs increase in size, the cell which contained them becomes too small; and by their exertions to be more at ease its thin sides are split. The workers, which stand constantly by to watch when their services may be wanted, apply a patch of wax to fill up these breaches as fast as they are made. The cells are thus daily increased in size, in order to accommodate the growing grub. When the larva is about to change into the pupa, the workers cluster over the cocoon, and thus cherish the tender inhabitant with that heat which is necessary to its existence. Mr. P. Huber put a dozen humble bees under a glass case, and gave them a piece of comb composed of ten silken cocoons, so uneven that it had no foundation on which it could rest firmly. The bees were sorely disquieted, as they could not, on account of the unsteadiness of the comb, cluster on the young. Their affection suggested, however, an ingenious expedient. Several of them mounted upon the comb, and fixing their hindermost feet on its edge, and the foremost on the table, they succeeded in rendering the mass sufficiently steady to allow their comrades to cluster on the cocoons. For three days sets relieved each other; at the end of which time they had prepared wax enough to build pillars to fix the comb. By some accident these pillars were displaced, when the affectionate creatures resorted a second time to the same means, and assumed the same constrained posture. At last, compassionating their distress, Huber did that for them which they had been endeavouring so earnestly to do for themselves. It has been very naturally asked, " If, in this instance, these little animals were not guided by a process of reasoning ?" If this question be answered in the negative, it would be difficult to show the difference between reason and instinct: for it may be assumed as a certainty, that the circumstances under which our rustics were placed had never occurred to them during the course of their short existence, nor probably to ten of their species since the creation.

There are some species of bees which lead a solitary life, and seem to exercise a mechanical art. The first of these performs the labours of a carpenter, the next those of a mason, and the third may be termed the upholsterer. The wood-boring or *carpenter-bee* is almost as large as the humble bee, not so downy, but more deeply coloured. In spring it seeks out for some old post or withered part of a tree, to begin its habitation—sedulously shunning the sappy and green wood, which probably from its

toughness would not suit its purpose.   The position,
as well as the quality of the substance is also taken
into consideration; for it will not select a piece of
wood placed in a spot where the sun rarely shines.
As soon as a piece of dry rotten wood is found, our
workman begins to bore in an oblique direction (*fig.*
1), and after having gone to a certain depth, the di-

rection of the cavity is changed, and is now continued in the wood in an axis perpendicular to the
horizon.   This is a work which occupies our labourers not a few hours, but weeks.*   For days together
the carpenter-bee may be seen going in and out of
the hole, and shovelling out the sawdust, which has
resulted from its patient labour.   The cavity is from
twelve to fifteen inches in length, and often broad

* This, assuredly, is a great work for a bee, since it is not finished in
a day.   The insect is occupied about it for weeks, and even for months.
—Reaumur, vol. vi. p. 42.

enough to admit the forefinger of a man. A single
bee will make two or three of these holes in the
course of the season. After the length has been determined, the tube is divided into about twelve compartments, each of which is destined to receive an egg.
The bottom of the tube forms the base of the first
compartment. ·In this the bee piles up a quantity
of bee-bread till it reaches about an inch in height;
upon the surface of this one egg is laid, and over the
whole mass a roof is formed, which serves as a cover
to the bottom division, and a floor for the next above
it. Each of the partition planks is about the thickness of a crown-piece. It is to be observed, that,
in partitioning off the cells, the bee follows a system-
atic plan, and that a curious one. It begins by gluing the particles of sawdust round the outside of the
cavity, so as to make an annular projection. Inside
this ring she glues more, and thus she gradually
works from the circumference towards the centre;
at last, a covering of concentrical circles of sawdust
is formed (*fig.* 2).

Having completed her first cell, and deposited an
egg in it, she now proceeds to form another heap of
bee-bread on the annular horizontal partition, and,
depositing a second egg, she covers it with a similar
roof of glue and sawdust; a second cell being finished,
she continues her labours until the whole excavated
space has been filled up by a series of cells. The
insect not only knows the figure and capacity of each
of the cells necessary to accommodate her young,
but much more: she knows the exact quantity of
aliment which the grub will consume from the moment of its birth to the period of its maturity; and
deposites precisely that supply which it will want,
from its tenderest state to the time when it shall
come out as perfect as herself.

It will be recollected that the hive bee is furnished
with a species of basket to carry home the pollen
collected in the fields. The wood-boring bee, being

destitute of this apparatus, makes use of a different contrivance to convey provender to its nest. "I observed," says Reaumur, "several of these insects walking in the little forest of stamina which surrounds the flower of the poppy; by their bulk and weight they upset and pressed down all the filaments which crossed their path; during their progress, their hind legs became covered with the pollen or yellow dust which adhered to the downy hairs on their surface. After they had buried themselves successively in several flowers, each of the last pair of legs appeared as if enveloped in a footless boot." With this load the insect flew to the nest, brushed off the pollen adhering to its legs, which, mixed and tempered with a proper supply of honey, was then deposited in the cell.

Each of the circles visible in the piece of wood marks a pause in the labours of the architect; and the sum of their number bears testimony to that indefatigable industry which formed them, grain by grain, into a solid mass

The sawdust used for this purpose is a portion of that which the insect had thrown out while excavating the tube. When shovelled out by the bee, it falls on the ground, and forms a little heap near the plank or piece of dry wood in which the insect is at work. When the ingenious little carpenter wants materials to form the partitions between the different compartments in the tube, it issues forth, alights upon this heap of sawdust, selects a grain of this dust, and flies away with it to the interior of the cavity. This proceeding is regularly repeated until the whole work has been completed

From the order in which the eggs are placed, it follows, that the worms are of different ages in the different cells; consequently the lowest emerge the first. But how is it to get out? Does it wait till all those above it have escaped from their cells? A provision is made for this emergency. The larvæ, or grubs, are placed with their heads downwards, so that, as the first effort to walk is forwards, their progress is not towards the superior cells. The mother-bee makes a hole at the bottom of the tube communicating with the lowest cell, and through this opening the inhabitant comes out. When the food in the cell next above is consumed, its tenant gnaws away its under partition, and then, through the cell which has been just vacated, finds the way clear to the outlet made by the mother. Hence it appears, that all the young come out through this back door, which is provided for them by their anxious parent.

Natural history, abounding as it does in the most interesting facts, presents few things more striking than the industry of this insect. Consider its labour—boring out a tunnel fifteen or twenty times its own height; descending and then ascending to carry off the sawdust, and then, after having cleaned out the tube thoroughly, returning to this heap of sawdust, and collecting, grain by grain, a sufficient quantity to partition off the number of nurseries which its young may require.

Lumps of mortar may frequently be seen stuck against a garden-wall, exposed to the sun; whenever an attempt happens to be made to remove them, they will be found to resist the impression of the strongest knife. These have not been formed by a careless bricklayer, who may have left a dab of his material to disfigure the wall. Each lump is the work of care, and constitutes the habitation of the *mason-bee*. One of these lumps, when detached from the wall, will be found to contain eight or ten cavities, in each of which is deposited a larva with its supply of food. At first sight these cells might be imagined simply bored in the lump; and truly, in giving solidity to its workmanship, this bee may, indeed, be said to conceal the skill which it has exercised.

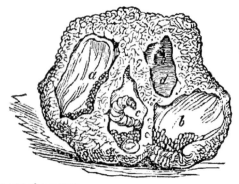

a A cell with the cocoon.
b Ditto.
c A cell in which the worm has not spun its cocoon; the excrements
   are seen in black dots.
d A cell from which the perfect insect has escaped.

As soon as the mason-bee has discovered, in some
old wall, a site suitable for its future habitation, it
sets about collecting the material requisite for its
construction. This material is a mortar chiefly composed of sand. The insect seems to be well aware
that all kinds of sand are not equally calculated to
produce good cement: the grains must neither be
too large nor too fine. The little creature, therefore, takes especial care to select, grain by grain,
what may suit its purpose; a few such grains only
being apparently contained in a heap of sand, the
whole of which a human plasterer would willingly
appropriate to the execution of his work. "I cannot understand," says Reaumur, "why the mason-
bee did not at once take the whole of its load from that
part of the gravel walk on which it had first settled.
Having collected a few grains on one spot, it flew
off and alighted on another: but, for my part, I
could not see that the gravel of one spot differed in
the slightest degree from that of the other; both
places abounding in large and small grains, inasmuch as the whole walk was covered with the same
kind of sand. Hence I infer that this insect pos-

sesses some sense which enables it to discover advantageous peculiarities of form which escape human observation." It felt each grain with its strong teeth: it did not, however, carry them off one by one; this would have occasioned a waste of time inconsistent with its usual habits of economy: it contrived to collect together a sufficient number of grains to form a heap of the size of a small shot, and cemented the mass together with a viscid liquor ejected upon it from the mouth. With the gravel and cement it mixed a little earth, which rendered the whole firmer and more tenacious. The little pellet of well-tempered mortar thus formed was instantly conveyed by the bee to the spot selected for the nest, where the foundation was formed by a circle of these little balls deposited in regular succession. On this circular foundation it proceeded to raise a round tower of very small dimensions. Every time that a fresh supply of mortar had been brought to the spot, the insect was seen to twist and twirl it about between its teeth and first pair of legs; it was then laid in the place destined to receive it, and moulded into the proper shape. As the tower or circular hollow increases in height, the insect is seen thrusting its head into the interior of the cell, for the purpose, no doubt, of ascertaining whether the material has been properly applied; as the inside comes in contact with the tender and unprotected skin of the cherished offspring, it is indispensable that it should be rendered perfectly even; and on this account it is smoothed with all the assiduity and skill of the provident and tender parent. The outside, being destined for no such purpose, is left in a rough state. Each cell is separately formed, and the whole, when completed, is enveloped in a common covering made of sand.

After a cell has reached a certain height, and before it has been quite finished, the mason-bee, like the carpenter-bee, goes in quest of honey and pollen, which it deposites as a support for its young. To facilitate the execution of this task, it is taught by instinct the exact quantity of food required to supply each grub with nourishment. It enters the cups of flowers, and daubs itself all over with pollen, and then flies to the nest, where the vegetable dust is brushed neatly off, and deposited in the store cell; on this it disgorges from its honey-bag a small portion of honey. These materials, well mixed and kneaded together, are formed into bee-bread; the requisite quantity of this substance having been prepared, and nicely packed, an egg is then laid in each cell, the top is carefully closed, and the labour of the mason-bee terminates. The scene of its industry, and the objects of all its care and tenderness, seem to be then all at once forgotten; the purposes of nature having been answered, and the perpetuation of the race having been provided for, the individual insect dies.

These insects have frequently been observed to appropriate the labours and usurp the rights of one another. While a mason-bee was on the wing in search of materials for finishing a cell, Du Hamel saw another enter and take possession of it without the slightest ceremony. It turned about in every direction, examined every part, and then began to proceed as if the whole had been raised by its own industry. When the real owner of the dwelling returned, the stranger would not budge a jot; in order to obtain possession of its own, the former insect laid down its load of mortar and offered battle; which was readily accepted by the trespasser. These combats, although curious and long, seldom prove mortal. The insect which gets soonest fatigued by the contest retires, leaving its victorious antagonist in possession of the cell which formed the subject of dispute.

The mason-bee, like other insects, is exposed to the attacks and depredations of various natural ene-

mies. Notwithstanding the strength of the habitation which had been formed for the young of the
mason-bee, some insects pierce, while others steal
into these stony towers, and, in the very recesses
of this mansion, devour the offspring of the industrious mason. But of all the enemies of this insect
the most destructive is the ant. When one of these
strolling marauders has discovered the hidden treasure of the mason-bee, information of the welcome
prize is speedily communicated to the whole tribe,
who repair in long files towards the spot which contains the booty. The poor bee makes every effort
to resist its antagonists; but, fatigued at last with
unavailing slaughter, and unable to drive off the advancing host, it gives up the contest in despair, and
abandons the produce of its labours to its hungry and
unrelenting foes.

The worms enclosed in their stony prison undergo
the usual metamorphosis, and bite their way through
the hard substance without the aid of the mother.

Du Hamel put one of these nests into a glass fun-
nel, and covered the orifice of the handle with gauze.
He saw three young bees pierce through three inches
of the nest, and yet they were unable to cut the gauze
which prevented their escape, and so they perished.
Such are creatures impelled by instinct, often tran-
scending rational beings in some things, as much as
they fall below them in others.

The ancients, not content to admire the actual qualities and instincts of the hive bee, imagined others,
to which it had no just pretension. Seeing bees flying
with little gravel-stones, the older naturalists thought
that they did so to prevent their being carried away
by the wind; but there can be little doubt that in
these instances, the mason-bee was mistaken for the
hive bee. There are other kinds of bees which build
their nests in the hollow of stones, or in other
ready-made cavities. Their manners may be passed
over.

The insect which Reaumur has denominated the
upholsterer-bee, is about the size of the hive bee; its
nest is composed of leaves, formed into a tube, sometimes eighteen inches long, in shape resembling a
toothpick-case, with its ends rounded: this it lays
sometimes horizontally, sometimes vertically, in a
hole in the ground. The boring of the hole is a
work of pure labour; but the construction of the
nest deposited in it manifests the most consummate
skill. The bee first of all hovers about a leaf, examines it well, and then settling, begins to clip off
a portion shaped to suit its purpose; the most dexterous milliner could not handle her scissors with
the quickness and precision with which this bee executes its task.

The shape of the cut pieces is either semi-ovoid
or circular; occasionally it makes a mistake in the
size, but this only happens in a number of instances,
just sufficient to remove the impression, that the

a The bee cutting
b The diameter of a large piece of leaf used for the sides of the cell
c The dimensions of a piece of leaf used in corking up the cells

insect is a mere machine. As it clips with its sharp
teeth, it folds the morsel under its belly, bestriding
and squeezing it between its six legs, so that at the
last bite it would fall to the ground with its load, if
it were not prepared for flight.

The pieces of leaf first used in lining the earthen
apartment are the largest. These large bits it rolls

into a tube, lining the whole length of the hole it has made, rounding off and closing one end of it by doubling the pieces one upon another.   This is the outermost coating, laid on to prevent the earth from falling in.   Within this is made the number of cells which the insect requires.   Three semi-ovoid pieces of leaf, rolled in such a manner that the edge of one piece overlaps a little the edge of the next, form the hollow of the cell, its height being less than an inch. The ends of these three pieces are then turned up to form the bottom.   The bee, however, is not contented with one layer only, but adds to the thickness of the lining of the cell by applying three additional pieces within it; and again within that three others, so that there are at least three cells put one into another, each made of three pieces of leaves, the bottom of which, being formed of the turning up of the extremities of all the morsels used, is ninefold.

One cell being thus completed, an egg is deposited within it, and the empty space around the egg is filled with food nearly liquid.   The cell being placed horizontally, and its contents not being very viscid, it is necessary to cork it up: this operation the bee executes by cutting several circular portions of leaf which precisely fit the mouth of the cell: they are as exactly measured as if a compass had been used in cutting them.

The second cell is placed on the first, the third on the second; the whole, when completed, very much resembles a set of thimbles put one upon another, and enclosed in a large toothpick-case (*fig.* 1, 2).

This is a very extraordinary result of instinct: how many trials would a human artificer require be-

I.—1

fore he should succeed in cutting a circular piece of
card to close up the mouth of a thimble so exactly,
that, if placed horizontally, no honey should escape!
—yet the bee accomplishes this in a few seconds,
and at a distance from the tube; acting as if it had
preserved the idea of its diameter in its head.   The
other pieces, entering into the composition of the
body of each cell, must also have their exact size;
the outermost must be the largest in every direction,
and have a determinate figure; while the inner ones
must be of a less size.

"If," says Reaumur, "these bees act mechanically,
they are very surprising machines; for they not only
cut out certain regular figures, but make them subservient to after-use.   Whether this be attained by
instinctive or intellectual means, the glory is due to
that Intelligence which made them and us."   In these
habitations, the young of the leaf-cutting bee remains
during the whole winter, and emerges a perfect insect
early in the ensuing spring.

The bee just described, though ingenious in the
furnishing of its humble dwelling, always ·chooses
the leaf of certain trees of a modest colour; for there
are various kinds of leaf-cutters, using various kinds
of leaves.   There is, however, another species which
may much more strictly be called the upholsterer
than the leaf-cutter; for it literally lines its dwelling,
which is a perpendicular hole in the ground, with
tapestry of the brightest flame-coloured scarlet

The nest of this little creature is usually to be
found by the side of the paths which traverse corn-
fields, and it begins to construct its habitation when
the wild poppy is young and fresh in flower, cutting
out bits from its thin and crimson leaf, to line a hole
which it has dug to the depth of three inches; the
last inch is wider than the first two; the bottom is
first overspread with the tapestry, and the cylindrical sides are next lined; the whole being composed
of several layers.   After this has been accomplished,

1 The cell before the egg is deposited within; it is lined the whole
   length with the leaf of the red poppy.
2. The red poppy lining depressed.

one egg is deposited in it, with a quantity of honey
and pollen, or bee-bread, piled up an inch high; the
lining of the two upper inches of the hole is then
thrust down, and pressed on the mass, so as to form
a sort of cork; and, to complete the work, the bee
shovels in the earth which had been dug out, so
neatly, that Reaumur was puzzled to make out what
had become of the nest he had seen only a short time
before.   It would appear that all this labour is required to form one cell and to receive one egg;
doubtlessly there are others, but the same vicinity is
not chosen by the same insect for the rest of its offspring; the nature of the ground, probably, decides
the location, for it must be dry, otherwise the crimson leaves and the honey become putrid, and the little inhabitant, instead of a cradle, finds a tomb.

CHAPTER VI.

THE COMMON WASP.

The Nest—Construction and Materials—Form of the Combs—Affection for its Young—Manner of feeding them—Solitary Wasps—Hornets.

AFTER considering the peaceful community of bees, few perhaps will be tempted to observe the manners and habits of wasps. The one may be looked upon as a highly-civilized and humane tribe, resorting to arms in self-defence alone, and seldom gaining their bread by violent means—the other as a ferocious tribe, subsisting solely by rapine and murder, fearlessly attacking most other insects, and giving no quarter to the bee or the fly. The habits of the common wasp will serve as an example of the rest of this species which live in society.

The vespiary, or wasp's nest, contains three classes of wasps; females, neuters armed with stings, and males destitute of this weapon. They are all workers. Different kinds of wasps choose different places to construct their nests; some exposing them to all the inclemencies of the weather, others sheltering them in a hollow of a tree, or a hole carefully dug in the ground. The latter is the case with the common wasp. A kind of covered and tortuous gallery leads to the subterranean city; in this there are large spaces, which may be likened to our public places, streets, and houses, all symmetrically arranged, and though not evincing the exquisite economy of the bee, yet deserving much commendation: the city itself is surrounded by a wall, composed of a substance which in texture very closely resembles the paper in ordinary use; this

frail material is, however, so artfully arranged and
compacted, as effectually to exclude the rain.

The mode in which this envelope is fabricated deserves attention: when the wasps wish to thicken it,
they build another layer upon the one already formed;
each of these layers is about as thick as a sheet of
ordinary paper; several wasps are simultaneously
employed in extending or thickening the layer, and
this is done without confusion and with great celerity.   Having procured from abroad the material
required for their work, they moisten it, convert it
into a paste, and roll it into a ball; this ball is then
taken to the part of the edifice which stands in need
of repairing; the insect then lays it down, and
running backwards, extends the ball into a thread;
this thread it then unites to the rest, by repassing
over it and consolidating it with great care.   The
exterior figure of the vespiary is not unlike a large
Indian-rubber bottle; the surface, however, instead
of being polished and smooth, seems as if composed
of oyster-shells tacked to one another.   It is not
uniform in colour, owing to the variety of vegetable
fibre used in fabricating the substance of which it is
formed; and when finished is about two inches thick.
There are generally two holes, each large enough
to admit only one wasp at a time; these are the
gates of the city, and, according to Reaumur, one
of them serves for ingress, the other for egress;
such is the order observed, that the uses of the respective doors are rarely if ever changed.

If a section of the nest be made, the first thing to
be observed is, that the envelope or wall is not solid,
but formed of layers of paper, between which there
is a considerable interval.   By this means, not only
economy of materials is consulted, but the rain cannot penetrate so easily as if the whole were solid.

The combs are parallel to each other, and to the
horizon; they are composed of the paper-like material already described; the cells are hexagonal;

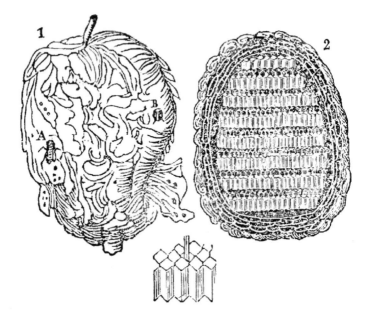

1 The exterior of the vespiary.
2 Interior of the same.
3 The position of a pillar.

but differ in this respect from those of the bee, that one comb contains only one set of cells, whereas, it will be remembered, the bee contrives to have a double row in each comb.   The cells contain neither honey·nor wax, but are solely constructed to lodge the young; the combs are of unequal dimensions, regulated by the diameters of the various parts of the globular envelope, the uppermost not being perhaps more than two inches, while that which is placed in the middle measures twelve inches in diameter.   It is calculated that, on an average, a vespiary may contain about sixteen thousand cells, which, as they are filled thrice in each year, will give some idea of the prodigious fertility of these creatures.

There is an interval of half an inch between each comb. Although the combs are fixed to the side of the nest, they would not be sufficiently strong without farther support; the ingenious builders, therefore, connect each comb to that below it, by a number of strong cylindrical columns or pillars, having, according to the rules of architecture, their base and capital wider than the shaft, and composed of the same paper-like material used in other parts of the nest, but of a more compact substance. A rustic colonnade, consisting of no less than forty or fifty such columns, connects the middle combs; for the upper and lower combs being of less dimensions and weight, a smaller number suffices. In order to get at these combs, the wasps take care to leave a void space between them and the extreme envelope.

Cruel and ferocious as these insects may appear, still their affection for their habitation and young is very striking. Whatever injury may be done to the nest, if it should be even broken to pieces, they will linger about the cherished spot, or quit it only to follow the combs wherever they may be transferred. "Those," says Reaumur, "which were absent when I removed the nest, finding, on their return, neither companions nor home, knew not where to go, and for days together hovered around the hole before they determined to abandon the spot." The material from which the nest is constructed is vegetable fibre. The wasp will not use sawdust; but, knowing that a filamentous material, like linen rags, is necessary for the fabrication of its paper, it amasses pieces of some substance possessing this quality. As the first step in the process of paper-making is to soak the vegetable fibre in water, so the wasp takes special care to select the filaments which it intends to use from wet wood which has rotted in the rain. These are worked up with a glutinous secretion, and thus the material is prepared. When the wasp can get its paper ready-made, it makes no scruple to appropriate it. Reaumur, being once disturbed by a noise in his study, found that it arose from the gnawing of a piece of paper which these insects had attacked. A few only of the community are architects; the rest having other appropriate employments. The females, for there are as many as three hundred, unlike the queen-bee, do not pass their lives in receiving the homage of their subjects, but perform every species of labour. The neuters, however, as among bees, are the true workers. They build the nest, and forage for food for the males, females, and the young. The worms are not locked up in a cell surrounded with food, but require to be fed, like the young of birds. " I saw," says Reaumur, " a female wasp, which had entered the vespiary with the belly of an insect; this she contrived by degrees to swallow, after which she ran to various cells, and, disgorging that which she had eaten, distributed it among the brood of worms." Hence it appears, that it not only procured the food, but prepared it by a partial digestion. The wasp is particularly fond of the belly of the bee; it is a choice bit which it eagerly seeks. It will watch for hours at the door of a bee-hive, pounce upon some unfortunate bee which is about to enter, and tumbling it to the ground, in a trice separate, with its two serrated teeth, the tender abdomen, containing the soft intestines and the honey-bag, from the dry and hard chest of the insect. having secured its prey, it hurries away to its habitation. The large blue-bottle fly is another delicate morsel greatly coveted by the wasp; and so well aware are some butchers of the service done by the wasps in preventing the fly from blowing their meat, that they bribe them to their stalls with pieces of liver. As soon as its appetite is satisfied, either by flesh or fruit, the worker carries to the nest a portion of its prey. When the insect enters the common dwelling, those whose labours kept

them at home surround it, and take their share
without dispute or combat. Those which feed on
fruit seem to return empty-handed, as they do not
carry off solid substances. However, Reaumur observed that even these had not forgotten the necessities of their comrades. Having entered the nest,
they disgorged a clear drop, which was sucked with
avidity by one or two hungry workers; when this
was consumed, a second, and even a third supply
was furnished. They seem to vary the quality of
the food according to the age of the larvæ. Reaumur mentions a young Comte de Chatelu, who en-
deavoured to bring up some young wasps by hand,
feeding them with honey; but a great mortality
took place among them, from the want of knowledge
as to the quantity and quality of the food fit for
them. As soon as the young become large, they
prepare for their metamorphosis, and they themselves like the larva of the hive bee, clothe the cell
with a silky covering. About three weeks elapse
between the laying of the egg and the evolution of
the perfect insect. As soon as the cell is vacated,
the males, who are the scavengers of the community, cleanse and prepare the habitation for a new
tenant.

All this mass of building, the columns, and the
walls, though the labour of several months, lasts
but one year: thronged as it is in summer, its thousands quickly perish; a few only linger there in a
torpid state during the winter. Those which survive the cold are females, destined to continue the
species. These are born in the autumn, at the same
time as the males, and, becoming impregnated, lay
in spring. Each founds a new republic. Alone,
unattended by a single guard or friend, the female
wasp builds a few solitary cells, and lays in them
the eggs of neuters. These are necessary to carry
on the labour of the nest, and commence their toils
within a few hours after their last metamorphosis.

If the queen-bee be compared with the mother-wasp, the latter will gain by the contrast. "If glory be known to insects," says Reaumur,—"if solid glory be measured among them, as among us, by the difficulties surmounted, the female wasp is a heroine to whom the queen-bee is in no way comparable. When the latter leaves her hive to seek a new sovereignty, she is accompanied by many thousand workers, industrious, laborious, and ready to execute all that is necessary for the welfare of the new establishment; while the female wasp, alone and single-handed, lays the foundations of her new republic. It is she who has to seek or make a hole, when she cannot find one ready-made to her purpose, to build in it cells to receive the eggs, and to nourish the young after they have been evolved."

It might perhaps be thought natural that several females, born in the same hive, should assist each other in laying the foundations of the new city. But for some unknown reasons this consorting of females is alien to the genius of these insects; and in the present case nothing would be gained by it. Each female is under the necessity of providing for her own eggs ; hence she could not help her neighbour. The neuters all perish when the first cold weather sets in ; nay, all the young, which have not arrived at maturity, are, on the approach of winter, dragged from their cells and massacred, to prevent perhaps a more cruel and protracted death by famine or frost.

The ferocity of the wasp is otherwise rarely exercised on its own kind; the nest never presents those terrible combats and massacres which take place in the hive. Occasionally the neuters fight with each other; or a neuter sometimes fights with a male ; but, according to Reaumur, the result is rarely fatal.—Even towards man, this tribe of insects is peaceably disposed. The celebrated naturalist just mentioned states, that they will not attack those who are content to observe them simply; and he adds, that he has seen ladies who had become familiar enough with them to allow them to settle on their hands.

The hornet is the largest of the wasp tribe, and were its motions at all equal to its strength, ferocity, and the venom of its poison, it would be a tiger among insects. It is a most unmerciful enemy of the hive bee, whose carcass forms the food of its young; and its sting is very dangerous even to the human race. Reaumur states, that " Don Allan Chartreux, having imprudently disturbed a hornets' nest was stung by one, which caused so much pain as to almost make him faint. He reached his convent with difficulty, and remained for three days in a state of fever."

The manners, habitation, &c. of these and the other social wasps are essentially the same. They all build their nests from a sort of paper more or less fine, and in all several females live peaceably together.

The *Vespa Nidulans* of Fabricius, a foreign species of wasp, appends its nest to a branch (*fig.* 1). It first forms a thick pasteboard case, which completely withstands the seasons, and within this it places layers of combs partitioned off with surprising regularity. The access to the cells is by means of a hollow and round passage, which runs along the centre of the whole nest.

To make cells is the same thing as to make a comb, with the hornet and the wasp; not so with this species. the mere juxtaposition of cells does not constitute a comb. After making the outside covering, they partition it off into shelves, and to these it is that the cells are appended (*fig.* 2).

The *Vespa Gallica* of Linnæus attaches its nest to a stubble, or a small branch in a bush; the form is elegant, being composed of one or two cakes, and twenty or thirty cells; it is placed vertically, and

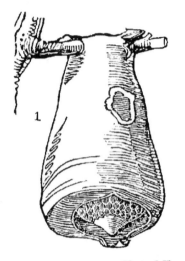
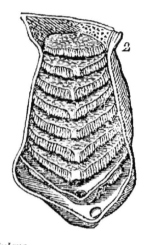

Nest of *Vespa Nidulans.*

Fig. 1 gives a miniature representation of one of these curious re
ceptacles : the bottom has been torn off, so as to show one of the cakes.

Fig. 2 shows the internal arrangement of the combs, as well as the
centrical orifice perforating all of them, serving as a door of admission
to the little wasp.

the whole bears a considerable resemblance to the
centre of the sunflower. The vertical position appears to be the best adapted to guard against rain;
but as an additional security, the little architect
carefully covers its paper habitation with a varnish
insoluble in water; and thus protected, it can dispense with the precaution of concealing its nest,

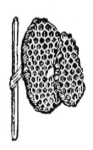

like the other species of wasps. It may be remarked that the cells of all the wasps we have described are not perfectly hexagonal, being wider at their orifice than at their base.

If the wasps which live in society may dispute with the hive bee in genius, address, in the patient endurance of labour, and in tenderness to rear their young, those which lead a solitary life yield in nothing deserving of admiration to bees of analogous habits.

The solitary wasps, like the social ones, feed on fruits or flesh, and are for the most part what may be emphatically termed insects of prey.

There is a little creature called *Vespa muraria* by Linnæus, which builds a curious nest for its young, and supplies them in a very singular manner with living food; it is about the size of a common worker-wasp.

Towards the end of May, and during the whole of the month of June, it is busily employed in building cells. Its whole object is to form a circular hole a few inches deep, and in diameter not much exceeding that of its own body. In this cavity only a single egg is deposited; several of these cells are of course necessary for the purposes of the same female.

The spot chosen by this mason-wasp is usually a wall or some sandy place; sometimes, however, the cell is dug in the earth.

On a particular occasion, Reaumur had constructed a set of boxes, which he had filled with sand for the purpose of observing at leisure the manners of the *formica leo*, or ant-lion; in one of these the sand had become quite hard, so that, although he made every possible allowance for the excellent teeth of the little wasp, yet he thought that to gnaw into that which was as hard as a common stone, was an undertaking which exceeded its power. He observed, however, that the little crea-

I.—K

ture did not trust to its teeth alone; but first voided a liquid drop on the spot, and by this means softened the material which it wanted for use. Then having recourse to its teeth, it detached a morsel from the mass, and taking it up in its two fore-legs, kneaded it into a mortar. With such materials, and so gathered, the insect commences its operations.

In the following figure several tubes are seen jutting out of the mass; although formed with great care and art, and evidently manifesting design, they are not made to last; they are no more than temporary elevations raised over the excavation in the wall or sand, and are destined to be destroyed as soon as the latter is completed.

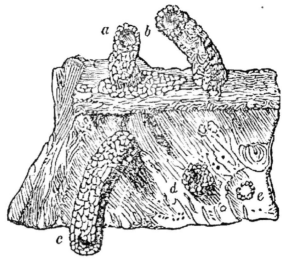

a, b, c, d, e, exhibit the formation of the tubes in various stages.

The little pieces of moistened sand and earth first gathered, are placed in a circle, which serves to mark out the dimensions of the hole. As the insect continues to dig, it adds to the length of the tube, and when it has completed the excavation, it has also completed its tube. The egg is then laid, and the hole carefully filled up and covered with the very sand with which the projecting tube had been made; the worker is sometimes compelled to leave its work, for the little stock of fluid with which the sand was moistened becomes frequently exhausted, and both Reaumur and Latreille conjecture that it fetches a fresh supply from a neighbouring rivulet, or perhaps sucks a gluing juice from some plant or tree.

"I have remarked," says the former naturalist, "that in about an hour a wasp excavated a hole as long as its body, and raised above it a cylinder of equal length: it does not appear that there is a determinate depth for every hole, nor are the tubes either of the same length; some are carried on to the length of two inches, and some fall short of one."

The wasp, no doubt, has a reason for all this: the very fact of the diversity proves a choice; but what are the reasons which impel it to take the trouble of building a hollow tube out of the material excavated? why not throw away the rubbish?

The following are Reaumur's conjectures :—

"In following this wasp while at work, we can discover at least one of the uses to which the tube is subservient: the materials of the tube are to the mason-wasp what the heap of mortar is to the brick-layer; the whole depth of the hole is not necessary to lodge one egg, a portion of it being sufficient for that purpose. It is proper, however, that the depth should be considerable, lest the rays of the sun should impart too much heat to an egg placed too near the surface. The wasp knows how much of it ought to be left unfilled, the rest is closed with the same sand which had been abstracted in digging it; and it is in order to have this, as it were, at hand, that the insect takes the pains of forming the tube.

"But it may be asked, why take the trouble of

making a tube? why not simply heap up the sand
dug out? When you see the work, you perceive
that it has scarcely more trouble in fixing the little
heap of mortar to the tube, than would be encoun-
tered in casting it out; and it is more easy to
arrange the little mass in the cylindrical form, than
to construct a pyramid on a vertical wall, where for
the most part these tubes are found.

"This tube has perhaps other uses. While the
wasp is absent, some ichneumon fly might come
and deposite in its nest an egg enclosing an insect
fatal to its young. The ichneumon will not so
readily enter a hole, when, to approach it, it is necessary to make a long journey, and pass a tube which
prevents it from seeing if the wasp be absent. I
have observed one, which, after much hesitation,
turned and re-turned around the mouth of the tube,
and at last ventured in; I also saw that this was
very *mal à propos*, for the wasp happening to be at
home, presented itself before the ichneumon, who
had believed it out of the way, so that there was
nothing left for the latter but to take speedily to
flight."

If the hole be opened after the wasp has closed it,
it will be found filled with a number of caterpillars,
neatly rolled and packed together, but these, though
alive, have not the power of motion. Thus, from
the moment it is evolved from the egg, the little
carnivorous offspring of the wasp can attack its
prey, and eat into them without any danger or dis-
turbance from creatures, which, in comparison to
itself, are giants in size.

Being lodged at the bottom of the cell, with a
dozen worms packed up over its head, the larva of
the wasp begins to attack the one immediately
above; it sucks with such avidity, that Reaumur
experienced some difficulty in withdrawing it from
the caterpillar. Indeed, all that the voracious worm
has to do, until the period of its metamorphosis, is

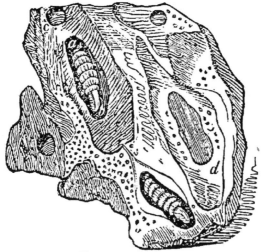

a The green caterpillar.
b The grub feeding on one.
c The orifice leading to a cell.
d A vacated cell.

to eat.   Reaumur took the trouble of ascertaining
the quantity consumed, and found that, taking one
day with another, one caterpillar a day was not too
much.

Here we meet with another instance of that singular faculty, by which the mother wasp is enabled
to apportion the exact quantity of food to the wants
of her offspring.   To some she gives twelve caterpillars, to others a less number, but in this case
they are of a larger size.   Moreover, the food is
always of the same kind; for during the twelve
years in which Reaumur observed their manners, he
invariably found the same species of caterpillar enclosed by these insects.

The caterpillars are entombed alive; but the poison of the sting appears to render them insensible;
at least this is the conjecture: some, therefore, must
remain without food for a fortnight, the period

which the larva of the wasp takes to prepare for its
metamorphosis. How is it that they do not perish?
It is a circumstance well worth remarking, that
these caterpillars are all of the same size, and
all therefore of the same age. It is not to save herself the trouble of multiplying her journeys that the
mother wasp chooses them of a large size, for it is
evident that a greater degree of trouble is required
to select, than to take at hazard worms of any size.
Reaumur conjectures that the wasp is guided by her
instincts to choose only those caterpillars which
have attained their full growth, and are capable, in
consequence, of sustaining a longer fast. Had they
been placed in the nest at a younger age, when their
appetite called for a plentiful supply of food, it is
evident they must have perished; and thus the mother-wasp would have enclosed the cherished worm
in an offensive sewer instead of a cradle furnished
with an ample store of appropriate food.

The mode, too, in which the caterpillars are deposited is worthy of observation. Had they been
huddled together, the worm, instead of finishing the
one immediately above, before it attacked the rest,
might have nibbled and killed the whole batch, without consuming any one entirely, and thus have destroyed the caterpillars, and consequently brought
on the putrefaction of the food, and so have been
doomed to live on carcasses or perish among them.
The entrance to the nest is just wide enough to admit the mother-wasp· when she carries in a caterpillar, she first unrolls it, and holds it in a line under
her own belly, and then depositing it at the bottom
of the cell, the creature of itself rolls into a ring,
the wasp merely taking care to press it down.
Reaumur found that the larva spins a cocoon, and
remains in it ten or eleven months; it then eats its
way through the nest, and comes forth a perfect
insect.

There are various species of American wasps

which feed their young with spiders, cock-roaches, flies, and other perfect insects. An observer, who had carefully studied their habits, says, that their mode of working is much alike, and it is very diverting to see them at it· their art and contrivance are wonderful, and appears as if they were given them to cheer them at their labour. They make a very particular musical noise, the sound of which may be heard at ten yards' distance. Their manner of working is, to moisten clay and temper it up into a little lump of the size of swan-shot. This they carry to build with. They begin first at the upper end of the cell and work downwards till it is long enough to contain the nymph or chrysalis: after they have spread out, their little lump in a proper manner to form their little fabric, they set up their musical notes, and return to temper and work up more clay for the next course. Thus they continue alternately singing and working until a cell is finished, which is made delicately smooth withinside. then, at the farther end of each cell they lay an egg: after this, by a surprising instinct, they go and catch spiders and cram the cell full of them; but it is farther wonderful to observe, that they only in some manner disable the spiders, but do not kill them, which is to answer this purpose, that they are preserved alive till the egg is hatched. The spider is the food of the embryo; having stored up a sufficiency of this provender, the insect closes the cell and proceeds to build the next in the same manner. The maggot, having eaten up all its provisions before October, prepares for its change. It lies all the winter in its chrysalis state, and in the spring eats its way out of its clay dwelling.

Cassigni furnished Reaumur with an interesting account of the mode in which another of these wasps attacks and kills the cock-roach, so injurious to the housewives of tropical countries. The wasp is seen walking or flying about in various directions, evidently on the look-out for game; as soon as it discovers a cock-roach, it remains fixed for a few seconds, during which the two insects appear to eye each other. The wasp, then pouncing on its prey, seizes it by the muzzle; it then insinuates its body under that of the cock-roach, and inflicts a wound. As soon as the wasp feels sure that the fatal poison has been introduced into the body of its enemy, the insect appears to be aware of its effect, and takes a turn or two to give it time to work. Having thus departed for a few instants, it returns, and is sure to find the cock-roach motionless on the spot where it had been left. Naturally timid, the cock-roach appears to be at this juncture totally incapable of resistance, and suffers its enemy to seize its head and drag it backwards towards a little hole situate in the next wall. Sometimes the way is long, and then the wasp stops and takes a turn or two to breathe and recruit its strength ere it proceeds to finish its task. Sometimes it lays down the unresisting cock-roach and makes its way alone to the nest, probably to reconnoitre whether any obstacles impede the way: returning in a few moments, it again lays hold of its prey. M. Cassigni, having, during the absence of the wasp, removed the cock-roach to a little distance, was highly amused with the restless embarrassment of this creature, when the prey seemed to have been thus snatched from its gripe. But the cock-roach having been ultimately dragged to the den of the insect, the hardest part of its task was yet to be accomplished; for the aperture by which the wasp could enter was by no means roomy enough to admit the larger frame of the cock-roach: the insect, however, went in, and applied its utmost force to drag its prey in after. But these efforts were too often quite unsuccessful. The remedy adopted in this dilemma would not have disgraced a reasonable creature. It quietly lopped off the wings and legs of the cock-roach, and thus diminished the bulk of the animal, without depriving the young worm of any part of the food destined for its support. Those solitary wasps effect every thing by main force; they seldom or never resort to stratagem, but boldly, and with the most impetuous courage, pounce at once upon their prey. Sometimes they light upon certain species of spiders which fabricate no web, but hunt about fields in pursuit of game. In the hope of catching some unwary fly, the treacherous spider counterfeits death; when the wasp darts on it with a blow, and rising into the air, amputates all the limbs of its victim.

There is one species of these insects which carry on an exterminating warfare against the honey and the solitary bees. As soon as one of these bee-devouring wasps has prepared in the sand a little hole destined to become a habitation for its own young, and a grave for the bee, it makes towards those flowers to which its prey resort; the moment one of these little creatures has been perceived by the wasp, it darts on its victim with the rapidity of lightning, and with one blow of its sting puts an end to its industrious and useful career.

As each female, says Latreille, lays five or six eggs, it follows that she destroys as many bees. In a space one hundred and twenty feet long, he counted fifty or sixty females preparing their nests; consequently they would kill three hundred bees. Now supposing a surface of ground of two square leagues infested in fifty places by a small number of these apivorous females, they would destroy within this range fifteen thousand bees.

Reaumur says, that in the woods and plains of the Isle of France no hive-bees are to be found—while they abound and yield much honey in the Isle of Bourbon; and the absence of this useful insect is perhaps justly attributed to the great number of wasps which infest the former island.

CHAPTER VII.

ANTS.

*Their Industry—Affection for their Young—Courage—Their Anger—
Unite in Myriads for War and Extermination—The Fallow Ants—
The Sanguine Ants—The Legionary Ants—Attack other Ants, and
reduce them to Slavery.*

THE history of the insects now to be described
presents examples of an industry which has become
proverbial, and traits of affection and feeling which
would do honour to our own species. Love and
courage, patience and perseverance, almost all the
higher virtues of human nature, when arrived at
the highest pitch of earthly perfection, seem to be
the ordinary springs of action in the ant.

Of ants, as of other social insects, the largest
portion of the community consists of neuters; beings possessing the most exquisite sentiments of
maternity unalloyed by passion; so that from their
birth to their death they live, think, and act only for
the offspring of another.

The instincts of this insect are, indisputably,
more extraordinary than those of any other in the
whole range of animated nature. The ancients
magnified them into fabulous miracles. Pliny talks
of an Indian ant as big as an Egyptian wolf, of the
colour of a cat, which entered the bowels of the
earth in search of gold, of which they are said to
have been plundered during the winter by the human
inhabitants of those regions.

But exaggeration and credulity apart, the real
habits and proceedings of these insects are so extraordinary, that they would stagger our belief, if
not confirmed by such observers as Huber and Latreille.

Their nests contain three kinds of individuals—

males; females, which have wings; and neuters,
which are destitute of these appendages.

" In the warm days which occur from the end of
July to the beginning of September, and sometimes
later, the habitations of the various species of ants
may be seen swarming with winged insects; these
are the males and females, preparing to quit for ever
the scene of their nativity and education. Every
thing is in motion; and the silver wings, contrasted
with the jet bodies which compose the animated
mass, add a degree of splendour to the interesting
scene. The bustle increases, till at length the males
rise, as it were, by general impulse into the air, and
the females accompany them· the whole swarm alternately rises and falls with a slow movement, to
the height of about ten feet; the males flying obliquely with a rapid zigzag motion, and the females,
though following the general movement of the
column, appearing suspended in the air, like balloons; and having their heads turned towards the
wind."

Sometimes the swarm of a whole district unite
their infinite myriads, and seen at a distance, says
M. Gliditsch,* produce an effect very much resembling an aurora borealis, when from the border of
the cloud appear several columns of flame and va-
pour, attended with a variety of luminous rays and

---

* A species of ant, called by Linnæus the *formica sacchivora*, appeared in such torrents in the island of Granada, and destroyed the
sugar-canes so completely by undermining their roots, that a reward of
£20,000 was offered to any one who should discover an effectual mode
of destroying them.

They descended from the hills in a flood, and filled not only the plan-
tation, but the roads for miles   Domestic quadrupeds perished, and
rats, mice, and reptiles, were devoured by them, and even birds were
so harassed when they alighted as quickly to die. Nothing opposed
their march they blindly rushed into the streams and were drowned
in such countless myriads, that the aggregation of their tiny carcasses
dammed up the waters, and formed a bridge for others to pass over.
The large fires lighted in their paths were speedily extinguished by the
rush of their masses, and had not Providence swept them away in the
torrents of a terrible hurricane in 1780, every thing must have fallen
before them —*Introduction to Entomology,* vol. i. p. 185

lines, resembling forked lightning confined in its brilliancy. The noise emitted by the countless myriads of these creatures is not so loud as the hum of a single wasp, and the slightest breath scatters them abroad. In the midst of these numberless males the females become fecundated, and the greater portion of the former sex immediately perishing, become the food of birds or of fish. So numerous are they, that Dr. Bromley says they formed a column on the water where they had fallen, five or six miles long, eight or ten feet broad, and six inches deep.

The females which escape are destined to found new colonies, and at first to do all the work of neuters ; in this particular resembling the mother wasp : but prior to their constructing a new habitation, they make themselves voluntary prisoners, by throwing off their wings. So extraordinary a dismemberment requires to be supported by the testimony of an eye-witness.

Accordingly, Huber, who made the experiment, states, "that having induced an ant to mount a straw, he placed it on a table sprinkled with a little earth, and covered it with a glass bell ; scarcely did she perceive the earth which covered the bottom of her abode, when she extended her wings, with some effort bringing them before her head, crossing them in every direction, throwing them from side to side, and producing so many singular contortions, that her four wings fell off at the same moment, in his presence. After this change, she reposed, brushed her corslet, traversed the ground, evidently seeking a place of shelter ; she partook of the honey he gave her, and at last found a hiding-place under some loose earth."

Huber might well be astonished at the coolness with which the female ant appeared to throw off her wings : one would have thought that as much proportionate suffering would have been felt in her tiny frame from the loss of these members, as in ours from the amputation of all our limbs; but insects in general do not appear to be sensible of much pain. A wasp will walk about and even eat after its body has been cut into two, and a dragon fly will voraciously devour its prey after the removal of its abdomen.

Having cast off her wings, the fecundated female begins to prepare a habitation for herself. In some cases, however, the workers do not allow all the females to quit the old nest; but detaining some of those which have been impregnated, clip their wings and keep them close prisoners so long, that at last they become reconciled to their fate, and prepare to lay eggs. As if still afraid that the impregnated female should depart, a single ant is appointed to watch her motions and supply her wants; no Argus appears to be more vigilant· it mounts on her abdomen, resting its two posterior legs on the ground: these sentinels are constantly relieved. As soon as an egg is deposited, the female becomes the object of the tender care of the neuters, and as a mother she receives those attentions which she would in vain have solicited as a virgin. A court, composed of from ten to fifteen individuals, says Huber, continually follows her; she is unceasingly the object of their care and caresses; all are eager to collect around her, offer her nourishment, and assist her with their mandibles in making her way through difficult and ascending passages; they also lead her through all the different quarters of the ant-hill. The eggs taken up by the labourers at the instant of their being laid, are collected around her. When she seeks repose, a group of ants environ her; several females live in the same nest, and show no rivalry; each has her court, they pass each other uninjured, and sustain in common the population of the ant-hill; but they possess no power, which it would seem is lodged exclusively with the neuters.

I.—L

" In whatever apartment," says Gould, " a queen
condescends to be present, she commands obedience
and respect; a universal gladness spreads itself
throughout the whole cell, which is expressed by
particular acts of joy and exultation. They have a
peculiar way of skipping and leaping, and standing
upon their hind-legs, and prancing with the others.
These frolics they make use of, both to congratulate
each other when they meet, and to show their regard
for their queen; some of them gently walk over
her, others dance around her, and she is generally
encircled with a cluster of attendants."

Their affection is extended, it would appear from
Huber, even beyond life; for when a pregnant female dies, five or six labourers rest near her, and for
some days lick and brush her constantly, either with
a hope to revive that little particle of cherished dust,
or as a tribute of their instinctive love for the departed.

If we observe the ant-hill, we shall see so many
traits of this affection of the worker towards the
female, as to satisfy us that the imprisonment and
mutilation she had undergone at the hands of the
former are dictated alone by that instinct which
prompts the ant to continue its kind. The republic
of ants is not annually dissolved like that of bees
and wasps.

Attachment to the female is not the only instance
of affection evinced by these insects; they, as well
bees, appear to recognise each other even after a long
absence. Huber, having taken an ant-hill from the
woods, placed it in his glass hive; finding that he
had a superabundance of ants, he allowed some of
them to escape, and these formed a nest in his garden. Those which were in the hive he carried into
his study, and observed their habits for four months,
after which period he placed the hive in the garden
within fifteen paces of the natural nest. Immediately, the ants established in it recognised their for-

mer companions, with whom they had held no communication for four months; they caressed them
with their antennæ, and taking them up in their
mandibles, led them to their own nest. Presently
others arrived in crowds and carried off the fugitives
in a similar manner ; and venturing into the artificial
ant-hill, in a few days caused such a desertion that
it was wholly depopulated.

The above anecdote seems to prove that ants have
a language of dumb signs, of which the organs are
the antennæ. As yet, the proofs of this antennal
language have been drawn from the affections of
these creatures, but more striking ones are derived
from their passions. For there are few animals
in which the passions assume a more deep and
threatening aspect; they unite them in myriads for
the purposes of war and extermination.

It would perhaps be too much to say, that the warfare which takes place among ants calls forth bright
traits of character, and occasions the exercise of
virtues, which under no other combination of circumstances could be exhibited. Yet Latreille, after
he had cut off the antennæ of an ant, saw another
approach it as if compassionating the loss of a
member as dear to the owner as the pupil of our eye
to us, and after caressing the sufferer, pour into the
wound a drop of a liquid from its own mouth.

The causes which give rise to these wars are, no
doubt, as important to them as those which urge
human monarchs to devastate, and human heroes to
struggle for victory. The ants will dispute furiously
about a few square feet of dust ; and such an object
is of equal magnitude and importance to them, as a
river, or a mountain, to an emperor. Sometimes a
straw, the carcass of a worm, a single grain of
wheat, will cause myriads to engage in deadly strife,
and leave the miserable inches of surrounding earth
thickly strewed with the pigmy dead. Sometimes
a nobler aim will cause them to defend to the utter-

most their homes and their young, from the marauding ambition of a neighbouring hill. "Alas!" says Bacon, "the earth with men upon it will not seem much other than an ant-hill, where some ants carry corn, and some carry their young, and some go empty, and all to and fro around a little heap of dust."

"If we wish to behold," says P. Huber, "regular armies wage war in all its forms, we must visit the forests in which the fallow ants establish their dominion over every insect within their territory: we shall there see populous and rival cities and regular roads, diverging from the ant-hill, like so many radii from a centre, and frequented by an immense number of combatants; wars between hordes of the same species, for they are naturally enemies, and jealous of any encroachment upon the territory which surrounds their capital. It is in these forests I have witnessed the inhabitants of two large ant-hills engaged in a spirited combat; two empires could not have brought into the field a more numerous or more determined body of combatants.

"Both armies met half-way from their respective habitations, and the battle commenced: thousands of ants took their stations upon the highest ground, and fought in pairs, keeping firm hold of their antagonists by their mandibles; while a considerable number were engaged in the attack, others were leading away prisoners; the latter made several ineffectual endeavours to escape, as if aware that upon reaching the camp a cruel death awaited them. The field of battle occupied a space of about three feet square: a penetrating odour exhaled on all sides; and numbers of dead ants were seen covered with venom. The ants composing groups and chains laid hold of each others legs and pincers, and dragged their antagonists on the ground; these groups formed successively. The fight usually commenced between two ants, who, seizing each other

by the mandibles, raised themselves upon their hind-
legs, to allow of their bringing their abdomen forward, and spurting their venom upon their adversary:
they were frequently so wedged together, that they
fell on their sides, and fought a long time in that
situation in the dust: shortly afterward they raised
themselves, when each began dragging its adversary;
but when their force happened to be equal, the
wrestlers remained immoveable, and fixed each
other to the ground, until a third came to decide the
contest.   It more commonly happened that both
ants received assistance at the same time, when the
whole four, keeping firm hold of a foot or antenna,
made ineffectual attempts to win the battle.   In this
way they sometimes formed groups of six, eight, or
ten, firmly locked all together; the group was only
broken, when several warriors from the same republic advanced at the same time, and compelled
the enchained insects to let go their hold, and then
the single combats were renewed: on the approach
of night, each party retired gradually to their own
city.

" On the following day, before dawn, the ants returned to the field of battle—the groups again formed
—the carnage recommenced with greater fury than
on the preceding evening, and the scene of combat
occupied a space of six feet by two: the event remained for a long time doubtful; about midday the
contending armies had removed to the distance of a
dozen feet from one of their cities, whence, I conclude, that some ground had been gained: the ants
fought so desperately, that they did not even perceive
my presence, and though I remained close to the
armies, not a single combatant climbed up my legs.

The ordinary operations of the two cities were
not suspended, and in all the immediate vicinity of
the ant-hills order and peace prevailed; on that side
on which the battle raged alone were seen crowds
of these insects running to and fro, some to join the

combatants, and some to escort the prisoners. This war terminated without any disastrous results to either of the two republics; long-continued rains shortened its duration, and each band of warriors ceased to frequent the road which led to the enemy's camp."

The astonishing part of this singular detail is, the instinct which enables each ant to know its own party. Of the same species, alike in form, size, faculties, and arms, it yet rarely happens that two of the same side attack each other; and when this takes place, says Huber, " those which are the objects of this temporary error caress their companions with their antennæ, and readily appease their anger." We can comprehend the existence of an instinct which shall, at all times, cause an animal to build its habitation after a distinct fashion, but a spontaneous combination of faculties seems to take place in the conduct of these wars. The insects march, countermarch, take prisoners, distinguish each other, retreat; in short, do all that man would do under similar circumstances. Nothing like the fatality of instinct is perceptible. These wars were accidental, might never have happened, and perhaps only happen in one community out of ten. Neither are they conducted alike in all cases, but are obviously modified according to the varying circumstances of time and place. These very fallow ants, when they attack the sanguine ants, for example, adopt a system of ambuscade and stratagem; and the sanguine ants, if too hardly pressed, send off a courier to their ant-hill for farther assistance, and immediately, says Huber, a considerable detachment leaves the sanguine city, advances in a body, and surrounds the enemy.

That ants, being such determined warriors, should occasionally have games of mimic war is not surprising. "I visited," says Huber, "one of the fallow ant-hills, exposed to the sun, and sheltered to

the north : the ants were heaped on one another,
enjoying the temperature of the surface of the nest ;
none of them were at work.   This immense multitude of insects presented the appearance of a liquid
in a state of ebullition, upon which the eye had some
difficulty in resting : but when I examined the conduct of each ant, I saw them approach each other,
moving their antennæ with astonishing rapidity ;
with slight movements of their fore-feet they patted
the lateral parts of the head of the other ants.   After
these gestures, resembling caresses, they were observed to raise themselves on their hind-legs by
pairs, struggle together, seize each other by a man-
dible, foot, or antenna, and then immediately relax
their hold to recommence the attack.   They fastened on the thorax, or abdomen, embraced and
overthrew each other, then raised themselves by
turns, taking their revenge without producing any
mischief.   They did not spurt forth their venom as
in their hostile combats, nor retain their adversary
with the obstinacy which they manifest in their serious quarrels.   I frequently visited this ant-hill,
which almost always presented the same spectacle,
but I never saw any quitting it wounded or maimed :
thus there is reason to believe that, industrious as
they are, the ant has its hours of repose, and its
season for enjoyment ; its serious duties, and its
pleasurable gambols."
     Connected with the subject of the warfare of ants
is the history of a species of this insect, not exist-
ing in these islands, called, by Huber, the Amazon,
or Legionary Ant, the *Formica rufescens* of Latreille.
It is both warlike and powerful, and, unlike the rest
of the tribe, its habits are far from being industrious.
Enough has been said to show that the proceedings
of some insects so nearly resemble human actions,
as to excite our greatest wonder : but the habits of
the legionary ant are still more surprising than
the proceedings of the chiefs which we have just

described; it is actually found to be a slave-dealer, attacking the nests of other species, stealing their young, rearing them, and thus, by shifting all the domestic duties of their republic on strangers, escaping from labour themselves. This curious fact, first discovered by Huber, has been confirmed by Latreille, and is admitted by all naturalists. The slave is distinguished from its master by being of a dark ash-colour, so as to be entitled to the name of Negro, —an epithet now appropriated to the *Formica fusca*, or ash-coloured ants. Their masters are light in colour. The negro is an industrious, peaceable, stingless insect; the legionary, a courageous, armed, and lazy one. The relation between them is not, however, that which subsists between a task-master and his bondsman, but a strong attachment is mutually felt—another instance of the modification of instinct, education obliterating in the ash-coloured ant all its natural antipathy to another species. All that we know concerning these extraordinary creatures being derived from Mr. P. Huber, the following is a short summary of his account.

While walking near Geneva, between four and five in the evening of the 17th of June, 1804, this distinguished naturalist observed an army of the rufescent or legionary ants traversing the road. The column occupied a space of ten inches in length, by four in breadth; they rapidly quitted the road, passed a thick hedge, entered a pasture-ground, wound through the grass without breaking the line of march, and approached a nest inhabited by the negro or ash-coloured ant. Some of its inhabitants were guarding the entrance, but on the discovery of an approaching army, they darted forth on the advancing party. The alarm was communicated to the interior, whence their companions rushed in numbers to join in the defence of their underground residence. The bulk of the army of the legionaries being about two paces off, now quickened their

march, and in an instant the whole battalion fell
upon and overthrew the negroes, who, after a short
and obstinate conflict, retired and took refuge in the
lowest parts of their nest. The legionaries now
mounted the hillock; some took possession of the
principal avenues, while others effected a new breach
with their teeth, so as to admit the remainder of the
army. Having thus taken the city by assault, they
remained in it only a few minutes: returning by the
apertures through which they had entered, each
carried in its mouth either a larva, or a pupa, and
scampered away without order or regularity. M.
Huber followed them for some time, but lost sight
of them in a cornfield. Wishing to observe the
assaulted city again, he retraced his steps, and saw
a small number of ash-coloured labourers perched
on the stalks of plants, holding in their mouths the
few larvæ which they had succeeded in rescuing
from pillage.

The next morning, Huber, taking the same road,
with the hope of once more seeing a similar scene,
discovered a large ant-hill tenanted by legionaries.
At five in the evening, provided the weather be fine,
and the temperature 67° Fahrenheit in the shade,
these sally out. During the other part of the day
they appear to do little; but at this hour they become restless, assemble on the outside of the city,
move round it in circles: a signal is then given,
which they pass from one to the other, striking, as
they proceed, with their antennæ and forehead, the
breasts of their companions; these, in their turn,
approach those advancing, and communicate the
same signal—it is that of departure—as the result
satisfactorily proves. Those which receive the
intimation are instantly seen to put themselves on
the march; the column becomes organized; and
not a single amazon remains near the garrison.
There is no commander-in-chief, every ant is in turn
first, each seeking to be foremost. A small number

may, however, be observed constantly returning to
the rear   this is probably the means by which the
whole army is governed.

With such dispositions, manœuvres, and disci
pline, Huber saw an army of legionaries set out
for a negro city.   With their usual impetuosity of
attack, one party soon entered, and returned laden
with the young of the assailed ant-hill; a second
detachment, not meeting with equal success, separated from their companions, and fell on another
negro colony, where they met with ample booty;
after which the whole number of legionaries marched
to their nest in two divisions.   As they approached,
Huber saw, to his astonishment, a great number of
the very same species which had been pillaged, all
around the nest of the legionaries.   Was this a di-
version made by carrying the war into the enemy's
territory?   No: the return of the legionaries excited no alarm; on the contrary, the negro ants
were seen to approach these warriors, caress them
with their antennæ, offer them nourishment, as is
the custom among their own species, while the
legionaries consigned their prisoners to them to be
carried to the interior of the nest.

In this way the same negro colony was observed
to be attacked three several times, and each time
with complete success; the last attack, however,
was made under different circumstances from the
first two: the negroes, as if conscious of their exposed situation, had lost no time in throwing up
trenches, barricading the several entrances, and re-
inforcing the guard of the interior; " they had moreover, brought together all the little pieces of wood
and earth within their reach; with these they had
blocked up the passage to their habitation, in which
they had posted themselves in full force."

" The legionaries at first hesitating to approach,
rambled about or returned to the rear; they then on
a given signal rushed forward *in masse*, with great

impetuosity, removing with their teeth and feet the
many obstacles which impeded their progress:
having succeeded, they entered the ant-hill by hundreds, notwithstanding the resistance of its inhabitants, and carried off their prize to the garrison."

In these attacks the legionaries never take the
old negroes prisoners, knowing perhaps that at an
adult age the love of home, with all its associations,
would be sad obstacles to transplantation; nor is
their contest attended with loss of blood; they seek
the young, and these being obtained, they speedily
decamp with their booty. Nor do they ever begin
their predatory warfare before the end of May, or
beginning of June; if they commenced at an earlier
period to purloin the young negroes, they might
secure a large supply of captives, but then it would
principally consist of males and females, and these
it seems nature does not permit them to seize: for
she has ordained that, in the ant-hills destined to
pillage, the males and females shall be produced
earlier than the males and females of the legionaries; and it is only after their own males and females
have undergone the last change, that the instinct
which prompts them to steal the young of others
begins to operate. Hence, Huber has distinctly
ascertained, and Latreille has confirmed the discovery, that the legionary ant-hill contains male, female,
and neuter amazons, together with negro-neuters,
but never negro males or females. The *amazon*
female, after having cast off her wings, lays the
foundation of her own nest, and performs all the
duties of a labourer. There is no doubt that these
creatures have the ability to work, and do so; but
as soon as they obtain slaves to do that for them
which they ought to do themselves, they relinquish
every domestic duty, and during the day " tranquilly
wait, at the bottom of their subterranean abode, the
hour of departure, reserving their strength, courage,

and the address which they so well know how to display, for the purposes of war."

On the negroes reared among them they depend not only for house and home, but even for food; and these faithful and affectionate servants begrudge neither labour nor pains, in providing for their masters. Huber enclosed thirty amazons with several pupæ and larvæ of their own species, and twenty negro pupæ, in a glass box, the bottom of which was covered with a thick layer of earth; honey was given to them, so that, although cut off from their auxiliaries, the amazons had both shelter and food: at first they appeared to pay some little attention to the young; this soon ceased, and they neither traced out a dwelling, nor took any food; in two days one-half died of hunger, and the other remained weak and languid: commiserating their condition, he gave them *one* of their black companions: this little creature, unassisted, formed a chamber in the earth, gathered together the larvæ, put every thing into complete order, and preserved the lives of those which were about to perish.

In order to obtain a more intimate knowledge of the facts, the same observer of nature opened and deranged an ant-hill in which the negroes and amazons dwelt together; in doing so, the aspect of their city was so altered as not to be recognised by the amazons, and they were seen wandering at random over its surface. The negroes, however, appeared to be well acquainted with the new localities of the ant-hill, and relieved them from their embarrassment, by taking them up gently in their mandibles, and conducting them to the galleries already pierced. "An amazon was frequently seen to approach a negro, and play upon its head with its antennæ, when the latter immediately seized the former in its pincers, and deposited it at one of the entrances; the amazon ant then unrolled itself, caressed once more its kind friend, and passed into the interior of the nest; now and then the negro lost its way too, and wandered about carrying the amazon.

"I observed one," continues Huber, "after ineffectual windings, take the precaution of laying its burden on the ground: the amazon remained on the same spot until the negro returned to its assistance, which, having well ascertained and examined one of the entrances, resumed its load, and bore it into the interior."

If the entrance to any gallery happened to be obstructed, the negro, depositing its burden, went to remove the obstruction, and again taking up the amazon, introduced it into the nest. It often happens that the ant-hill is not sufficiently commodious; in this case the negroes alone decide upon the expediency of a removal, and choose a spot for the new dwelling; they set about building, and as soon as the works are sufficiently advanced, appear eager to conduct the legionaries to the new city: for this purpose, each negro takes up an amazon, which it carries to the chosen spot, so that a long line of these faithful creatures may be seen extending all the way from the old to the new town; their charges are then deposited at the various entrances, when other negroes come out, welcome their arrival, and usher them into the interior of their new abode.

The negro is not the only species of ant subjugated by the legionaries. The mining ants are attacked for a similar purpose; but as these are a much more resolute race than the pacific ash-coloured tribe, the legionaries are obliged to vary their tactics.

"In one of these forays, the amazons," says Huber, "proceeded like a torrent along a deep dike, and marched in a more compact body than ordinary, and in a short time reached the nest they proposed to attack. As soon as the legionaries began entering the subterranean city, the miners rushed out in

I.—M

crowds, and while some fell upon the invaders with
great spirit, others passed through the scene of contest, solely occupied in bearing off to a place of
safety their larvæ and pupæ."

The amazon army was often despoiled of its
booty, but their superior address and agility at length
gave them the advantage, and in a quarter of an hour
they were seen returning homewards loaded with
prey—not, however, straggling, and in a file, as after
an assault upon the negroes, but in a compact mass;
a precaution so much the more necessary, as the
courageous miners disputed every inch of ground,
following and attacking them until they arrived
within ten paces of the amazonian citadel.

Besides the amazons, there is another slave-
making species, called the *formica sanguinea;* a
species which has not as yet been discovered in this
island.   They are larger than the legionaries; unlike
them, however, they share the labour with their
slaves.   Their mode of attack is very different from
that of the legionaries; the latter carry every thing
by sheer impetuosity; the former never pour in immense masses, but attack in small divisions: they
sometimes go one hundred and fifty paces, to attack
a negro habitation, and the various divisions succeed each other by means of couriers, which are
evidently sent off to fetch assistance from the garrison.

"On the 15th July, at 10 A. M.," says Huber, "a
small division, of sanguine ants was despatched
from the garrison, and arrived in quick march near
a nest of negro ants, situated twenty paces distant,
around which they took their station.   The inhabitants perceiving the strangers, rushed forth, and
made several prisoners; the sanguine ants advanced no farther: they appeared to be waiting for
reinforcements; from time to time, little companies
arrived from the garrison to strengthen the brigade:
thus reunited they advanced a little nearer, and

seemed more willing to run the risk of a general
engagement; but in proportion as they approached
the negro dwelling, the more solicitous did they
seem to despatch couriers to the garrison, who, arriving in great haste, produced considerable alarm,
when another division was immediately despatched
to join the army. The negroes took up a position
of about two feet square, in front of their nest,
where nearly their whole force was assembled,
awaiting the enemy." In the interim, the pupæ
were removed to the side of the nest facing the field
of battle, so that they might be conveyed away at a
moment's warning, affording a trait of what Huber
calls prudence, and certainly a marvellously singular
one it is. When fighting with the amazons, the impetuosity of the attack leaves the negro-ant no time
for thought, but in their contests with the sanguine
ants, they vary their tactics so as to meet the new
circumstances. The latter insects being sufficiently
reinforced, make the attack, and band after band pillage and carry away their booty, not in a few minutes,
as is done by the amazons, but during the whole day;
and if the pillaged city should suit them better than
their own, they remove to it on the following morning; at least so it appears in an instance observed
by Huber. It is rare, according to that author, that
they do not change at least once during the year.
They certainly inspire the negroes with great terror,
for these, once attacked by them, generally forsake
their nest for ever.

"To their own slaves they are much attached;
the sanguine ants are often besieged by the fallow
ants: on these occasions they carry their servants
to the lowest chambers, and these, as if aware of
the intention of their removal, immediately begin
barricading the different entrances, with every species of material lying within their reach.

" The sanguine ants evince extraordinary foresight
in these engagements; for while one party is fight-

ing, another is engaged in bearing away the negroes, who immediately begin constructing a new dwelling at a considerable distance from the scene of combat."

Such is the extraordinary recital contained in that delightful work of Huber's, every fact of which has been confirmed by the subsequent observations of the accurate and learned Latreille. It would seem that the negro and miner ants are both occasionally enslaved and dwell together in the sanguine ant-hills. And Huber has brought up legionaries and sanguine ants, which are both slave-makers, with negroes, in one common dwelling.

The wonders of the ant-tribe are far from being exhausted; we have seen them subjugating their own species, and reducing them to the condition of domestic slaves. But a more singular trait in their manners remains to be stated. They keep and feed certain other insects, from which they extract a sweet and nutritious liquid, in the same manner as we obtain milk from cows. There are two species of insects from which the ant-tribe abstract this juice—the aphides, or plant-lice, and the gall-insects. Linnæus, and after him other naturalists, have called these insects the milch cattle of the ants; and the term is not inapplicable. In the proper season, any person, who may choose to be at the pains of watching their proceedings, may see, as Linnæus says, the ants ascending trees that they may milk their cows, the aphides. The substance which is here called milk is a saccharine fluid, which these insects secrete; it is scarcely inferior to honey in sweetness, and issues in limpid drops from the body of the insect, by two little tubes placed one on each side just above the abdomen. The aphides insert their suckers into the tender bark of a tree, and employ themselves without intermission in absorbing its sap; which, having passed through the digestive system of the insect, is discharged by the organs

just described. When no ants happen to be at hand
to receive this treasure, the insects eject it to a distance by a jerking motion, which at regular intervals
they give their bodies. When the ants, however,
are in attendance, they carefully watch the emission
of this precious fluid, and immediately suck it down.
The ants not only consume this fluid when voluntarily ejected by the aphides, but what is still more
surprising, they know how to make them yield it
at pleasure; or, in other terms, to milk them. On
this occasion the antennæ of the ants discharge the
same functions as the fingers of a milk-maid: with
these organs, moved very rapidly, they pat the abdomen of an aphis first on one side and then on the
other: a little drop of the much coveted juice immediately issues forth, which the ant eagerly conveys
to its mouth. The milk of one aphis having been
thus exhausted, the ant proceeds to treat others in
the same manner, until at length it is satiated, when
it returns to its nest.

A still more singular fact, connected with this
branch of the natural economy of these insects,
remains to be stated. These cows are not always
considered the common property of a whole tribe;
on the contrary, some of them are appropriated to
the exclusive use of the inhabitants of a particular
hill or nest; and to keep these cows to themselves,
they exert all their skill and industry. Sometimes
the aphides inhabiting the branches of a particular
tree, or the stalks of a particular plant, are thus appropriated; and if any vagrant foreigners attempt
to share this treasure with its true owners, the latter, exhibiting every symptom of uneasiness and
anger, employ all their efforts to drive them away.

Some species of ants go in search of these aphides
on the vegetables where they feed; but there are
others, as the yellow ant, which collect a large herd
of a kind of aphis, which derives its nutriment
from the roots of grass and other plants. These

milch kine they remove from their native plants and domesticate in their habitations, affording, as Huber justly observes, an example of almost human industry and sagacity. On turning up the nest of the yellow ant, this naturalist one day saw a variety of aphides either wandering about in the different chambers, or attached to the roots of plants which penetrated into the interior. The ants appeared to be extremely jealous of their stock of cattle; they followed them about and caressed them, whenever they wished for the honeyed juice, which the aphis never refused to yield. On the slightest appearance of danger, they took them up in their mouths, and gently removed them to a more sheltered and more secure spot. They dispute with other ants for them, and in short watch them as keenly as any pastoral people would guard the herds which form their wealth. Other species, which do not gather the aphides together in their own nest, still seem to look on them as private property; they set sentinels to protect their places of resort and drive away other ants; and, what is still more extraordinary, they enclose them as a farmer does his sheep, to preserve them not only from rival ants, but also from the natural enemies of the aphis.

If the branch on which the aphides feed be conveniently situated, the ants have recourse to a very effectual expedient to keep off all trespassers: they construct around the branch containing the aphides a tube of earth, or some other material, and in this enclosure, formed near the nest and generally communicating with it, they secure their cattle against all interlopers.

The brown ant has been observed by Huber to build a chamber around the stem of a thistle, in such a way that the stalk passed through the centre, so that from their ant-hill they had only to climb the thistle-stalk, in order to enter this cattle-fold, which was suspended in mid-air. The interior, smooth

and compact, was entirely formed of earth; it contained an extensive family of insect-cows, sheltered
from the inclemencies of the weather, and protected
from their enemies.   These edifices are not always
constructed near the bottom of the thistle-stalk;
once Huber saw one at the height of five feet from
the ground.   " These proceedings," says he, " are
by no means common : we cannot attribute them to
an habitual routine."   Indeed, the modes of preserving their cattle seem to be as various as those
practised by man.   Some ants receive their food
from the aphides which suck the juices of the common plaintain, and these at first take their station
near the flower of the plant ; as soon as the flowers
wither, these insect-cows take shelter under the
radicle leaves; upon which the ants, which before
had climbed up to them, now surround them with a
mud wall, and, making a covered gallery by way of
communication between their nest and the "pad-
dock," extract food from them at their convenience
and pleasure.

During autumn, winter, and spring, many species
of ants keep aphides.   Indeed, in winter they would
be exposed to the horrors of a famine, did they not
rely for food on their cattle ; for though they become
torpid when exposed to intense cold, yet, for the
most part, the depth of their nests preserves for
them a temperature sufficiently high to prevent this
contingency.   Their milch cows are then kept on
the roots of the plants which penetrate the interior
of the nest, and furnish an abundant supply of liquid
in which their keepers delight.   And not only is the
full-grown animal kept, but its eggs are watched
and guarded with that care which warrant us in
supposing that the ant knows their full value.

It is of real consequence to the ants that the hatching of the eggs of the aphides should take place as
early in the spring as possible, in order to ensure an
early supply of food for their colony; and with the

view of hastening this event, they deposite them in the warmest part of their dwelling.

The mode in which the habitations of the ants are constructed varies according to the species of this insect. Some excavate their dwellings, and are hence denominated *mining* ants; others build them on the surface of the ground, and are, in consequence, termed *mason* ants; and a third species take up their residence in hollow trees. But whatever may be the mode in which they form their habitations, they always contrive to shelter themselves completely from the rain. The longest and loftiest chamber is placed near the centre of the nest, and here all the galleries terminate; the subterranean chambers are horizontal. In the evening, the aperture of the nests of some ants is always closed, and in the morning reopened; but according to Huber, the brown ant has been seen to work during a moonlight night.

Having in the daytime noticed some aphides upon a thistle, he examined it again in the night about eleven o'clock, and found his ants busy milking their cows. At the same hour, another night, he observed, on an elder-tree, the little negro-ant engaged in the same employment.

From the result of their labours, it might be inferred that they were actuated by a common mechanical instinct, yet this is by no means the case: no two apartments are alike in the same nest; and no two nests have exactly the same arrangements. Each ant seems capable of conceiving a particular plan, which is in some manner made intelligible to the rest, and practically executed. If pieces of straw be placed conveniently for its purpose, an ant, after careful examination, proceeds to make use of this appropriate supply of materials. In another case it would have to drag bits of stubble, then arrange them, and then build. The operations of these insects vary very much from the beautiful and

geometrically precise labour of bees. Indeed they
seem to act so completely according to the exigencies of each case, that the moving power which
impels and guides their operations approaches so
closely to human reason, that to establish a distinc-
tion appears extremely difficult.

The strength and perseverance of ants are perfectly wonderful. Kirby states, that he once saw
two or three horse-ants hauling along a young snake
not dead, which was of the thickness of a goose-
quill. St. Pierre relates, that he saw a number of
ants carrying off a Patagonian centipede : they had
seized it by all its legs, and bore it along as work-
men do a large piece of timber. Nothing can divert
them from any purpose which they have undertaken
to execute. In warm climates they may be frequently seen marching in columns which exceed all
power of enumeration ; always pursuing a straight
course, from which nothing can cause them to
deviate : if they come to a house or other building,
they storm or undermine it ; if a river cross their
path, they will endeavour to swim over it, though
millions perish in the attempt.

It is related of the celebrated conqueror Timour,
that being once forced to take shelter from his enemies in a ruined building, he sat alone many hours :
desirous of diverting his mind from his hopeless
condition, he fixed his observation upon an ant which
was carrying a grain of corn (probably a pupa)
larger than itself, up a high wall. Numbering the
efforts that it made to accomplish this object, he
found that the grain fell sixty-nine times to the
ground ; but the seventieth time it reached the top
of the wall. " This sight," said Timour, " gave me
courage at the moment, and I have never forgotten
the lesson it conveyed."

The Jesuit Dobrizhoffer, in his History of the
Abipones, gives the following very singular account
of the ravages of ants known in Paraguay. He

furnishes no means of ascertaining the species
whose proceedings he describes. "The largest
ants which I had an opportunity of seeing are
formidable on account of their undermining buildings. They make burrows, with infinite labour,
under churches and houses, digging deep, sinuous
meanders in the earth, and exerting their utmost
strength to throw out the loosened sods. Having
got wings, they fly off in all directions, on the approach of heavy showers, with the same ill fortune
as Icarus, but with this difference, that he perished
in the sea, they on the ground, to which they fall
when their wings are wetted by the rain. Moreover
those holes in the earth by which the ants used first
to pass admit the rain-water, which inundates the
caves of the ants, and undermines the building,
causing the wooden beams that uphold the wall and
roof, first to give way, and, unless immediately supported, to fall along with the house. This is a common spectacle in Paraguay. The whole hill on
which St. Joachim was built was covered with ant-
hills, and full of subterranean cavities. Our house
and the one adjoining suffered much from these
insects. The chief altar was rendered useless for
many days; for, it being rainy weather, the lurking
ants flew in swarms from their caves, and not being
able to support a long flight, fell upon the priest, the
altar, and sacred utensils, defiling every thing. Ten
outlets by which they broke from their caves being
closed up, next day they opened twenty more. One
evening there arose a violent storm, with horrible
thunder and lightning. A heavy shower seemed to
have converted our court-yard into a sloping lake,
the wall itself withstanding the course of the
waters. My companion betook himself to my apartment. Meantime, an Indian, the churchwarden,
arrives, announcing that the floor of the church was
beginning to gape, and the wall to open and be inclined. I snatched up a lamp and ran to the place,

but had hardly quitted the threshold of my door,
when I perceived a gap in the earth; and before I
was aware of any danger, sunk up to the shoulders
in a pit, in the very place of the chief altar, but
scrambled out of it, by the help of the churchwarden, as quickly as I had got in, for under that
altar the ants seemed to have made their metropolis:
the cavern was many feet long and wide, so that it
had the appearance of a wine-cellar. As often as
earth was thrown in by the Indians to fill it, so often
was it dug out by the ants. In this universal trepi-
dation, all the Indians were called to prop the gaping
wall of the church with rafters and planks. The
greatness of the danger rendered it impossible to
remain quiet, whatever arts were adopted. That
same night I removed from my apartment, which
was joined to the church with the same beams and
rafters, in such a manner, that if one fell, the
other could not avoid being involved in the ruin. I
have read that in Guiana, rocks and mountains
have been undermined, walls thrown down, and
people turned out of their habitations by ants, which
I can easily believe, having myself witnessed similar or even more incredible events.

"In Paraguay I was made thoroughly acquainted
with the powers of ants. They are weak and, compared with many other insects, diminutive, but numbers, labour, and unanimity render them formidable,
and endow them with strength superior to their
size. In the plains, especially those near the Paraguay, I have seen ant-hills, like stone pyramids,
three or more ells high, with a broad base, and composed of a solid material as hard as stone: these
are the storehouses and castles of the ants, from
the summits of which they discern sudden inunda-
tions, and safely behold the floating carcasses of less
industrious animals. Elsewhere I have seen an immense plain, so covered with low ant-hills, that the
horse could not move a step without stumbling. In

the plains you may often observe a broad path, through which you would swear the legions of Xerxes might have passed. The Spaniards hollow out these pyramidal heaps, and use them for ovens, or reduce them to a powder, which, mixed with water, serves admirably to floor houses. Pavements of this kind resemble stone in appearance and hardness, and are said to prevent the breeding of fleas and other insects. But hear what mischief ants commit within doors. They flock in a long and almost endless company to the sacks of wheat, and in a journey uninterrupted by day or night (if there be a moon), carry off by degrees some bushels. They will entirely strip fruit trees of their leaves, unless you twist a cow's tail round the trunk to hinder their ascent, and eat away the crops so completely that you would think they had been cut with a sickle. Moreover, ants of various kinds are extremely destructive both to vineyards and gardens, devouring vegetables and pulse to the very root. Set a young plant in the ground, and the next day you will seek it in vain. They refrain from pepper on account of its pungency. If you leave meat, either dressed or raw, in your apartment, you will soon find it blackened with swarms of ants. They devour all sorts of trash, the very carcasses of beetles, toads, and snakes. On returning to my apartment, I found a little bird which I kept in a cage devoured by ants. Nor do they abstain from the bodies of sleeping persons. In the dead of the night an army of ants will issue from the wall or pavement, get upon the bed, and unless you instantly make your escape, sting you all over. This happened so frequently in the Guarany colonies, that we were obliged to burn a candle at night; for lighted sheets of paper thrown upon the swarm are the only means of driving them away. The Portuguese have an old saying, that the ants are queens of Brazil. Certainly we have found them the sovereigns of Paraguay. There may be said to be more trouble in conquering these insects, than all the savages put together; for every contrivance hitherto devised serves only to put them to flight, not banish them effectually."

CHAPTER VIII.

TERMITES, OR WHITE ANTS.

Their Destructiveness—Clear the Ground of all dead vegetable Matter —Societies composed of four sorts of Individuals—Eaten as Food by the Indians—Appear in countless Myriads at the end of the Rainy Season—Prodigious Fertility of the Queen—Size, Form, and Interior Arrangements of their Hills—Marching Ants.

ALMOST all that we know concerning the habits and instincts of these curious animals is derived from an account published by Smeathman, in the " Philosophical Transactions" for 1781. The proceedings of this insect-tribe, as detailed in that paper, are so singular, that they cannot fail to prove interesting to the reader.

The termites are represented by Linnæus as the greatest plagues of both Indies, and indeed, between the Tropics, they are justly so considered, from the vast damages and losses which they cause · they perforate and eat into wooden buildings, utensils, and furniture, with all kinds of household stuff, and merchandise; these they totally destroy, if their progress be not timely stopped. A person residing in the equinoctial regions, although not incited by curiosity, must be very fortunate if the safety of his property do not compel him to observe their habits.

" When they find their way," says Kirby, " into houses or warehouses, nothing less hard than metal or glass escapes their ravages. Their favourite

I.—N

food, however, is wood, and so infinite is the multitude of assailants, and such the excellence of their tools, that all the timber work of a spacious apartment is often destroyed by them in a night. Outwardly, every thing appears as if untouched; for these wary depredators, and this is what constitutes the greatest singularity of their history, carry on all their operations by sap or mine, destroying first the inside of solid substances, and scarcely ever attacking their outside, until first they have concealed it and their operations with a coat of clay."

An engineer having returned from surveying the country, left his trunk on a table; the next morning he found not only all his clothes destroyed by white ants or cutters, but his papers also, and the latter in such a manner, that there was not a bit left of an inch square. The black lead of his pencils was consumed, the clothes were not entirely cut to pieces and carried away, but appeared as if moth-eaten, there being scarcely a piece as large as a shilling that was free from small holes; and it was farther remarkable, that some silver coin, which was in the trunk, had a number of black specks on it, caused by something so corrosive, that they could not be rubbed off, even with sand. "One night," says Kemper, "in a few hours, they pierced one foot of the table, and having in that manner ascended, carried their arch across it, and then down, through the middle of the other foot, into the floor, as good luck would have it, without doing any damage to the papers left there."*

The destructiveness of these insects is, perhaps, one of the most efficient means of checking the pernicious luxuriance of vegetation within the tropics; no large animals could effect in months what the white ant can execute in weeks; the largest trees which, falling, would rot, and render the air pesti-

* Hist. Japan, vol. ii. p. 177.

lential, are so thoroughly removed, that not a grain
of their substance is to be recognised. Not only is
the air freed from this corrupting matter, but the
plants destroyed by the shade of these bulky giants
of the vegetable world are thus permitted to shoot.

In those countries, the white ants answer another
purpose; they serve for food: in some parts of the
East Indies, the natives catch the winged insects
just before their period of emigration, in the following manner—they make two holes, the one to
the windward, the other to the leeward: at the leeward opening they place the mouth of a pot, the
inside of which has been previously rubbed with an
aromatic herb, called Bergera: on the windward
side they make a fire of stinking materials, which
not only drives these insects, but frequently the
hooded snakes also, into the pots, on which account
they are obliged to be cautious in removing them.
By this method they catch great quantities, of which
they make with flour a variety of pastry, which they
can afford to sell very *cheap* to the poorer ranks of
people: when this sort of food is used too abundantly, it produces cholera, " which kills in two or
three hours."

It also seems that, in some form or other, these
insects are greedily eaten in other countries: thus,
when, after swarming, shoals of them fall into the
rivers, the Africans skim them off the surface with
calabashes, and bringing them to their habitations,
parch them in iron pots over a gentle fire, stirring
them about as is usually done in roasting coffee;
in that state, without sauce or any other addition,
they consider them delicious food, putting them by
handfuls into their mouth as we do comfits. " I
have," says Smeathman, "eaten them dressed in
this way several times, and think them delicate,
nourishing, and wholesome; they are something
sweeter, though not so fat and cloying, as the cat-
terpillar or maggot of the palm-tree snoutbeetle

(*curculio palmarum*), which is served up at all the
luxurious tables of the West Indian epicures, particularly of the French, as the greatest dainty of the
Western world."

The different species of this genus resemble each
other in form, in their manner of living, and in their
good and bad qualities, but differ as much as birds
in the manner of building their habitations, and in
the choice of the material of which they compose
them.

Some build on the surface of the ground, or partly
above and partly beneath, and some on the stems or
branches of trees, sometimes aloft at a vast height.

Their societies consist of five different descrip-
tions of individuals.

1. Workers or *larvæ*, answering to the neuters of
bees.   These constitute the most numerous division
of the community; they construct the nest and take
charge of the young, until the latter are capable of
providing for themselves.

2. Nymphs or pupæ: which differ in nothing
from the larvæ, except in possessing the rudiments
of wings.

3. Neuters: which are known by their large
heads, armed with very long mandibles.   These
exceed the labourers much in bulk, and are in nu-
merical proportion to the latter as 1 to 100.   They
are the soldiers of the community.

4 and 5. A male and female arrived at their full
state of perfection.   Each community contains but
one of each of these, and they are strictly king and
queen; they are exempt from all the ordinary duties
falling upon their subjects: when first disclosed
from the pupa, they have four wings; but like the
ants, they soon cast off these members.   They are
known from the blind larvæ, pupæ, and neuters, by
their having two large eyes.

" In this form," says Smeathman, " the animal
comes abroad during or soon after the first tornado

which at the latter end of the dry season proclaims
the approach of the ensuing rains, and seldom waits
for a second or third shower, if the first, as is generally the case, happen in the night and bring much
wet after it.

" The quantities that are to be found next morning all over the surface of the earth, but particularly
in the waters, is astonishing; for their wings are
only calculated to carry them a few hours, and after
the rising of the sun, not one in a thousand is to be
found with four wings, unless the morning continue
rainy, when here and there a solitary being is seen,
winging its way from one place to another, as if
solicitous only to avoid its numerous enemies, par
ticularly the various species of ants which are hunt
ing on every spray, on every leaf, and in every possible place, for this unhappy race: hence probably
not a pair in many millions gets into a place of
safety to fulfil the first law of nature, and lay the
foundation of a new community.

" Not only all kinds of ants, birds, and carnivorous
reptiles, as well as insects, are upon the hunt for
them; but the inhabitants of many countries, and
particularly of some parts of Africa, eagerly seize
upon them."

On the following morning, however, they are to
be seen running upon the ground in chase of each
other.   From one of the most active, industrious,
and rapacious, from one of the most fierce and im-
placable little animals in the world, they are now
become the most innocent, helpless, and cowardly;
never making the least resistance to the smallest ant.

The ants are to be seen on every side in infinite
numbers, dragging to their different nests these
annual victims of the laws of nature.   It is wonderful that a pair should ever escape so many dangers, and get into a place of safety; some, however,
do in fact escape, and being found by some of the
labouring insects that are continually running about

N 2

the surface of the ground under their covered galleries, they are elected kings and queens of new states. All those who have not the good luck to be so preserved, certainly perish, and most probably in the course of the following day.

The manner in which these labourers protect the happy pair from their innumerable enemies, not only on the day of the massacre of almost all their race, but for a long time after, justifies the use of the term "election."

The little industrious creatures immediately enclose the favoured individuals in a small chamber of clay, suitable to their size, into which at first they have but one entrance just large enough for the workers and the soldiers to go in and out, but much too contracted to be used by either of the royal pair; and when necessity obliges them to make more entrances, they are never larger so that of course these subjects charge themselves voluntarily with the labour of providing for the offspring of their sovereigns, as well as of working and of fighting for them, until they shall have raised a progeny capable at least of dividing the task with them.

About this time a most extraordinary change begins to take place in the queen, to which nothing similar is known except in the chigoe, and in the different species of the coccus tribe: the abdomen begins gradually to enlarge, and at length acquires such an enormous size, that an old queen will have it increased to an extent which equals fifteen hundred or two thousand times the bulk of the rest of

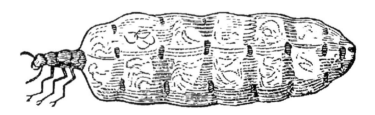

her body, and twenty or thirty thousand times the bulk of a labourer.

The skin between the segments is distended in every direction; and at last the segments are removed to the distance of half an inch from each other, though at first the length of the whole abdomen is not half an inch; they preserve their dark brown colour, and the upper part of the abdomen is marked with a regular series of brown bars from the thorax to the posterior part of the abdomen; while the intervals between them are covered with a thin, delicate, transparent skin, and appear of a fine cream-colour, a little shaded by the dark hue of the intestines and watery fluid seen here and there beneath.

Smeathman conjectures that the animal must be upwards of two years old when the abdomen is thus increased to three inches in length: he has sometimes found them of nearly twice that size: the abdomen is then of an irregular oblong shape, being contracted by the muscles of every segment, and is become one vast matrix full of eggs, which make long circumvolutions through an innumerable series of very minute vessels. This singular matrix is not more remarkable for its amazing extension than for its peristaltic motion, which resembles the undulation of waves, and continues incessantly without any apparent effort on the part of the animal; so that there is a constant protrusion of eggs to the amount, as Smeathman has frequently counted in the case of old queens, of sixty in a minute, or eighty thousand and upwards in twenty-four hours.

These eggs are instantly removed by her attendants, of which a sufficient number is always found waiting in the adjacent chambers, and carried to the nurseries, which, in a great nest, may be four or five feet distant, in a direct line, and consequently much farther by the winding galleries which conduct to them.

The nests of these insects are usually termed hills by natives, as well as strangers, from their outward appearance, which, being more or less conical, generally resemble the form of a sugar-loaf; they rise about ten or twelve feet in perpendicular height above the ordinary surface of the ground.

They continue quite bare till they reach the height of six or eight feet; but in time the dead barren clay of which they are composed becomes fertilized by the genial influence of the elements in these prolific climates; and in the second or third year, the hillock, if not overshaded by trees, becomes like the rest of the earth, almost covered with grass and other plants; and in the dry season, when the herbage is burnt up by the rays of the sun, it appears

not unlike a very large hay-cock. "But of all extraordinary things I observed," says Adanson, "nothing struck me more than certain eminences, which,
by their height and regularity, made me take them
at a distance for an assemblage of negro huts, or a
considerable village, and yet they are only the nests
of certain insects."*

Smeathman has drawn a comparison between these
labours of the termes and the works of man, taking
the termes' labourer at one-fourth of an inch long,
and man at six feet high.   When a termes has built
one inch, or four times its height, it is equivalent to
twenty-four feet, or four times the height of man.
One inch of the termes' building being proportionate
to twenty-four feet of human building, twelve
inches, or one foot, of the former must be proportionate to twelve times twenty-four, or two hundred
and eighty-eight feet, of the latter; consequently,
when the white ant has built one foot, it has, in
point of labour, equalled the exertions of a man
who has built two hundred and eighty-eight feet;
but as the ant-hills are ten feet high, it is evident
that human beings must produce a work of two
thousand eight hundred and eighty feet in height, to
compete with the industry of their brother insect.
The Great Pyramid is about one-fifth of this height;
and as the solid contents of the ant-hill are in the
same proportion, they must equally surpass the
solid contents of that ancient wonder of the world.

Every one of these hills consists of two distinct
parts, the exterior and the interior.

The exterior consists of one shell formed in the
manner of a dome, large and strong enough to enclose and shelter the interior from the vicissitudes
of the weather, and the inhabitants from the attacks
of natural or accidental enemies.   It is, therefore,
in every instance, much stronger than the interior

* Voyage to Senegal.

of the building, which, being the habitable part, is
divided, with a wonderful degree of regularity and
contrivance, into an amazing number of apartments
for the residence of the king and queen, and the
nursing of their numerous progeny; or appropriated
as magazines, to hold provisions.

These hills make their first appearance above
ground by a little turret or two in the shape of su-
gar-loaves, rising a foot or more in height. Soon

after, at some little distance, while the first turrets
are increasing in height and size, the insects raise
others, and so go on, increasing their number, and
widening their bases, till the space occupied by their
under-ground works becomes covered with a series
of these elevations; the centre turret is always the
highest; the intervals between the turrets are then
filled up, and the whole collected, as it were, under
one dome. These interior turrets seem to be intended chiefly as scaffolding for the dome; for they
are, in a great part, removed when that has been
erected.

When these hills have reached somewhat more
than half their height, they furnish a convenient
stand, where the wild bulls of the district may be
seen to station themselves, while acting as sentinels and watching the rest of the herd reposing and
ruminating below; they are sufficiently strong for

this purpose. The outward shell, or dome, is not only of use to protect the interior buildings from external violence and heavy rains, but to collect and preserve a regular supply of heat and moisture, which seems indispensable for hatching the eggs and rearing the young ones.

The royal chamber, occupied by the king and queen, is manifestly considered of the most consequence, being always situated as near the centre of the interior building as possible, and generally upon a level with the surface of the ground, at a pace or two from the hillock. Its interior shape nearly re-

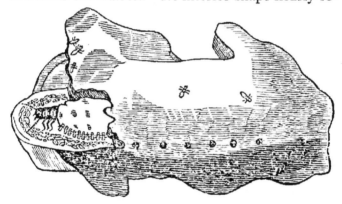

sembles half an egg, or an obtuse oval, not unlike a long oven. In the infant state of the colony it is scarcely an inch in length, but it is enlarged as the queen increases in bulk, until it reaches the length of about eight inches.

Its floor is perfectly horizontal, and about an inch thick; the roof is generally of the same solidity, being formed of one well-turned oval arch; the doors are made level with the floor, equidistant from each other, and just large enough to admit a labourer, but not to permit the exit of their majesties, who are imprisoned for life.

In a large hillock, the royal chamber is surrounded

by numberless others of different shapes and dimensions, all of them arched either ovally or circularly; these communicate with one another by means of passages, and are the waiting-rooms for the attendants employed in removing the eggs of the queen; they also lodge the soldiers engaged in the defence of the colony.

Next to these are the magazines, in which are deposited the inspissated exudations and juices of trees, of various colours and consistency. Intermixed with the magazines are the nurseries, differing totally in construction from any other part of the building, being composed of raspings of wood cemented with gum. They are compact, and divided into many very irregular-shaped chambers,

not one of which is half an inch wide. The nurseries are enclosed in chambers of clay; they are placed at first near the royal cell, but as the queen enlarges, they are removed to a distance, in order that room may be made for her increasing wants. In the early state of the hill, these nursery-chambers are not bigger than a hazelnut; but as it advances, they become enlarged to the size of a child's head.

The intervention of these various cavities is well

calculated to regulate the temperature of the interior. There are also large subterraneous galleries, to which the Roman sewers are not to be compared, when the size of the worker is taken into account. Some of these are thirteen inches in the bore, extending more than a hundred yards under ground, and forming the great thoroughfares of the community. The tender body of the termites, compared with the armour-like integument of their mortal enemies the ants, makes it necessary for them thus to conceal themselves in their covered roads.

These galleries wind spirally up to the top of the hill. By this contrivance the ascent is rendered easier to an insect toiling under its load. Let us only conceive a man carrying a heavy weight up a ladder two thousand eight hundred and eighty feet, and we shall have some notion of the labour saved by inclining the ascent. The distance too is shortened by another ingenious contrivance: an arch is thrown from one frequented spot to another; and one of these when measured has been found to be ten inches in length, half an inch in width, and one-fourth of an inch in thickness; and, according to Smeathman, it was not excavated, but projected from one point to another. It would be curious to know the site of these arches in different hills, as proving how far they might or might not be varied with the exigencies of each community.

Having thus described the city, some account shall now be given of its inhabitants. In the subjoined engraving:—the first (*fig.* 1) represents the king, which, after losing its wings, never seems to increase in bulk. The next (*fig.* 2) is a labourer magnified; it is less than a quarter of an inch in length. If its formidable jaws be examined, and its immense industry and activity be considered, the effects resulting from the labours of myriads of these insects will scarcely excite surprise. The next (*fig.* 3) is the soldier, with its huge head armed with

I.—O

awls, which may be seen magnified in the last figure
fig. 4).

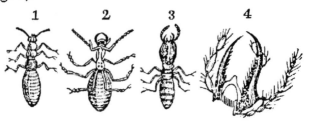

1. King.
3. A Soldier.
2. Labourer magnified.
4. The head magnified.

The workers and soldiers of all the different species of termites never expose themselves to the open
air, but travel either underground, or in the interior of
such trees and substances as they destroy. It sometimes happens that they cannot proceed by latent
passages, although they find it necessary to search
for plunder above ground; in this emergency they
make pipes of the same material with which they
build their nest.   With this material they completely line most of the roads leading from their
nests into the various parts of the country, and
travel outwards and homewards with the utmost
security in all kinds of weather.   If they meet
with a rock or any other obstruction, they will make
their way over the surface: for that purpose they
erect a covered way, or arch, still of the same materials, continuing it, with many windings and rami-
fications, through large groves; and, where such a
precaution may be practicable, they construct subterranean pipes running parallel with the surface
passages, into which they sink for security, whenever their galleries above ground may be destroyed
by violence, or they happen to be alarmed by the
tread of men or animals.

" When one chances to enter," says Smeathman,
" a solitary grove where the ground is pretty well

covered by their arched galleries, they give the
alarm by loud hissings, which we hear distinctly at
every step we make.   Soon afterward it is vain to
examine the galleries for these insects ; little holes
are found just large enough for them to escape
through.

Smith, in talking of a species of termes, says, " I
one day attempted to knock off the top of one of
the hills with my cane, but the stroke had no other
effect than to bring thousands of the insects out of
doors to see what was the matter; upon which I
took to my heels, and ran away as fast as I could."
" The first object which strikes one upon opening
their hills," says Smeathman, " is the behaviour of
their soldiers.   If you make a breach, in a few seconds a soldier will run out, and walk about as if to
reconnoitre.   It will sometimes go in as if to give
the alarm, but most frequently may be followed by
two or three others, who run straggling after one
another; and to them succeed a large body, who
rush out as fast as the breach will permit them;
and the number increases as long as any one continues battering the building.   It is not easy to de-
scribe the rage and fury they show.   In their hurry
they frequently miss their hold, and tumble down
the sides of the hill, but recover themselves as
quickly as possible, and, being blind, bite every
thing they run against, thus making a crackling
noise, while some beat repeatedly with their forceps
upon the building, and make a small vibrating noise
something shriller and quicker than the ticking of a
watch—it can be heard at three or four feet distance.   They make their hooked jaws meet at
every bite ; and if it should be the leg of a man, a
spot of blood, extending an inch on the stocking,
follows the wound.   Nothing can tear them away,
but they must be taken off piecemeal.   If, on the
other hand, you cease to batter, in half an hour they
retire into the nest, as if they supposed the won-

derful monster that damaged their castle to be beyond their reach. The labourers, who had fled on the first alarm, are now seen hastening to repair the breach, every one with a burden of ready tempered mortar in its mouth. This they stick on to the breach with such wonderful celerity and order, that although thousands, nay, millions, seem employed, yet they never embarrass one another. While the labourers are thus engaged, the soldiers retire, save here and there one, who saunters about, never touching the mortar. One, in particular, places itself close to the part undergoing repair; it may be seen turning leisurely on all sides, and every now and then, at an interval of a minute or two, lifting up its head, and with its forceps beating upon the building and making a vibrating noise, on which a loud hiss, apparently from the whole body of labourers, issues from withinside the dome and all the subterranean passages : that it comes from the labourers is very evident, for all these may be seen hastening at every such signal, redoubling their pace, and working as fast again. Attack the nest again, and with a loud hiss the labourers disappear, and the soldiers rush out; so that the experiment yields constantly the same result, of labourers at work and soldiers rushing to battle, the duties of each being as distinct as night and day."

Smeathman gives the following account of the marching termes.

While sauntering very silently in the hopes of finding some spoit, on a sudden he heard a loud hiss, which, on account of the many serpents in those countries, is a most alarming sound. The next step produced a repetition of the sound; and then he saw with astonishment and delight, an army of the marching ants (*termes viarum*) emerging from the ground : their march was orderly, and very rapid, and their numbers prodigious   they were divided into two columns sixteen abreast, composed chiefly

of labourers, with here and there a huge soldier
that appeared like an ox among sheep; other soldiers kept a foot or two from the column, apparently
acting as videttes, appointed to guard against surprise · others mounted the plants or blades of grass,
which flanked the main bodies, and, thus elevated
a foot and more, looked over and controlled the proceedings of the moving multitude.   They turned
their heads in the different directions whence danger might arise, and every now and then struck
their forceps against the plant and produced the
ticking sound already mentioned, to which the
whole army answered simultaneously with a loud
hiss, and quickened their pace: after proceeding
thus for about fifteen paces, the two columns united
and sunk into the earth.   The stream, however,
continued to flow on for more than an hour, during
which Smeathman watched their movements : the
rear was brought up by a large body of soldiers.

CHAPTER IX.

*Parasitical Insects—Gall-Insect—Cochineal-Insect—The Scarlet
Colour used in Dyeing.*

We shall now proceed to the habits and instincts
of a class of insects which may with a little lati-
tude be termed parasitical; some of these attach
themselves to the vegetable, others to the animal
kingdom.

The history of the gall-insects is curious, chiefly
from the power they possess of diverting the laws
of vegetation from their ordinary into an extraordinary track.   These insects are not all of one kind;
but, though differing in many respects, they have
this quality in common, that they deposite an egg

under the outward covering of a plant, whence a little mansion springs up which provides its inmate both with shelter and food.   Judging from the great number of plants attacked by them, it would appear that our insects are destined to fill a very important department in the economy of nature.   These excrescences are found in every part of a plant; there is scarcely a portion of the oak, for instance, whether it be root, branch, stalk, leaf, or bud, which is not capable of furnishing the gall-insects with a habitation.

Some of the galls are tenanted by only one embryo, others contain many in their larva state, so that these insect-houses consist either of one or many chambers; they vary in size from the minuteness of a pin's head to the bulk of a walnut; they sometimes resemble fruit, both in shape and colour: the gall of the oak, for example, is sometimes shaped like an apple, sometimes like a bunch of currants, and sometimes like an artichoke: but it were endless to enumerate the strange and beautiful diversities which are produced by a tiny insect in a space of time varying from a few hours to a few weeks.

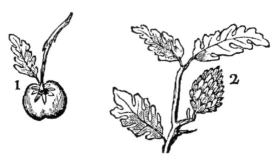

The older botanists mistook the trees in which these vegetable excrescences were produced for distinct species.   Thus, Gerard describes a willow which bore something like roses; he talks of it, as not only "making a gallant show, and being set up in houses for the decking of the same," but also as " yielding a most cooling aire in the heat of summer."

" This willow, however," observes Kirby, " is nothing more than one of the common species, whose twigs in consequence of the deposition of the eggs of a cynips in their summit, there shoot out into numerous leaves totally differing in shape from the other leaves of the tree, and arranged not much unlike the flower of a rose, adhering to the stem even after the others fall off."

In consistence, these excrescences have nothing in common with the plant to which they are attached. On the oak, some are found literally as hard as iron, so as to turn the edge of a knife, while others are as juicy and pulpy as fruit. It is not the tree but the insect which regulates this; for it is certain that, on the very same leaf, one species of gall-fly will invariably form a woody and hard gall-nut, while another as invariably produces a spongy and soft one—although both of these are formed from materials of the same texture. Persons who formerly saw insects emerging from little excrescences having no visible inlet, were induced to believe that they had either been sucked up by the roots with the juices, or generated by putrefaction.

Attentive observation, and the use of a lens of sufficient power, will explain the manner in which the gall-nut rises. The little fly may be seen settling on the part to which its instinct invariably leads it; and introducing a sort of sting, its ovipositor, under the epidermis or skin of the plant: it then moves it about as if to enlarge the orifice, and deposites the egg. These eggs, when examined first in the body of the fly, and afterward in the nut, are found to differ so much in size, that Reaumur supposes them to grow after they have been laid. If this be the fact, it is singular, as in that case the egg will not resemble so much that of oviparous animals as that of viviparous. The gall-nut will be, as that unrivalled naturalist has conjectured, a matrix or womb, from which juices are absorbed by the egg, in order to furnish the material of its growth.

The plant being alive, we can easily imagine that, if any part of it be wounded, the sap would flow from the orifice, and produce a knob, which would grow and harden into an irregular mass.

The gall-fly, however, has the art of altering the organization of the part: an egg, together with perhaps a most minute drop of fluid, is introduced into a plant; and a part which, under ordinary circumstances, would have expanded into a leaf or stalk, is seen to burst out under the form of a fruit or flower, as evidently organized, as if it had been transferred from the plant which it resembles, to that to which it has no natural affinity.

Why one insect should produce invariably one species of gall, and another insect a different species —why these should resemble the regular forms of parts of other plants, are mysteries extremely difficult, if not utterly incapable, of solution. When the egg is deposited in the young shoot, by a particular kind of gall-fly, instead of pushing forth a sprout, the irritation brings out an abundance of leaves, which gradually assume the figure of an artichoke.

The first general effect produced by the insertion of the egg is, therefore, to augment the vegetative powers of the part, and the next to alter their action. The hairy gall of the wild rose, formerly employed in medicine, under the name of Bedeguar, has a mossy appearance. Here the liquor of the gall-fly seems to have caused a disjunction of those fibres which, in their ordinary state, would have united and formed a leaf. The difference observable in the consistence of these various galls may possibly arise from the different power of absorbing juices possessed by the different insects inhabiting them; though it is just as possible, in this guess-work, to suppose that the irritation should cause a greater quantity of juices to flow towards the punctured part.

The gall-insects remain five or six months in the larva state, before changing to nymphs; some undergo all their metamorphoses within the gall-nut, and piercing their prison, come forth as perfect insects: others quit it and bury themselves in the earth, until they arrive at maturity; soon after which the female becomes impregnated and lays her eggs. Carefully concealed in the manner just described, they escape most of their natural enemies; but frequently some of the ichneumon tribe contrive to introduce their eggs into the same habitation, and the larva as it grows up feeds on the young of the gall-fly.

This shows that even insects, which nature seems to have gifted with the most surprising foresight, cannot provide against all the hazards to which their young are exposed. What could an anxious mother do more, than to conceal her offspring in so solid and secret a habitation, as that which envelopes the young gall-fly? But insects, as small or smaller than those into which the larvæ are transformed, know how to pierce the sides of the cells and to deposite within them an egg, which shall produce a carnivorous worm, for whom the rightful tenant of the mansion serves as food. When some of these galls are opened, two worms of different sizes will frequently be found, the least sucking the biggest, while

the latter sucks the gall-nut.   When the ichneumon,
for the small worm generally turns into that species
of fly, comes out, it is often found to be much bigger
than the creature it lived on, and here a difficulty
presents itself which requires to be explained.   How
does it happen that the ichneumon worm should be
so much bigger than the gall-insect, which is the only
substance on which it feeds?   Where does it obtain
the additional food required to produce this additional bulk?   Not from the gall-nut, for the ichneumon worm does not feed on a vegetable; and as
there is no living thing, save the larva of the gall-fly,
enclosed with it in the cell, it must in some way or
other obtain it from that.   The truth is, that Nature
has taught the young of the ichneumon not to kill
the larva of the gall-fly outright; it wounds only
certain parts which are not vital, and from these it
extracts its nourishment.   The gall-worm, therefore,
goes on sucking the vegetable juice, and elaborating
it into animal matter, and as fast as that process is
completed, the ichneumon worm abstracts and ap-
propriates it; and so well-timed are the operations
of nature, that the moment the ichneumon worm
has reached its perfect state, and requires no farther
supply of food, the gall-insect, which previously
furnished it with this supply, becomes exhausted,
and perishes.

While some persons have supposed that a plant
could be converted into a gall-fly, others, and those,
too, accustomed to entomological investigation, have
mistaken an insect for a gall-nut.   Some of our trees
appear as if covered with scabs of an oval shape:
these remain fixed, show no sign of motion, nor any
external mark by which an animal form may be recognised; nevertheless, they are true insects, and the
nearer they are to maturity, the less they exhibit
the character of animal life, and at the time they are
occupied in laying thousands of eggs, they present
the aspect of a gall-nut.

They vary in figure, some being globular, some flattened, or slightly convex like the bottom of a boat, or kidney-shaped. Some of these do not exceed in size a pepper-corn, others become as large as a pea.

These extraordinary creatures form the genus *coccus* of Linnæus, and are to be reckoned among the insects which are directly useful to man. Formerly, a species of these insects, the *coccus Polonicus*, formed a considerable article of commerce in Poland. The *coccus cacti*, or the cochineal-insect of South America, however, has now, by the superiority of the crimson dye it affords, superseded the other. In 1518, the Spaniards found it used by the Americans, for the purposes of dyeing; yet its true nature was not discovered for nearly two centuries after, when the observations of Hartsoeker, Leeuwenhoek, De la Hire, and Geoffroy clearly proved it to be an insect, and not, as was supposed, a grain, or seed. This insect feeds on the nopal, which is a species of fig-tree very common in New Spain, and in some parts of India: the leaves are thick, and full of saccharine juice. At the approach of the rainy season the cultivators sweep from the leaves several little insects, resembling a bug, which suck the green plant. They preserve them in their own houses, and feed them with the branches of the nopal. At the close of the rainy season twelve or fourteen of these insects, by that time grown strong, are put into little baskets made of moss or the down that covers the cocoa-nut. These baskets are placed on the nopal, and in a few days the cochineal insects spread themselves over the tree, and give birth to an infinite number of young.   In the immediate vicinity of Oaxaca, the cultivators of this insect feed it in the plains during the dry season, which extends from October to April. In the month of April the rain sets in, and continues until October.   At the beginning of this season they transport their stock of insects, and place them to feed on plantations of nopals in the neighbouring mountains, where the weather is more favourable. The dams live but a little time after they have laid their eggs, and are what may be called the first crop. The young, forsaking the baskets, disperse themselves over all the verdure of the nopal, and thrive to that degree, that in the space of three months they become prolific in their turn.   The second brood are permitted to live, but all the parents are carried home and killed: the new offspring on the tree have likewise their young at the end of about three months; but lest they should all be destroyed by the rainy season, the cultivators carry home the parents as well as their offspring, and this is the third produce. A sufficient number of the young insects are preserved to continue the species the next year, and all the rest are killed in hot water, or ovens, or upon the flat stones with which the American women bake their bread.   The inside of the insects thus destroyed is filled with the beautiful red dust so well known to dyers.   Plantations containing fifty or sixty thousand trees, growing in straight lines, may be seen in some districts of America.   The quantity of insects annually exported from South America is valued at £500,000.   The Spanish government are jealous of its being naturalized elsewhere, while a reward of £6000 is offered by the East India Company for its introduction into our territories.   The figures of the female cochineal-insect, magnified, will give a good idea of this genus generally.

Their trunk is so brittle that they cannot be moved from their place without breaking it; an accident which would prove fatal to them: the consequence is, that during the whole term of their life they remain fixed to the spot where they first settled, and to the vegetable nipple which feeds them. When the females have attained the age of puberty, the males are supplied with wings, and enabled to quit the plant on which they were hatched. The females remain stationary, and hatch their young on the spot; but the latter would soon become so numerous as to be at a loss for space to feed on, while they are so delicate, that it would be impossible for them to pass from one plant to another, if nature did not provide for them admirable means of emigration: at the period of their birth a multitude of spiders fasten their nets to the leaves of the nopal; and it is along these slender threads, which answer the purposes of a bridge, that the brood of the cochineal-insect emigrates to a neighbouring tree in quest of food.

The gall-nuts used in making ink are produced by an insect which punctures the leaves of a species of oak very common in Asia Minor, where they are collected in considerable quantities by the poorer inhabitants: from the different ports of the Levant they are exported to various parts of the world. The galls held in the greatest estimation are those

I.—P

known in commerce under the name of blue galls. These are the produce of the first gathering, before the fly has issued from the gall. Those which may have been overlooked in the first gathering, and from which the fly may afterward have emerged in its perfect form, are called white galls : these are of a very inferior quality, containing less of the astringent principle than the blue galls, in the proportion of two to three.

The true vermilion kermes, and a variety of other valuable colours or drugs have no other origin than the punctures of different insects : many plants are covered with them, and it seems probable that we daily import from other countries commodities which we might procure at home. The persons who gather the kermes take the insect when ripe and spread it upon linen, turning it at first while it abounds in moisture twice or thrice a-day, to prevent its heating. When there appears red powder among it, they separate it, passing it through a sieve, and then again spread out the grain upon the linen, until more red powder becomes visible; and the same process is repeated until it ceases to yield any more of this substance.

In the beginning, when the small red grains are seen to move, as they will do, they are sprinkled over with strong vinegar, and rubbed between the hands ; afterward, little balls are made of them, which are exposed to the sun to dry. If this powder should be let alone, without pouring vinegar or some other acid liquor upon it, out of every grain would come forth a little fly, which would skip and wing about for a day or two, and at last, changing its colour, fall down quite dead.

Another species of the cocci produce the article of commerce called gum-lac. The insect is of a deep red colour, of the general shape of this tribe, and not bigger than a louse. It infests certain trees of the fig kind in the large forests of Hindostan

in such innumerable multitudes, that their upper
branches appear as if covered with blood. About
November and December the young leave the shelter afforded by the carcass of the mother, and, after
wandering about the stems and branches, fix on the
succulent extremities of the newest shoots. Towards
the middle of January they are motionless, exhibiting
no signs of life, though as plump as before, and are
glued to the branch by a viscid and semi-transparent
liquor. In March, the cells, as Kerr calls them, are
completely formed; that is, the carcass of the insect is now an oval red bag, the size of a cochineal,
and full of a beautiful red liquor. In November or
December, about twenty or thirty oval eggs are
found within the red fluid of the mother. When
this fluid is expended, the young pierce a hole
through the carcass of their parent, and walk off one
by one, leaving the tattered remains of their old
covering behind them. This is the white substance
which is seen in stick-lac. These young, like their
parents, proceed to fix themselves on some tender
and juicy shoot. Kerr calculates that only one in
six can have room to complete its cell, the others
dying or being eaten by birds, which, should they
perch on any of the branches loaded with these insects, must with their feet necessarily carry off numbers to the next tree on which they may happen to
alight. The quantity of sap which they pump out
turns the branches of a dirty black.

There are four kinds of lac—the stick-lac, which
is the substance in its natural state, and from which
the others are all made. 2. Seed-lac, or the shells
separated from the sticks. 3. Lump-lac, or the seed
melted down and made into cakes. 4. Shell-lac, or
the shells liquefied, strained, and formed into thin
transparent layers. The gum-lac is principally gathered on the uncultivated mountains on both sides
of the Ganges, where it is produced in such astonishing quantities, that it would supply ten times the

demand which exists for it; and the only trouble required in gathering this substance consists in breaking down the branches and carrying them to market.

The shell-lac is used by the natives in making ornaments, rings, necklaces, and bracelets; when impregnated with cinnabar it forms sealing-wax, or, as the Dutch call it, segel-lak (seal-lac). When heated and mixed with a black powder, it may be spread on a box or other article for the purpose of japanning it. It also enters into the composition of various varnishes. It affords likewise a beautiful red colour by throwing the insect into water.

Of the insects which are common to various parts of Europe, it may be said that the cocci fix themselves to such plants as are hardy enough to pass the winter through. " All that I know," says Reaumur, " require a plant capable of nourishing them for one year, the natural term of the life of these insects." While young they attach themselves to the leaves, and as these wither away, descend to the branches, where they adhere during the winter. As spring returns, they become fecundated, and prepare to perpetuate their species. One of these insects, which sucks the juice of the peach, is boat-shaped; its skin, which is all that can be seen, is exactly like the fine bark of the cherry-tree. On looking at the peach, some of these gall-insects may be observed dry and dead, others alive, though immoveable; those on the old branches are for the most part of the former, those in the new shoots of the latter class. They may farther be known by the colour of the latter being more brilliant than that of the former; and also by the dead ones being easily pushed off with the finger or a penknife, while the live insect adheres: a more violent push kills them; and they yield a thick liquid substance, similar to that which is produced by crushing any other species of living insect. The spot from whence the coccus has been removed is covered with a downy cotton, which transpires or exudes from the abdominal surface of the insect."

If the coccus of the peach be examined about the end of May, it will be difficult to persuade ourselves that the little skinny globe which presents itself to the eye is an insect: there is no fleshy texture; it has the appearance of a little tortoise-shell, under which is concealed an infinite number of very diminutive grains; these are the eggs of the insect, which, when expelled, are hatched under the carcass of their dead parent. If these protuberances be removed, beginning at the top and proceeding downwards, so

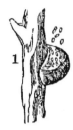

as not to let their eggs fall, they may readily be collected. In these figures the little dots represent the eggs; if, however, the gall-like protuberance be transversely divided with a penknife, both the contents and the arrangement of the eggs will be observed more readily. Hence it would seem, that at first these creatures have a form like many other insects, that after a time they fix themselves to the tree, and suck its juice, and that their extraordinary distention is owing to an innumerable quantity of eggs contained at first within the abdomen, and ultimately protruded. Nature has taught most other insects to protect their young by furnishing them in their period of helplessness with a habitation composed of silk or some other substance. The coccus, however, from the moment the eggs are laid, de-

fends them from the elements and their natural
enemies by its own body, and after death still shelters them with its carcass.   It may at first sight appear extraordinary that a fleshy body, when dead,
should not putrefy; this, however, will be intelligible, if the following figures be attended to.   The
first (*fig.* 1) represents the under surface of the in-

sect; this is nearly plane, and is exactly fitted to the
tree.   As the eggs are protruded, they are placed,
by a sort of peristaltic motion, between the skin of
the belly and the layer of cotton which covers the
spot of the tree to which the insect is attached.   As
more eggs are laid, the skin of the belly is pushed
nearer that of the back, till at length the two skins
are thrust close together by means of the eggs, and
the under part of the insect assumes a concave shape
(*fig.* 2).   Under the influence of this pressure, an
absorbing process goes on, which leaves no putres-
cible matter behind.   Hence it arises that, when our
little insect yields to the general law, and dies almost
immediately after perpetuating the species, its carcass is as sure a protection to its young, when dead,
as its body was when alive.

The time during which the young cocci remain
in the egg is not determined by Reaumur; he conjectures, however, that they take twelve days, and afterward remain several days under the skin of their
mother, before they emancipate themselves, and go
out into their little world of leaf or stem.   At this
period of their existence, they exhibit, in their activity, nothing of the peculiarities just detailed; they
soon, however, select and fix upon a suitable part

of a plant : the male insect, which is destined to become a small winged creature, as soon as it has its wings, crawls out backwards from its larval skin, which served it for a cocoon while undergoing its nymphine metamorphosis.

The opening by which they quit their maternal prison is provided also by nature. The posterior portion of the body of the mother is cloven, and cannot be exactly fitted to the tree—hence, the young can escape without lacerating those parental remains which had sheltered them even after death.

After having got abroad, they fix themselves to the leaves of trees, and their growth from June to October, when they enlarge a little, is slow, but it is only in the following April that they begin to assume perceptibly a globular shape. At the falling of the leaf, however, nature has taught them to retire to the stem of the tree, where they finish their life. As soon as the male has acquired wings, it does not fly away, but walks, and it is towards the females fixed on the tree that its steps are directed. The size of the former is so small, in comparison with that of the latter, that the globular body of the female appears a spacious territory, for the diminutive male to walk about.

There are other kinds of gall-insects, which do not cover their young with their bodies, but secrete a quantity of downy cotton, sufficient to form a species of cocoon, on which they perch themselves. The dark spot is the insect, the white bag the cocoon.

CHAPTER X.

APHIS, OR PLANT-LOUSE.

Every Tree, every part of a Tree has its peculiar Species—Suck Vegetable Juices—Shelter themselves from bad Weather in the concave parts of Leaves.

AMONG the most curious of those animals which are parasitical on plants, is the aphis, or plant-louse. It is an insect common enough in our fields and gardens, and there is scarcely a tree or shrub which is not attacked by one or more species peculiar to itself. Some are winged, and others have no wings; and some are black, green, brown, in short, all colours: but however they may vary in these non-essentials, their habits and instincts are similar. They live in society, and attach themselves to the stems, the leaves, and roots of shrubs and vegetables, the juices of which they suck by means of a tube, with which they are furnished for the purpose; and they frequently cling in such numbers to the sustaining plant, as to give it a most unsightly appearance.

If the rose-tree, or any other plant, be carefully examined, some portion of it will be found covered with little transparent insects of a green colour. They appear to be in a state of perfect repose: they are, however, in reality, diligently occupied in pumping out the juices of the plant. The following is a magnified figure of the insect. The length of the sucking pump or trunk, in some species, extends beyond the body; when they walk, it is folded under the belly: in the generality, however, the ordinary length of this member is about one-third that of the insect. While employed in using this instrument, they form at times two layers, one over the other;

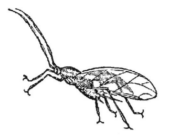

the second or upper layer walk freely over the first, and not being able to suck, are diligently employed in bringing forth young.

These immense societies of suckers must of course drain the leaf, and exhaust the juices of the plant to which they are attached: this is the fact, and, by Leeuwenhoek, they have been truly termed the pests of the garden. However, the effect is occasionally curious enough; for instead of withering, the parts to which the aphides are attached enlarge or twist, and by so doing furnish shelter to their enemies. The insect chooses the concavity of a shoot, for example, and this, through loss of juice, being diverted from its straight direction, assumes the shape of a corkscrew; in the concave folds of this diverted shoot it is that the aphis shelters itself from the weather.

Reaumur says that this curve takes place on the side from which the insects suck the juices, for the same reason that a piece of wood soaked in water,

and exposed to the action of the fire, is bent to the side acted upon by that element. Another effect of the curling of the shoot is, that the leaves, which, if extended, would stand far apart, are so drawn together as to form a complete covering, and thus the insects are at once defended from wind and rain, and concealed from the view of their natural enemies.

If shoots can be bent by insects which attach themselves to this portion of a plant, the leaves must of course be more easily susceptible of this operation.

Generally, they seek the under surface of the leaves, probably as that part which affords them most shelter. If the upper surface of a gooseberry, currant, or apple leaf be examined, it will be found studded with pale, reddish, or citron-coloured eminences; and on the under surface, cavities will be discovered answering to these eminences, and peopled with aphides. These portions of the leaf are thicker than the rest.

A still more remarkable change of form is caused in the plant by the developement of galls formed by the plant-louse. When opened, they will be found hollow, and filled with a colony of these creatures. In size they vary from that of a nut to that of the human fist.

It has been already stated, that the formation of
the true gall-nut is owing to the deposition of an
egg in some part of a plant. But in the formation of
the protuberances inhabited by the aphides there
is this remarkable difference; that the parent, instead of burying her offspring, buries herself, and
then, as the walls of her wonderful mansion rise up
around and enclose her, she begins to people her
abode. When Reaumur examined the smallest of
these at its first formation, he found it tenanted by
one old aphis only:—when he examined a larger
gall-nut he found, in addition to the old aphis, one
or two young ones—and in a protuberance of a
larger size still, he discovered a more abundant population. The mode by which the insect is at last
thoroughly enclosed is thus described by him :—" Let
us imagine that the mother-aphis, still young, pricks
the leaf; the punctured spot swells all around the
insect, and consequently it becomes enclosed within
a little cavity. If it continue to prick it at the lowest part of this cavity, this place will go on swelling
in length, so as to become oblong or cylindrical.
Let us conceive that the insect always continues to
puncture it forwards; as soon as the gall has risen
to a certain height above the superior surface of the
leaf, the insect is no longer in its original position;
viz. on the plane of the inferior surface of the leaf.
Here then it is that there is a small opening into the
incipient bladder; this aperture is only an indenta-
tion in the leaf. As soon as the insect removes from

the aperture towards the other end of the bladder, nothing tends to hinder the bent sides from meeting soonest at the narrowest part, and so at last closing it up entirely. Here then we have the insect shut up in an oblong sack or bladder. It brings forth young, these prick the gall, and suck the juice on all sides, so that being thus irritated in every direction, it grows in every direction, and consequently a glo- bular form results. And as the punctures are al- ways in a direction farthest from the original aper- ture, that part enlarges least; and consequently the gall appears to be attached to the leaf by a pedicle or foot-stalk."

Another class of aphides, which inhabit the poplar, instead of forming galls, contrive to double the leaf so nicely on the nerve which runs through the mid- dle, as to bring the two edges exactly together, and so construct a closed sack. This they effect by pricking the under surface in various places, so as to give rise to small galls, which cause the leaf to curve. Reaumur observes that these punctures must be made according to some definite measure on each side of the centre nervure, or else the edges of the two sides would not exactly meet. Besides these modes of protection, few species of aphides destined to live

in the open air have been discovered, which are not encased in a downy stuff.

The injury inflicted by the aphis may be estimated from the following extract:—" Our apple-trees here are greatly injured, and some annually destroyed by the agency of what seems to be a very feeble insect. We call it from habit, or from some unassigned cause, the 'American blight' (aphis lanata); this noxious creature being known in some orchards by the more significant name of 'white blight.' In the spring of the year a slight hoariness is observed upon the branches of certain species of our orchard fruit. As the season advances, this hoariness increases, it becomes cottony, and towards the middle or end of summer, the under sides of some of the branches are invested with a thick, downy substance, so long as, at times, to be sensibly agitated by the air. Upon examining this substance, we find that it conceals a multitude of small, wingless creatures, which are busily employed in preying upon the limb of the tree beneath. This they are well enabled to do by means of a beak terminating in a fine bristle; this being insinuated through the bark, and the sappy part of the wood, enables the creature to extract, as with a syringe, the sweet, vital liquor that circulates in the plant. This terminating bristle is not observed in every individual: in those that possess it, it is of different lengths, and is usually, when not in use, so closely concealed under the breast of the animal, as to be invisible. In the younger insects it is often manifested by protruding like a fine termination to the anus; but as their bodies become lengthened the bristle is not in this way observable. The alburnum or sap wood, being thus wounded, rises up in excrescences and nodes all over the branch, and deforms it; the limb, deprived of its nutriment, grows sickly; the leaves turn yellow, and the part perishes. Branch after branch is thus assailed, until they all become leafless, and the tree dies.

I.—Q

" Aphides in general attack the young and softer parts of plants; but this insect seems easily to wound the harder bark of the apple, and by no means makes choice of the most tender part of the branch. They give a preference to certain sorts, but not always the most rich fruits; as cider apples and wildings are greatly infested by them, and from some unknown cause other varieties seem to be exempted from their depredations. The Wheeler's russet, and Crofton pippin, I have never observed to be injured by them. This insect is viviparous, or produces its young alive, forming a cradle for them by discharging from the extremities of its body a quantity of long, cottony matter, which, becoming interwoven and entangled, prevents the young from falling to the earth, and completely envelopes the parent and offspring. In this cottony substance we observe, as soon as the creature becomes animated in the spring, and as long as it remains in vigour, many round pellucid bodies, which, at the first sight, look like eggs, only that they are larger than we might suppose to be ejected by the animal. They consist of a sweet, glutinous fluid, and are probably the discharges of the aphis, and the first food of its young. That it thus consumed I conjecture from its diminution, and its by no means increasing so fast as fæcal matter would do, from such perpetually feeding creatures. I have not, in any instance, observed the young to proceed from these globular bodies, though they are found of various ages at all times during the season. This lanuginous vestiture seems to serve likewise as a vehicle for dispersing the animal; for though most of our species of aphis are furnished with wings, I have never seen any individual of this American blight so provided, but the winds wafting about small tufts of this downy matter, convey the creature with it from tree to tree throughout the whole orchard. In the autumn, when this substance is generally long, the winds and rains of the season effectually disperse these insects, and we observe them endeavouring to secrete themselves in the crannies of any neighbouring substance. Should the savoy cabbage be near the trees whence they have been dislodged, the cavities of the under sides of its leaves are commonly favourite asylums for them. Multitudes perish by these rough removals, but numbers yet remain; and we may find them in the nodes and crevices, on the under sides of the branches, at any period of the year, the long, cottony vesture being removed, but still they are enveloped in a fine, short, downy clothing, to be seen by a magnifier, proceeding apparently from every suture, or pore of their bodies, and protecting them in their dormant state from the moisture and frosts of our climate. This aphis, in a natural state, usually awakens and commences its labours very early in the month of March; and the hoariness on its body may be observed increasing daily: but if an infected branch be cut in the winter, and kept in water in a warm room, these aphides will awaken speedily, spin their cottony vests, and feed, and discharge, as accustomed to do in a genial season.

" It is often very difficult to ascertain the first appearance of many creatures not natives of our climate, though from the progress of science, and more general observation, many things will be recorded. The first visit of this aphis to us is by no means clear. The epithet of American blight may be correctly applied; but we have no sufficient authority to conclude that we derived this pest from that country. Normandy and the Netherlands, too, have each been supposed to have conferred this evil upon us; but extensively as this insect is spread around, and favourable as our climate appears to be to its increase, it bids fair to destroy in progression most of our oldest and long-esteemed fruit from our orchards. The same unknown decree, which regulates the increase and decrease of all created beings, influences this insect; yet wet seasons, upon the whole, seem

genial to its constitution.   In the hot dry summer of
1825, it was abundant every where; in the spring of
1826, which was unusually fine and dry, it abounded
in such incredible luxuriance, that many trees seemed
at a short distance as if they had been whitewashed:
in the ensuing summer, which was a very dry and
hot one, this cottony matter so entirely disappeared,
that to superficial observation the malady was not in
existence; and it did not become manifest again
until September, when, after the rains of that season,
it reissued in fine, cottony patches, from the old
nodes on the trees."*

From the peculiar powers with which nature has
invested the aphides, and from their extraordinary
fecundity, for they are both oviparous and viviparous,
no rational man can doubt that they form an important link in the economy of the universe.   Their
inordinate increase is kept in check by other insects,
which appear to be born for no other purpose than
that of devouring them.   Such is the voracity of
this tribe, that naturalists term them aphidivorous
insects . they are of different species, having few
qualities in common except this faculty of devouring
the plant-louse; the same instinct which impels certain insects to deposite their eggs in the midst of the
food which is to support the yet unborn young, causes
others, in like manner, to place their eggs in the
midst of the habitations of the aphides.   In this
way the larvæ of some species of syrphus, and of
hemerobius, are, as Reaumur says, "born in the
midst of a people, pacific, and unprovided with
offensive or defensive arms, who patiently await the
mortal blow without suspecting the quarter whence
it comes."

The strength and size of the syrphus in comparison with its victim, the aphis, is that of a lion
to a kid.

* Journal of a Naturalist, p 347—352, 2d ed.

In the following magnified figure (*fig.* 1) it will be seen that the larva tapers from the head to the tail;

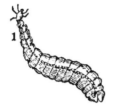

under the head is a mouth, which (*fig.* 2) appears armed with two horny pins, and a trident-like dart; between these is the orifice of the mouth. The creature has the power of emitting a glutinous secretion, by means of which it fixes itself to a spot well stocked with aphides, where, like a wolf in a sheepfold, it commits the most dreadful havoc: thus attached to a stem or a leaf, there is no other animal of prey which hunts with so much ease. It begins by turning its head in all directions, backwards, forwards, and sideways, until it meets with a plant-louse, which it instantly transfixes with its dart: it then contrives to adjust the body of the aphis over its mouth like a cork, and in an instant the victim, with its leg stretched out, is sucked dry.

Reaumur used to make these syrphi fast a few hours, and then placing one on his hand, he could with the assistance of a lens see the whole operation of feeding, and observe the juices, and even the young aphides sucked out of the body of their parent, go down the transparent gullet of the voracious larva. The drained skin of the aphis is then thrown aside.

It is easy to calculate, that if they ate incessantly they would destroy a prodigious number of aphides.

Reaumur has seen a piece of stalk seven or eight inches long, and covered with plant-lice, completely cleared in four days by two or three aphidivorous worms.

Q 2

After having eaten its fill, in its appointed time it
seeks the hollow of a leaf, glues itself to it, and contracting its body into an oval, undergoes that species
of metamorphosis in which the insect retracts itself
within its own skin, which, becoming hard, forms a
cocoon, and ultimately appears in its perfect form
of a fly.

Another enemy of the aphis is an insect, called by
Reaumur the lion of the aphides (hemerobius).
" We sow grain," says he, " in our land, for the purpose of providing ourselves with food. It appears
that nature rears aphides on plants for the purpose
of feeding other species of insects, which, without
them, would perish of hunger."

The following figure is a larva of the lion of the

aphides; a title which it well deserves from its voracity. The largest plant-louse is sucked by it in a
few moments; and, like its prototype, it is not inac-
tive, but hunts for its prey. They do not spare even
each other; for, if by chance one of its own species
should be found between its suckers, it makes not

the least objection to this substitute for its natural
food.

Reaumur shut up twenty of these ravenous creatures in a box, and supplied them with aphides for
food; they were reduced in a few days to three or
four, these having eaten the rest.

They spin a cocoon which is globular, and not
bigger than a pea, and yet the full-grown insect
comes out with a pair of such ample wings, that it
is a matter of astonishment how these, together with
the insect, could be packed up in so small a case.
These wings are so fine that the solar rays are
broken upon them as on a prism; indeed, the whole
form of the insect, with its large lustrous eyes, gossamer wings, the tender shining and golden green
of its body, is strikingly beautiful.

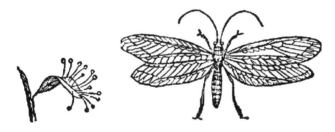

The eggs which it lays are remarkable, inasmuch
as they present the appearance of parasitical plants,
growing from the leaf to which they are attached;
the stalks are about an inch in length, white and
transparent. The mode in which they are attached
to the extremities of these hairs is thus explained
by Reaumur.

The egg is enveloped in a viscous matter fit for
forming silk. Being in part protruded, the insect
applies the end of the egg bedewed with this substance to the leaf, and a portion of the glutinous
stuff thus adheres to it. It then withdraws its abdomen, and by doing so, the viscid drop is length-

ened out; by the time the egg is expressed, and the
body of the insect withdrawn from it, it is found
attached to a thread formed of glutinous matter,
which now, being dry, is capable of supporting the
egg. In due time the worm pierces its aërial habitation, descends upon the leaf, and finds itself in the
midst of a colony of aphides, which it instantly
attacks. The obvious use of these stalks appears
to be to preserve the egg from being covered or injured by the aphides But whether this be the true
explanation is uncertain.

The larva of another kind of hemerobius clothes
itself in an artificial manner, and for this purpose
uses the skins of those unfortunate plant-lice which
it had previously sucked. Indeed it piles up such a
quantity of them on its back, as to look as if it carried a little mountain. This ostentatious exhibition of its trophies does not appear to arise from any
sentiment of vainglory; for when Reaumur removed these skins, the insect clothed itself with the
fragments of its cocoon; and on this coat too being
taken away, an abundant supply of paper-shavings
was placed within its reach: " Never," says Reaumur, " was so much convenient matter placed at the
disposal of any insect of this kind; and accordingly
a thicker, more complete, and a higher vest was
never borne, perhaps, by any other little lion."

The structure of the covering thus formed is rude
enough. The parts adhere for the same reason that
shreds of any thing adhere to one another. The
insect, however, places them on its back with much
address; it lays hold of the material or skin between
its horns, so that it rests on its head; it then gives
a toss, and pitches it to the desired spot; if not successful, a few contortions of its body bring it right.
The reason of this anxiety to invest their bodies
with such a strange covering appears to be to deceive the birds, which consider them as dainties—
at least this is M. Dumeril's opinion. It is more

easy to believe it when stated, than to know how the author of the assertion could find it out.

Another enemy of the aphis is the larva of the lady-bird. It is difficult to trace the origin of the popular custom which ensures protection to these insects. In France they are called Bêtes de la Vierge, or Vaches à Dieu, as if under the tutelary patronage of the Virgin herself. But they really deserve all the protection they receive; for while they leave our hops and valuable plants uninjured, they destroy the greatest enemy of these vegetables —the plant-louse. " If," says Kirby, " we could only discover a mode of increasing these insects at will, we might not only, as Dr. Darwin has suggested, clear out hot-houses of aphides by their means, but render our crops of hops much more certain than they now are." In 1827, the shore at Brighton, and all the watering places on the south coast, were literally covered with them, to the terror of the inhabitants: they being ignorant that these insects were emigrating after having cleared the neighbouring hop-grounds of the destructive aphis.

It furnishes a subject of serious consideration, as well as an argument for a special providence, to know, that the accurate Reaumur, and other naturalists, have observed, that when any kind of insect has increased inordinately, their natural enemies have increased in the same proportion and thus preserved the balance.

CHAPTER XI.

*Gnat—Bug—Fly-bug—Flea—Chigoe—Louse—Mites and Ticks—
Gad-fly.*

THERE are few insects with whose form we are
better acquainted than that of the gnat.   It is to be
found in all latitudes and climates ; as prolific in the
polar as in the equatorial regions.   In 1736 they
were so numerous, and were seen to rise in such
clouds from Salisbury cathedral, that they looked
like columns of smoke, and frightened the people,
who thought the building was on fire.   In 1766, they
appeared at Oxford in the form of a thick black
cloud; six columns were observed to ascend the
height of fifty or sixty feet.   Their bite was attended
with alarming inflammation.   To some appearances
of this kind our great poet Spenser alludes, in the
following beautiful simile :—

> As when a swarm of gnats at eventide,
> Out of the fennes of Allan doe arise,
> Their murmurring small trumpets sownden wide,
> Whiles in the air their clust'ring army flies,
> That as a cloud doth seem to dim the skies,
> Ne man nor beast may rest or take repast,
> For their sharp wounds and noyous injuries,
> Till the fierce northern wind, with blustering blast,
> Doth blow them quite away, and in the ocean cast

In Lapland their numbers have been compared to
a flight of snow when the flakes fall thickest, and the
minor evil of being nearly suffocated by smoke is
endured to get rid of these little pests.   Captain
Stedman says, that he and his soldiers were so tor-
mented by gnats in America that they were obliged
to dig holes in the ground with their bayonets, and
thrust their heads into them for protection and sleep.
Humboldt states, that "between the little harbour

of Higuerote and the mouth of the Rio-Unare, the
wretched inhabitants are accustomed to stretch
themselves on the ground, and pass the night buried
in the sand three or four inches deep, exposing only
the head, which they cover with a handkerchief."

After enumerating these and other examples of
the achievements of the gnat and mosquito tribe,
Kirby says, " It is not therefore incredible that
Sapor, king of Persia, should have been compelled
to raise the siege of Nisibis by a plague of gnats,
which attacked his elephants and beasts of burden,
and so caused the rout of his army; nor that the
inhabitants of various cities should, by an extraordinary multiplication of this plague, have been compelled to desert them; nor that, by their power of
doing mischief, like other conquerors who have been
the torment of the human race, they should have
attained to fame, and have given their name to bays,
towns, and territories."*

The instrument with which they inflict their tortures, simple as it appears to the eye, is nevertheless wonderfully complicated and ingenious: it
forms a set of lancets, consisting of five pieces,
enclosed in a case. This case is split from one end
to the other, and, as the creature sucks, it serves to
give steadiness to the instruments, while they are
thrust forward into our flesh. In the first figure
(*fig.* 1), the lancets alone are seen entering, and
their case forms an arc, supporting them. In the
second (*fig.* 2), the lancets are perceived to have
penetrated more deeply, while the case, not entering, is seen to form an angle.

In order to see the whole process of suction,
Reaumur courted what most others sedulously shun
—a sting or two: " After a gnat had done me the
kindness of settling on the hand I stretched out, I
saw that it protruded a very fine point from its pro-

* Mosquito Bay   Mosquitos, a town in Cuba   Mosquito country
in North America

boscis, with the extremity of which it felt four or five spots of my skin. It would appear that it knows where it can pierce through most easily, and reach a large blood-vessel. Having selected a spot for its operations, it soon causes the sufferer to feel its sting." The *fine point* when magnified presents the following formidable picture, of which some of the

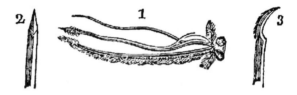

detached pieces seem admirably fitted for the gnat's purpose and our annoyance. It is not however, the introduction of these points, which, when combined, are as much less in size than the finest needle, as that is than a sword, that causes the irritation which, when extended over the limb, has in some cases rendered amputation necessary—the gnat introduces a little liquid, for the purpose, as Reaumur conjectures, of rendering our thick blood thin enough to be sucked through its proboscis. To allay the effects of this poison, there seems to be no better or readier means than sweet-oil, which, if applied to the wound within a few hours after it has been made, will remove the swelling, although when delayed five or six hours it has no effect.

The gnat undergoes many metamorphoses. If water be allowed for some time to stand still in a bucket, or if a quantity of that fluid be taken from a stagnant pool, it will be found to contain innumerable aquatic insects of the following shape (*fig.* 1): these are the larvæ of the gnat; they swim with the head downwards, a position which, to most animals, would be fatal; they retain the longest tube, which is their respiratory organ, on the surface; the other tube forms the anus. In this state they live on the contents of stagnant waters, and change their skins several times.

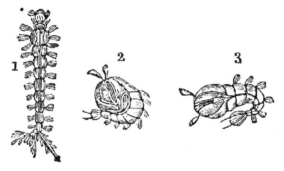

After having thrice got rid of its skin, the gnat appears in a new form, for, instead of being oblong, it is lenticular (*fig.* 2). The surface of the circle is vertical to the water. In this, which is its nymphine state, it is still capable of moving briskly after the manner of a shrimp, by expanding and elongating its body (*fig.* 3), and striking the water with the fins at its tail. In this stage of its metamorphosis, it has no organ for food, and it seems to require none; but a regular and abundant supply of air appears indispensable; it floats on the surface of the water, and only descends by efforts made with its tail. Two ears may be observed sticking out at the thickest part; these are its respiratory organs, and afford a curious instance of an important part. being re-

I.—R

moved from one extremity of the body to the other
during the progress of an insect through its different
stages of life.

Its last metamorphosis into a winged fly is
attended with curious circumstances.   When nature
has prepared the insect to change its element, instead
of lying rolled up on the surface of the water, it
stretches out its body, and by some mechanism,
puffs up its corslet so that it splits between the stigmata or the breathing-horns.   As soon as the fissure
is sufficiently enlarged to make way for it, the head
of the gnat appears in its perfect shape; but this is
the most critical period of its whole life; up.to this
time it was an aquatic animal; now it has nothing
to dread so much as the water.   It has, moreover,
the use neither of leg nor wing; these members are
as yet soft, moist, and bound up, and it only pro-
trudes itself from its skin, by means of a wriggling
action given to its body.   If at this critical juncture
the water should happen to touch its corslet or abdomen, the gnat would inevitably and instantly
perish.   In such circumstances, then, it requires the
prudence of an old gnat, at least, to escape the dangers which surround the young one.   Nature, however, has conferred upon the insect an instinct suitable to the emergency.   As soon as it puts out its
head, it elevates it above the water; and worming
itself out always perpendicularly, supported only by
the inequalities of the skin which it is about to cast
off, with no power to balance itself, surrounded by
an unfriendly element, it literally becomes a canoe,

of which its own body forms mast and sail. The skin floats, and when the observer perceives, says Reaumur, how much the prow of the little bark sinks, and how near its sides are to the water, he forgets at the moment that the gnat is an insect which at another time he would kill; nay, he becomes anxious for its fate, and the more so if the slightest breeze play on the surface of the water: the least agitation of the air suffices to waft the creature with swiftness from place to place, and make it spin round and round. Its body, folded in its wings, bears a greater proportion to the little skiff, than the largest mass of sail to a ship: it is impossible not to dread lest the insect should be wrecked; once laid on its side on the water, there is no escape. Reaumur has seen the surface of the water covered with creatures of this kind which had thus perished at their birth. Generally, however, all terminates favourably, and the danger is over in a minute. After having stood perpendicularly, it draws out its two fore-legs, and bending to the water, places them on its surface, which is terra firma for a gnat's weight; having secured this position, all is safe; the wings dry and expand, and the insect, quitting its natal element, mounts into the air.

It is supposed, that from the end of May to that of October, six or seven generations of these insects are born, and each gnat is capable of laying two hundred and fifty eggs. These are found agglutinated into a mass, and swimming about on the surface of water: they are individually olive-shaped, the large end being in the water, the rest in the air.

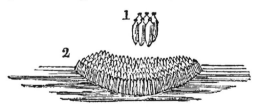

When conjoined, the upper surface of the mass presents to the eye the appearance of an infinite series of points. In arranging and floating this raft of eggs the gnat displays surprising ingenuity. They are discharged one by one, vertically, and not horizontally from the extremity of the insect; for this purpose it generally fixes itself on some solid substance, such as the bank of the water, or on a floating leaf. Standing on its four feet, it stretches out the two hindmost legs; these being crossed, form

an angle in which the first egg is laid; the second is placed next, and they adhere by means of a glutinous matter surrounding each. The gnat places them thus with the abdomen solely: when a sufficient number of eggs have been placed side by side, to render the base of the mass large enough to balance the height—for it is clear that a few eggs only could not float upright on so narrow a stem as they possess—the gnat launches its precious vessel, and fearlessly commits its cherished young to that little ocean which is fraught with so many dangers to itself.

The mass thus glued together, consisting of between two hundred and fifty and three hundred eggs, is of an oblong form, and considerably resembles a little boat in shape. And it possesses not only the form, but also most of the other properties of a boat; its fore and hind parts being sharp and higher than the middle; the lower part on which it always floats being convex, and the upper part concave. It is likewise so buoyant that no agitation of the water, however violent, can sink it; and what is still more deserving of admiration, although hollow, it never

becomes filled with water, even when exposed to
the violence of the torrents which frequently accompany a thunder-storm. "To put this to the
test," says Kirby, "I yesterday (July 25, 1811) put
half a dozen of these boats upon the surface of a
tumbler, half-full of water. I then poured upon
them a stream of that element, from the mouth of a
quart bottle, held a foot above them. Yet after this
treatment, which was so rough as actually to project
one out of the glass, I found them floating as before
upon their bottoms, and not a drop of water within
their cavity."

Another of our tormentors is the bug, which as it
would appear has not been long known in this island.
Had the insect been common, as Kirby justly observes, the two noble ladies mentioned by Mouffet
would scarcely have mistaken their bites for plague
spots. They were first known by the name of
wall-louse. It was not until the middle of the last
century that they began to be styled bugs, or gob-
lins; the word being of Celtic origin, and used in
old versions of the Bible, in the sense of spirit:
thus, in Matthews's Bible, Ps. xci. 5, the passage
translated in our modern version, "Thou shalt not
be afraid for *the terror* by night," is rendered, "Thou
shalt not nede to be afraide of any *bugs* by night."
Horrible as these disgusting creatures are, it would
appear that, at Surat, there was, or perhaps there
still is, a Banian hospital, containing not only horses,
pigs, mules, oxen, sheep, goats, monkeys, pigeons,
and poultry, but also an extraordinary ward appropriated to rats, mice, and bugs; and Forbes, upon
the authority of whose Oriental Memoirs this is
stated, adds, that beggars are hired, who, for a sti-
pulated sum, agree to pass a night at this institution,
in order to afford "the fleas, lice, and bugs" an un-
molested feast!

A species of bug, described by Geoffrey unde
the name of fly-bug (*reduvius personatus*), is an in-
R 2

habitant of our dwellings.   It prowls about in disguise, at night, and, among other insects, shows itself the uncompromising enemy of the loathsome bed-bug.   Kirby thinks it ought on this account to be encouraged ; but its own bite, as painful as the sting of the bee, and its supposed power of communicating an electric shock on the slightest contact, would render the remedy somewhat worse than the evil.   In its three states of grub, nymph, and winged insect, it is ever on the look out for food.   Being slow of motion, though capable, like a crab, of walking backwards, sideways, or forwards, it is obliged to entrap its prey by masking itself: hence its cognomen, " personatus."   Knowing that the insects for which it is on the hunt are accustomed to the sight of dirt, cobwebs, flue, and such other materials as are usually found in the habitations of man, the reduvius piles upon itself bits of hair, flour, down of feathers, sawdust or plaster, so as to enlarge its own dimensions to twice or thrice the natural size ; and thus accoutred it is scarcely to be recognised by its prey, or by its own enemies, as any thing but a ball of flue.   When it sees a bug, or spider, or any soft-bodied insect, it approaches its destined victim with the most guarded caution. Sometimes the little lump of gathered dust seems to be blown about the room in a zig-zag direction : sometimes it is puffed into the air, and falls as if a chance gust had acted on it.   These motions, however, are any thing but unintentional.   After stealthily sideling, or making little leaps, followed by intervals of motionless repose, the better to deceive its prey, the creature at last contrives to secure, paralyze, and suck its victim's juices to the very last drop.   When it has acquired the wings of its perfect state, it doffs its cassock, and boldly flies about without disguise.

The flea is another of our pests, yet it has been domesticated by some curious persons.   Thus, the naturalist Willoughby kept a tame one, which was fed not only with, but literally out of, his own hand, being permitted to suck his blood.   Others have contrived a pigmy chariot, cut from the cherry-stone, to be dragged by a team of these nimble creatures.   Wherever they swarm it is no easy matter to get rid of them.   In order to prevent being eaten up by these insects and lice, the Hungarian shepherds are said to grease their bodies and linen with lard, so that even these unscrupulous tormentors are deterred from the filthy banquet.   They abound so much in the Missouri country, that the natives are often obliged to shift their quarters. Once when th late Dr. Clarke was rejoicing at the thought of passing one night free from vermin, his expectations were speedily dissipated by the sheikh of the district, who assured him that the " king of the fleas held his court at Tiberias."

The chigoe or jigger is a species of this genus. The female lodges under the skin, where it breeds

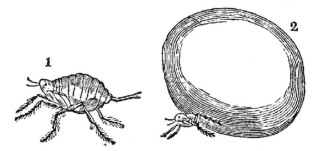

its young.   Formerly the genus of the insect was a subject of dispute ; and a capuchin friar suffered one to breed in his great toe, for the purpose of bringing it up to determine the point.   His scientific zeal, however, cost him a foot, for the member containing the precious deposite having mortified, its amputation became indispensable.   The male is not very unlike the common flea.   The abdomen of the female,

nowever, like that of the queen of the white ants,
the cocci, &c., enlarges to an enormous size when
full of young.

A greater abomination than any of these is the
louse. It is said that on the third day of the disease
called *plica Polonica*, in which the hair of the head
becomes painful and distended with blood so as to
drain the patient if cut, they appear in myriads.
Leuwenhoek has calculated that a female lays at
least sixty eggs in six days; that in six days more
the young appear; that in eighteen days more they
are capable of propagating; so that, according to
his calculation, two families of lice would, in sixty
days, have fifteen thousand descendants.

Since the days of Pharaoh, Herod, Scylla, and
Philip II., these horrid infesters of our race, three
species of which attach themselves as parasites to
man, have given a name to a disease, which, though
extremely rare, is not fictitious—the *phthiriasis*, or
morbus pedicularis.

The mite tribe (*acari*) is another class of insects,
which sometimes cause the most horrible maladies
to man.   They are oviparous, and those which
swarm in rotten cheese will give a correct notion of
the general form of the whole class.   Heberden and
Willan, in modern times, have recorded dreadful instances of the sufferings which they have inflicted
upon the human race.   They penetrate under the
skin, and multiply in little tumours, which, when
opened, swarm with these creatures.   Mouffet states
of the Lady Penruddock, that mites swarmed on
every part of her body; on the eyes, nose, gums,
head, soles of the feet, putting her to daily and
nightly torture; so that all the flesh of her body
being consumed, she at length had the happiness to
die !

It has been also asserted that the itch is caused
by the presence of a mite.   The insect, says Linnæus, insinuates itself under the skin, and there

produces a little vesicle from whence it never moves. An experienced eye will readily detect its lurking place, and an experienced hand as readily remove it with the point of a pin. If it be placed on the nail it remains immoveable until warmed by the breath, when it runs with great agility.

Almost all the vegetable and animal matter used by man is infested by some species of this insect: dried meat, old bread, flour, sweetmeats, cheese, soon swarm with an extremely minute and active race of mites, any of which, when viewed with the microscope, appear covered with hair; and, what is curious, each hair is as moveable as the quills of the porcupine · consequently in an animal invisible to the naked eye, it is probable that each hair has a muscle attached to it. These insects multiply both in winter and summer, and as they arrive at perfection in a week, it may be imagined what myriads must be generated. In fact, to these little creatures is intrusted the task of clearing away much of the dead matter which would otherwise annoy us. As they are imperceptible, says Latreille, an infinite number must enter into the bread we eat, especially if it be made of old flour.

Our domestic quadrupeds furnish a lodging for acari. They appear, in the first instance, to be generated in the woods, and whenever the dog, the ox, or even man, comes into contact with them, they bury their trunk in the skin, and suck the blood with avidity.

Their body is smooth, and their shape a little oval sac or cup,—a reservoir for the vital fluid. The trunk or pump is furnished on each side with a set of teeth like those of a saw, and it is by means of the hold these afford that the acarus is enabled to fix itself so firmly. The mite known to the older naturalists by the name of reduvius fixes itself to cattle and sheep, by a similar trunk, the teeth of which are turned backwards. These, like several of their tribe, have a sort of vesicular enlargement on their feet: this bladder seems to be moved in various directions, and assumes various shapes; and as the animal can fix itself or walk upon the most polished mirror, it is not improbable that they effect their object, after the manner of the fly, by exhausting the air.

The woods of the southern provinces of both the Americas are infested by a species of acarus, which proves a terrible pest to man and beast. They who sit down on the stumps of trees, or heaps of dried leaves; they who happen to walk barefoot, are soon covered with little slow-moving creatures, which, fixing on the naked skin, suck the live blood, and become distended to the size of half an inch in length, and a quarter of an inch in height and breadth. They swarm in such multitudes on cattle, and inflict such wounds, that these often perish. At first the sensation is scarcely perceptible, afterward a pleasant itching comes on; which is succeeded by acute pain. If the part be examined, the insect will be found half buried in the flesh, and its place marked by a swelling of the size of a pea. In endeavouring to extract this pest, the utmost care must be used; for it will sooner be pulled asunder than loose its hold; and should this accident happen, the portion of the insect which is left in the skin will cause a deep and ill-conditioned sore, accompanied with intolerable itching, which, it is said, has sometimes rendered it indispensable to amputate the limb. Kalm says he has seen them fixed to the bellies of horses, in such numbers, that the point of a knife could not be insinuated between any two tumours, and the wretched animals, after being drained and weakened, died in the greatest tortures. He adds, that, like leeches, when they have sucked their fill, they will drop off; having taken two of these, and enclosed them in a box, he found that they began to lay, and he counted upwards of a thousand eggs, which each had deposited, and still they had not finished.

Sparrman asserts, that he found several acari, of the largest dimensions, on three rhinoceroses recently killed; and that when these were gorged with blood, they became distended to an enormous size.

Birds are infested with acari: the domestic fowl, the sparrow, the peacock, are worlds for minuter creatures, which attack them as parasites, like the species already mentioned. Some others of this family, besides having their extremities terminating in bladders, capable of being inflated and contracted at will, are furnished with a crotchet or hook, on the under part of each bladder. This mechanism renders it extremely difficult to dislodge them when they have once settled. Not only man, and the giants of the creation, whether vegetable or animal, are subjected to the attacks of these tiny depredators, but insects themselves must furnish nourishment to still smaller insects; and even the smallest of those which are visible to the naked eye, present a wide range for some puny parasite. The bee, the beetle, and the dragon-fly may be seen covered by these creatures. The spider, at all times offensive, becomes loathsome when its body is eaten up with acari. The common fly must yield up its juices to its parasites, and the gnat which steals a minute drop from man, provides an ocean of nourishment for the little hexapodes, which lodge under the ample folds of its body. The minute plant-lice, which drain the vegetable world, are themselves drained in their turn. But there are some species of insects, which are infested by acari whose habits are perfectly unique. De Geer observed a heap of small acari piled on the body of a species of beetle (*leptura*), which prevented it from walking, and appeared to inflict upon it the greatest torment. On examining this heap with a lens, what was his astonishment in discovering that the acari composing it formed a chain of suckers! The first sucked the leptura, the second sucked the sucker, and the third drained the second. Each of these acari has a sort of tube issuing from its tail, which is funnel-shaped at both ends. The loose extremity is applied so firmly to the insect to be sucked, that it cannot be removed even by the acarus itself without great exertion.

Of the mites which infest vegetables, our gardens furnish innumerable examples. The little greenish creatures which cover the leaves with a thin film, and lodge in it in myriads, ruining our fruits and garden-stuff, are too well known to require description.

Besides these various species of stationary acari, which perish when the animal or vegetable on which they feed perishes, there are others called wanderers, which are common both to plants and animals. Of this description is the *acarus autumnalis*, or harvest-bug. This is a little red insect, which creates a furious itching wherever it buries itself.

What the gall-fly does to a plant, the gad-fly (*œstrus*) does to our cattle: it deposites its egg under the skin of the animal, and thus gives rise to what may be justly termed an animal gall. These tumours are to be found most frequently on young and well-fed calves; and far from being any drawback in the estimation of the purchaser, cattle-breeders prefer those animals in which they exist, being well aware that the instinct of the parent insect causes it to place its young only where its food is most abundant—that is, under the skin of such of our cattle as are full of juices and health. The tanners also prefer those skins which abound in bot-holes, because

they are the thickest and strongest. As soon as the worm has quitted the egg, it finds itself in a nest,

which affords it shelter, food, and an equal tempera
ture in all seasons.

The egg, having been introduced, gives rise to a
tumour, which gradually enlarges with the growth
of its inhabitant; during this period, the hole perforated by the insect to deposite its egg, so far from
closing, becomes wider.   The bot, or worm, requires
a constant supply of fresh air; and its stigmata, situated at its posterior extremity, are constantly applied to the orifice.   In this it acts like a skilful surgeon, who desires to keep an issue open; for the application of its tail to the orifice keeps up the irritation and prevents its closing.   Not only must there
be an opening for the admission of the air, but, as
the bot subsists on the pus which arises from the interior of the tumour, if there were no outlet for the
excess, its too great accumulation would convert the
nest into an abscess, in which the animal, instead of
being nourished, would be destroyed.

When it has acquired its full growth, its old habitation becomes unfit for its approaching metamorphosis; accordingly, it dilates the orifice of the tumour by using its own body in the same manner as
a surgeon applies a sponge-tent.   It thrusts a ring or
two through the hole, and then withdraws them, and
so on, until it crawls out backwards.   This operation, according to Reaumur, is usually completed in
the cool of the morning.   The worm, having escaped from its den, rolls off the animal on which it
has fed, and falling on the ground, seeks the shelter
of some fissure, or stone, and there its own skin har-
dens into a black cocoon, within which it undergoes its last change, when it comes out a perfect
insect.

J.—S

Other species of the *œstrus* infest the intestinal cavity of the horse. The *œstrus equi* is found in the stomach; the parent insect deposites its egg about the shoulder of the horse, where it can be easily reached by the tongue; the irritation causes the animal to lick the part; and by this means the bot is introduced into the only place which affords the viscid nutriment and due heat requisite for its full developement.

The *œstrus hemorrhoidalis* chooses the anal extremity of the horse to deposite its egg. According to Clark, the egg is deposited on the edge, and the larva creeps through the whole length of the intestines. Dr. Gaspari saw the perfect insect hover about one of his horses apparently for the purpose of laying its egg; its attempts caused the animal to plunge, kick, and run, and, in short, excited that furor, which induced the ancients to give these insects their designation of *œstrus*. Not being successful, the creature insinuated itself with less noise under the tail of another horse which was feeding quietly by itself. Its attack seemed at first to excite itching, and the fly profited by the irritation thus produced to effect a lodgment. Soon after this happened, the horse ran about, plunged, and then threw himself on the ground; and did not recommence feeding until after the lapse of a quarter of an hour. The worm is provided with hooks, by means of which it retains its place. It also, when sufficiently developed, falls off the horse, and, like the œstrus bovis, undergoes its metamorphosis on the ground.

A third species of œstrus is found in the nostrils of sheep, goats, and various other animals. The egg is lodged in the frontal sinus, in the midst of the mucus which they contain.

"In Lapland," says Linnæus, "there is a fly covered with a downy hair, called the rein-deer gadfly; it hovers all day over these animals; their legs tremble under them, they prick up their ears and flee

to the mountains covered with snow and ice; with
so much horror do they avoid so minute an insect
hovering in the air. This fly endeavours to lodge
its egg on the back of the deer, which being effected
the worm perforates the skin, remains under it the
whole winter, and in the following year becomes a
fly."

Although Linnæus has attributed the perforation
of the skin to the larva, it is probable that the same
process which has already been detailed in treating
of the œstrus bovis, is also followed by this species.
But another kind of œstrus lodges near the gullet
of the deer, and there the larvæ take up their abode
in families consisting of one hundred or more individuals.   At each side of the root of the tongue
there is, according to Reaumur, a slit, in the pharynx
or gullet of the deer, which leads to two fleshy cavities, which he calls purses.   We do not know,
says he, of what use they are to these large animals,
but they are essential to the worms which are developed within them.   If they are not made for these,
if they are useful to the deer, at all events, He who
constructed the cavities, and formed the insects,
knew that they were necessary to the existence of
these worms, and so taught them to lodge in their
destined repositories; for all that is essential to their
nourishment and growth is contained within these,
and is not to be found elsewhere.   The question is
how the perfect insect contrives to deposite its young
in a spot which none but an anatomist can detect,
and to reach which requires the boldness and dexterity of a creature which is regardless of its own
life.   If we consider that nature has endowed the
deer with the power of ejecting any substance an-
noying the nostrils, by sneezing—the power of en-
veloping any thing irritating the palate in a viscid
saliva, or crushing it by means of grinder teeth, we
must give due credit to a fly, which, in spite of these
obstacles, manages to reach the cavities in question.

If, however, we recollect the boldness with which
the œstrus of the horse enters the intestine of that
animal, we shall not be astonished to find that a fly,
as full of care and foresight for its young, should,
with equal courage, enter the nostril of the deer.
According to Reaumur, the creature boldly walks
into the cavities, and proceeding to the extremity,
comes at once on the fleshy purses at the root of the
tongue: in these the female fly deposites her eggs,
and leaves them in a matrix furnished with a supply
for every want.

Humboldt, Bonpland, and Gmelin have discovered
a species of gad-fly which attacks man. It is a native of South America, and is about the size of a
common house-fly. It deposites its egg under the
skin of the abdomen, where it forms a swelling of
the nature of that on oxen, and other animals, in
which the grub remains for six entire months. If
molested, it sinks deeper and deeper, and, creating
ulcers or inflammation, often causes death.

CHAPTER XII.

*Ichneumon-fly—Deposites its Eggs in the Bodies of other living In-
sects—Thirty or Forty in the Body of a Caterpillar—Dragon-fly—Its
Voracity—Ferocity.*

To the numerous tribes of Ichneumons is allotted
by nature the task of restraining the superabundance
of the rest of the insect world. They were called
by the more ancient authors *Muscæ tripiles*, on account of their abdomen being terminated by an ovipositor, composed of three hair-like pieces, or *Muscæ
vibratoriæ*, from their habit of constantly vibrating
their antennæ or feelers.

The most interesting portion of their history is
the mode in which they are propagated. Other in-

sects either nourish their young themselves, or place them in the midst of an element which contains the food which they require; but these present the anomaly of cradling their offspring in the living bodies of other insects.

They vary in size, from the minutest to the largest among insects. They deposit their eggs sometimes on the outside, but mostly on the inside of the insect which they attack; and it is only to the three first insect forms of egg, larva, and pupa that they choose to commit their offspring. By means of their long ovipositor they pierce the cell of the gall-fly, or the nest of the solitary and the social humble bee; in short, when pressed to lay their eggs, nothing can escape them. Neither the vigilance of the parent nor the solidity of the habitation can defend the young of other insects from their attacks. These grow up just so long as is requisite to supply the young ichneumon which is feeding on their vitals; and when it is ready to emerge, they die.

Those which are obliged to pierce the nests of insects, in order to deposite their eggs, are provided with a long ovipositor; those which simply pierce the insect itself have only short ones.

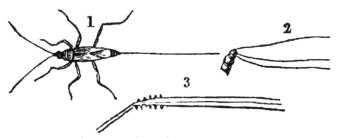

Fig 1. The ichneumon fly, with its ovipositor.
2. The ovipositor, seen to consist of three pieces.
3. The centre piece or tube through which the egg is transmitted. It is serrated at the end, and the two lines which run from it ought to have represented a string of mucus, which is lodged with the egg, wherever the latter is deposited.

S 2

The preceding (*fig.* 1) is a figure of an ichneumon of the first kind. The long tail consists of three hairs, as in the second figure; the two lateral enclose the middle one as in a sheath; the central fillet is round throughout the greater part of its length, but at the end pointed like a pen, flattened and serrated as in the third figure.

The following figure represents the short ovipositors of those ichneumons which pierce the insect only. It lies concealed in a groove under the abdomen.

Reaumur gives the following account of the operations of the ichneumon (*Comitator, F.*) while piercing the cell of that species of solitary wasp which feeds its young with green caterpillars. He had covered a wall with sandy mortar for the purpose of enticing these wasps to make their nests under his eye; they did so in great numbers.

" I saw," says he, " this ichneumon at the very moment it settled on the spot under which so many little animals were hidden. Its long tail, which it dragged after it, appeared to form but one thread, though in reality it was composed of three. It soon, however, put it to use: it showed me that it was not only capable of raising or depressing it, but also that it could bend it in various directions, and that in different portions of its length." It bent its tail, and carried it under its body, so as to protrude it considerably beyond its own head; and it directed it to the spot which its instinct pointed out as the place in which the young wasp was concealed.

" Although," continues Reaumur, " the creature did not seem disturbed by my observations, still I could not see whether the serrated point protruded beyond the case which contained it: this, however, I did see—that it gave the whole apparatus movements well adapted to make way even in this mortar. It turned it half round from right to left, and then back from left to right. I looked on for a full quarter of an hour before the ichneumon had succeeded."

The following figures will perhaps serve to give a clearer insight into the manœuvres of this insect, while driving its ovipositor deeper and deeper.

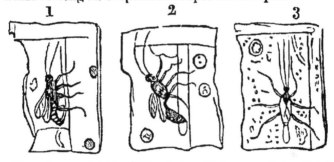

The cuts represent an ichneumon fly settled on a wall, in which it has discovered the nest of the mason-wasp.

In the 1st figure, the ovipositor, or instrument with which the insect pierces the cells of the wasp, is seen to be directed under the belly of the ichneumon

In the 2d figure, the insect's head being too near the point of the wall which is to be pierced, the long ovipositor is obliged to be thrown back into a curve; and, being thus shortened, it is seen to pass under the belly of the ichneumon.

In the 3d figure, the ovipositor, being still too long, is curved behind the insect It is then passed under its belly, and is seen like a thread supported by the right fore-leg of the ichneumon In order to prevent this instrument from bending, while the insect immerses it into the mortar, it is obliged to support it with the end of its leg. The other two hair-like lines are intended to represent the antennæ of the insect.

The three figures convey a good notion of the great flexibility of the ovipositor, and the facility with which the insect can use it under any circumstances.

The manœuvres of those ichneumons which attack the insect itself are as curious. The body of the caterpillar is the matrix destined to receive the eggs of this species. The little fly may be seen

pouncing upon a caterpillar, walking over its body,
stopping at certain parts, and wounding it with the
little sabre-like ovipositor.   It is in vain the caterpillar turns and twists itself about; the ichneumon
is not at all discomposed, but reiterates the wounds
in thirty or forty different places, and in each deposites an egg.   These are placed deep enough to
allow the caterpillar to change its skin without getting rid of the parasitical young of its enemy.   After
a time, the caterpillar is covered with little inequalities, which grow higher and higher, so that it pre-

sents a hideous figure.   Its body is studded with the
larvæ of the ichneumon, protruding themselves perpendicularly as soon as they emerge ; the pain occasioned by thirty or forty larvæ thus boring into its
carcass at one time soon causes the caterpillar to
die in a sort of convulsion.   The larvæ set about
spinning their cocoons round the carcass, and afterward undergo their allotted changes.
    These are gregarious; and when the caterpillar
is opened, may be found equally developed and regularly arranged in its interior.   The miracle is, that
the caterpillar, thus perforated, should not die : were

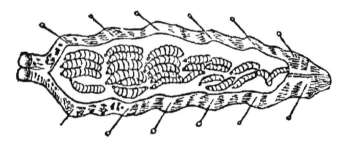

this to take place, nature would be defeated. These
little worms never attack a vital organ; they consume only the fat that surrounds the alimentary
canal. The caterpillar goes on feeding as usual,
and thus continues the supply necessary for the full
growth of the larvæ of the ichneumon till such time
as these are fit to emerge. The instinct of those
ichneumons which deposite only one egg in one insect is still more extraordinary. If another perches
on one which has already had an egg confided to it,
by some sense it discovers the fact that it has been
anticipated, and flies off, as if aware that there is
just food enough for one larva, and that if two were
deposited, both would starve.

Another and a most destructive enemy of the
living insect is the tribe of *libellula*, or dragon-fly, a
name which they well merit from their voracious
habits.

The French have chosen to call them "demoi-
selles," from the slim elegance and graceful ease
of their figure and movements. But, although their
brilliant colouring, the beauty of their transparent
and wide-spread wings, may give them some claim
to this denomination, yet they scarcely would have
received it had their murderous instincts been observed. So far from seeking an innocent nurture in
the juice of fruits or flowers, they are (says Reaumur) warriors more ferocious than the Amazons.
They hover in the air only to pounce upon other insects, which they crush with their formidable fangs;
and if they quit the banks of the rivulet, where they
may be seen in numbers during an evening walk, it
is only to pursue and seize the butterfly or moth,
which seeks the shelter of the hedge.

The waters are their birth-place; their eggs are
protruded into this element at once, in a mass which
resembles a cluster of grapes. The larva which
comes out of these eggs is six-footed. The only
difference between the larva and nymph is, that the

latter has the rudiments of wings packed up in small cases on each side of the insect.

In this latter state it is supposed that the creature lives at the bottom of the water for a year. It is equally voracious then as in its perfect state. Its body is covered by bits of leaf, wood, and other foreign matters, so as to afford it a complete disguise, while its visage is concealed by a prominent mask, which hides the tremendous apparatus of serrated teeth, and serves as a pincer to hold the prey while it is devoured.

Its mode of locomotion is equally curious; for though it can move in any direction, it is not by means of feet or any direct apparatus that it moves, but by a curious mechanism, which has been well illustrated by Reaumur and Cuvier. If one of these nymphs be narrowly observed in water, little pieces of wood and other floating matters will be seen to be drawn towards the posterior extremity of the insect, and then repelled; at the same time that portion of its body will be observed alternately to open and shut. If one of them be placed in water which has been rendered turbid by milk, or coloured with indigo, and then suddenly removed into a more limpid fluid, a jet of the coloured water will be seen to issue from the anal extremity of the libellula, to the extent sometimes of several inches; at the same time the force with which the column is ejected propels the insect in the opposite direction, by virtue of the resistance with which it meets. Hence it appears that it is by means of its respiratory system that the creature walks—a strange and anomalous combination of functions in one organ.

If the insect be taken out of the water, held with its head downwards, and a few drops of that fluid poured on its tail, that which was a mere point will immediately open and display a cavity; at the same

time the body of the insect, which was before flat, will be observed to be enlarged and inflated, and if held up to the light, semi-transparent: moreover, something solid will appear to be displaced by the water, and driven towards the head. This solid mass will shortly descend, obscure the transparency of the lower portion of the body of the insect, lessen its diameter, and, when it does so, a jet of water will issue from the vent. It is clear, then, that the abdomen of the libellula is a syringe, the piston of which being drawn up, of course the pressure of the fluid fills up the vacuum, and, when pushed down, expels the water. To ascertain the fact, Reaumur held the insect in his hand, and when he saw its body inflated, cut it immediately with a pair of scissors, and found it unoccupied with solids. He watched when the jet of water was expelled in another, and as soon as the body was darkened and lessened in diameter, he clipped it, and found the cut portion occupied by solids. There is no doubt, then,

that the abdomen contains a moveable piston, and
this piston is composed of the air tubes.   There are
four of these longitudinal trunks, although two only

are represented, they terminate in innumerable
smaller ones, and, according to Reaumur, perform
the functions of respiration, as well as locomotion,
in the ways detailed.

After the voracious creature has lain in ambuscade, devouring the larvæ of the gnat and other
aquatic insects, till its appointed hour of change, it
leaves its natal element for the shore, to undergo its
last metamorphosis: for this purpose it usually
fastens itself to some friendly plant, and begins the
important process which is to convert an aquatic animal into an inhabitant of the air.

Any person who should at this period choose to
seize a number of them, and, taking them into his
chamber, fix them to a bit of tapestry, would be re-
warded for his trouble by witnessing the conversion
of an aquatic into an aërial insect.

It may easily be seen by the eyes of the nymph
whether it is about to change its form; for, instead

of remaining tarnished and opaque, they suddenly
become transparent and brilliant.   This change is
owing to the visual organ of the perfect insect, which
is amazingly lustrous, shining through the mask of
the nymph.   If the eye of the nymph be removed,
that of the perfect insect may be seen beneath.   As
soon as the nymph has fixed itself to any object by
means of its claws, the first sign of the commencing
metamorphosis is a rent in the upper skin, extending along the corslet to the head.   When it approaches this latter part, another rent, perpendicular
to the first, runs across the face from eye to eye.

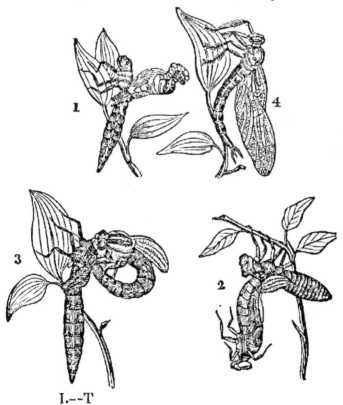

These rents are brought about by a power which
the insect possesses of inflating its body and head.
This last organ, ultimately destined to become fixed
and solid, is at this period capable of contraction
and dilatation, like a membrane.

The head and corslet being exposed, the legs are
drawn out from their nymphine cases. At this period
every part of the insect is soft. The four figures in
the preceding page illustrate its mode of exit.

In the first (*fig.* 1), it is partially out; in the second (*fig.* 2), after having protruded itself thus far,
it hangs with its head downwards, and remains motionless, so as to lead the observer to believe that
the efforts which it had hitherto made had exhausted
its strength, and that it had thus perished in the act
of being born. However, it remains in this position
just so long as to permit its body and limbs to be
hardened and dried by the air, and then it reverses
it to that of *fig.* 3, forming an arch; this enables the
insect to draw out its tail from the mask.

When it has just cast off that tenement in which
it had till now existed, the body of the libellula is
soft, has not attained its full length, and the wings
are still folded. It remains, therefore, tranquil and
motionless till these important operations have taken
place, which are finished sooner or later, according
to the heat or moisture of the atmosphere. The
operation may be completed in a quarter of an hour,
or take up several hours, according to circumstances.
The wings unfold themselves in every direction;—
it is supposed that this curious mechanical effect is
brought about by means of the fluids, which rush
into and distend them; for they remain drooping as
wet paper if the insect die in the act of metamorphosis; so that something more than drying is necessary. During the time that the wings, from
being shrivelled and flexible, are becoming firm and
glistening as talc, the dragon-fly takes care not to
allow even its own body to obstruct their expansion

in the proper direction, and for this purpose bends it from them, as in *fig.* 4; for if they took a wrong fold at this moment, they would for ever retain the deformity. Provision is even made to prevent the wings from coming in contact with each other; for, instead of being all in the same horizontal plane, as they subsequently are, they are perpendicular to the insect, and thus ranged side by side.

CHAPTER XIII.

THE ANT-LION.

Forms a Funnel-shaped Excavation in the Sand—Uses its Leg like a Shovel to remove the Sand—Secures its Prey by Stratagem—Its Ingenuity and Perseverance in getting rid of Impediments—Spins a Cocoon, and is transformed into a beautiful Fly.—The Lion-Worm.

Of all the creatures which secure their prey by stratagem, there is perhaps none more singular in its manners and habits than the ant-lion (*Formica-leo*). It is an inhabitant of the south of Europe. When full grown, its length is about half an inch: and in form it in some degree resembles a wood-louse; it has six legs, and the mouth is furnished with a forceps, consisting of two jaws curving inwardly, which give it a very formidable appearance.

But looking at its form alone, a person imperfectly acquainted with its habits and economy would be apt to set it down as the most helpless of all created animals. Its food consists solely of the juices of other insects, particularly ants; but at first view it appears impossible that it should ever secure a single meal; for its powers of locomotion are so feeble, that it can walk only at a very slow pace, and that backwards; he never follows his prey, and would sooner perish with hunger than advance one step towards it. Thus accomplished for the pursuit, it stands but a poor chance of being able to hunt down an active ant; nor would his prospects be mended by standing still; its grim and forbidding aspect is such as to deter every vagrant insect from venturing within its reach. In the choice of its food the insect shows itself a finished epicure; however pressed by the calls of appetite, it will taste no carcass except what it has itself killed: and of this it only extracts the finer juices. Thus delicate in its appetite, and thus apparently incapable of securing a supply of food, what is to become of the poor ant-lion? How does an insect, thus to all appearance unfitted by its natural habits to provide a supply even of the coarsest food, contrive to secure a succession of delicacies? It accomplishes, by the refinement of art and stratagem, what would utterly baffle all its open exertions—it excavates a conical pit, and, concealing itself at the bottom, calmly lies in wait for any unlucky insect which may chance to stumble over the margin and fall into its den.

For the purpose of excavating this trap, it seeks a spot of loose and dry sand, under the shelter of an old wall, or at the foot of a tree. Two circumstances incline it to select a spot of this description; in such a soil its snare is constructed with the least possible trouble; and the prey most agreeable to its appetite particularly abounds in such places. Having fixed upon a spot proper for its purpose, it

traces in the sand a circular furrow which is to determine the extent of its future abode. The outline
of the hollow which it intends to excavate being
drawn, it proceeds with its task. Placing itself on
the inside of the circular furrow previously traced,
it thrusts the hind part of its body like a plough-
share, under the sand; and using one of its fore-
legs as a shovel, it deposites a load of sand upon
its head, which is flat and square: it then gives its
head a jerk, sufficiently strong to toss this load to a
distance of several inches beyond the outward circle. All this is executed with a wonderful degree
of celerity and address. Always going backwards,
the same process is repeated, until it reaches that
part of the circle where it commenced its operations. Another furrow is then excavated inside of
the first circle; this is succeeded by others, until at
last the insect arrives at the centre of its intended
hollow. One peculiarity deserves to be pointed
out; the insect neither uses its outward leg nor dis-
turbs the sand lying on the outside of the circle;
using the inner leg only, it loads its head with sand
taken from the inside of the circle. It seems to be
well aware that the sand within the circle is all that
requires to be removed, and also that this can be
effected only by using the inside leg. If both the
legs were used at the same time, the excavation
would assume the shape of a cylinder, and not that
of a cone; which is the only form that can suit the
purpose of the insect. It must, however, be obvious,
that if, throughout the whole of this laborious process, one leg continued to be exclusively used, the
limb would get tired. To obviate this inconvenience, nature has taught the little pioneer to adopt an
apt expedient. one furrow having been completely
excavated, another is traced in an opposite direction;
this brings into play the leg which had been previously at rest. It frequently happens that small
stones impede the progress of its labours; these

are all, one by one, placed upon its head, and jerked
beyond the outer margin of the excavation. But
when arrived near the bottom, it sometimes en-
counters a pebble too large to be removed even by
this process, its head not having sufficient breadth
and strength to bear so bulky and so heavy a substance : while the hole is too deep to admit of its
being projected over the margin. In this dilemma
the little engineer is not destitute of resources. A
new mode of proceeding is adopted, suitable to the
difficulty which the insect has to overcome. By a
series of the most ingenious movements, it contrives to lift the pebble upon its back, where it is
kept in a steady position by means of the segments
which compose that part. Having thus secured the
pebble from the chance of falling, the indefatigable
labourer resolutely walks, tail forwards, up the
slope of the excavation, and deposites its burden on
the outside. When the stone to be removed happens to be round, the insect's task becomes more ar-
duous and difficult : in this emergency, the proceedings of the little ant-lion cannot fail to excite the
deepest sympathy. With incredible exertion it lifts
the pebble on its back ; it then commences its re-
trograde ascent up the slope of the den : but at every
step of its progress, the load may be seen to totter
to one side or the other; but the expert porter elevates the segments of its back in order to restore
the balance. It sometimes occurs, that, when it has
very nearly reached the top of the excavation, a
false step causes it to stumble : in this unlucky case,
all its efforts are frustrated, and the stone rolls
headlong to the bottom. Mortified, but not despair-
ing, the unwearied ant-lion returns to the charge ;
again places the stone on its back, and again ascends the sloping side, artfully availing itself of the
channel which had been formed by the rolling stone
—the sides of this channel frequently serving to
support the load. Throughout the whole progress

of the work, the insect shows itself a most expert engineer. It describes a perfect circle, and traces out a volute, without the assistance of a pair of compasses; and gives the slope of earth which it hollows all the solidity of which it is susceptible.

Desirous to witness the ingenuity and try the perseverance of one of these creatures, M. Bonnet threw a good-sized pebble into the den; its removal seemed to be quite essential, for the ant-lion left its work to effect it. To toss it out was beyond its power; it therefore determined to carry it up the declivity. For this purpose it insinuated its tail under the offending impediment, and by moving the rings of its body, hoisted it gradually on its back; thus loaded, it set off with its burden, walking backwards up the sloping side of the hole. Of course every step made the stone shake and over-balance; but it was righted in a trice by a due adjustment of the body of the insect, or a proper movement of the rings which compose it. Five or six times successively, the stone fell off in spite of all the skill and patience of the creature, and five or six times, Sysiphus-like, it renewed its efforts. In some instances, success attended his patient labours; in others, its efforts proved unavailing; but rather than submit to the inconvenience of a pebble which could offer the means of escape to its prey, the insect chose to quit the den and begin a new one. Another, however, acting with more sagacity simply drove the stone into the sandy walls of the den, and thus effectually abated the nuisance with little trouble.

All difficulties having been at length surmounted, the pit is finished; it is a conical excavation, rather more than two inches deep, and about three inches in diameter at the top, gradually diminishing in its dimensions until it becomes no more than a point at the bottom. It is at this narrow part of the den that the ant-lion now takes its station; and lest its

uncouth and forbidding appearance should scare
away any prey which might happen to approach its
lurking hole, it conceals its whole body under a layer
of sand, except the points of its expanded forceps,
which stick out above the surface. It seldom happens
that much time elapses before some vagrant
ant, unsuspicious of danger, arrives upon the margin
of the den. Impelled by some fatal motive, it is
prompted to explore the depth below; and bitterly
is it made to rue its prying intrusion. The treacherous
sand gives way under its feet; the struggles
which it makes to escape serve but to accelerate its
descent; and it falls headlong into the open forceps
of its destroyer. The ant, however, sometimes succeeds
in arresting its downward progress half way,
when it uses every effort to scramble up the sloping
side. Furnished with six eyes on each side of the
head, the ant-lion is sufficiently sharp-sighted to
perceive this manœuvre. Roused by the prospect
of losing the expected delicacy, it instantly throws
off its inactivity; shovels loads of sand upon its
head, and vigorously throws it after the retreating
victim. The blows which the ant thus receives
from substances comparatively of great size, soon
bring it down within the grasp of the terrible pincers
which are extended to receive it. If one shower
should fail, another soon follows, and lucky indeed
must be the insect which can effect its escape.

Very few species of insects, not excepting its own,
come amiss to this voracious creature. Reaumur
cut the wings of a bee, and threw it thus irritated
into the den of an ant-lion. The creature, seizing
the bee by the back, and holding it suspended in the
air, disabled it from using its sting. It made, however,
a terrible struggle, but on every motion the
ant-lion dashed it forcibly against the sand. Thus
beaten and wounded, the bee yielded up the contest
with its life, and was sucked at leisure by its enemy.
When its prey has been drained dry, it casts the

skin with a jerk far from its cave, lest the relics should embarrass it in its future contests, or deprive it of future visits, by bringing its place of residence into bad repute. Any damage which the den may have sustained during these struggles is carefully repaired; when the ant-lion resumes its station at the bottom, and patiently awaits the approach of more prey.

The ant-lion will not take a dead insect, however recently killed. Reaumur tempted it with fine, fat blue-bottles, but these it would not touch. Those insects, too, whose instincts teach them to simulate death when danger is near, escape the fangs of the ant-lion.

If it has long missed its necessary supply of game, it concludes its place of ambuscade to have been badly selected, and moves to another spot; or, if the hole has been so long occupied that the frequent crumbling of the sides has rendered the descent too easy, it is forsaken. Its progress on these occasions may be seen in the following figure.

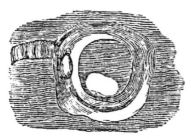

To this species of life the ant-lion is destined for about two years; after this period it passes from its state of larva into that of nymph. It then buries itself entirely in the sand. With a kind of viscid substance, which appears to exude from the pores of its skin, it glues together a crust which encompasses its whole body; this covering is round, and about half an inch in diameter, which affords the

insect sufficient space for motion: but it is not content with the shelter of a bare wall, which would
inevitably chill it; it therefore spins out of its own
bowels a thread, which in fineness infinitely sur-
passes that of the silk-worm.   This thread it fastens
first to one place, and then extends it to a second,
crossing and interlacing it   by this means it hangs
all its apartment with a satin tinged with the colour
of pearls, and exquisite both in beauty and delicacy.
In this work all the propriety and convenience is
confined to the inside, for nothing appears without
but a little sand, which confounds and incorporates
the mansion with the contiguous earth.   Here, in a
state of oblivion and tranquillity, it remains secluded
from the world for the space of about two months,
when it divests itself of its eyes, horns, paws, and
skin: its spoils sink to the bottom of the ball like a
heap of rags· all that now remains is a nymph,
which has other eyes and paws; other entrails and
wings, enveloped in a second skin, and a nutritious
liquor which gradually strengthens the new animal.
When its new limbs have acquired their necessary
tone and activity, it tears away the tapestry of its
apartment and pierces through the walls, for which
purpose it employs a couple of teeth like those with
which the grasshopper is furnished.   Its efforts to
escape become now more strenuous; the opening
gradually enlarges; half the body is first thrust out,
and at last the whole emerges.   Its long body, which
at this moment winds like the volute of an *Ionic* capital, and fills only a space of about a quarter of an
inch, begins to unfold and expand itself, and in an
instant stretches to the length of an inch and a quarter.   Its four wings, which were contracted in little
folds, and whose dimensions did not exceed the sixth
part of an inch in the film that sheathed them, begin
to expand, and in the space of two minutes shoot
into a greater length than the whole body.   In a
word the ravenous and malignant ant-lion assumes

the form of a large and beautiful fly, very closely
resembling the dragon-fly, which, after it has for
some time continued immoveable and apparently
astonished at the prospect of nature, flutters its
wings and enjoys a liberty unknown to it in its
former obscure condition.   And as it has cast off
the spoils and cumbersome weight of its first form,
so is it likewise divested of its barbarity and pernicious inclinations, it comes forth an entirely new
creature, full of gayety, alacrity, and vigour, and
graced with a noble and majestic air.   It then proceeds to deposite an egg in some sandy spot; from
this egg an ant-lion emerges, which in its turn becomes changed into a fly.

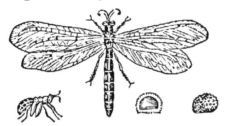

The lion-worm (*Leptis*) is a curious and voracious
little creature, having a tapering form; the head
being more pointed than the tail.   Its instincts are
very similar to those of the ant-lion; for, like that
formidable insect, it makes a species of cavity in
the loose earth, and there waits in ambuscade for its
prey.   A portion of its body lies concealed under
the sand—the rest stretches across the bottom of the
den, and appears so stiff and motionless, that, at first
sight, it might be taken for a bit of straw, half an
inch in length.   If, however, any insect, in search
of food, should happen to walk into the cave of the
lion-worm, the little morsel of stubble in an instant
becomes all animation—falls like a serpent on its
prey, and winding its body in coils around its victim,

compresses it to death, and sucks out the juices by
means of a couple of hooks fixed to its head. When
a strong insect happens to be thus captured, it might
fly away with the lion-worm if nature had not furnished the latter with means of fixing itself suitable
to the emergency. It bends a part of its body into
the shape of a hook; this is then thrust under the
sand, and serves as an anchor to hold the insect,
while the upper part of the body remains at liberty
to master and devour the prey. If the prey, eluding
its serpent-like grasp, should begin to make its way
up the sides of the den, the cunning hunter resorts
to the very same expedient as the ant-lion; by means
of its head, it sends forth a shower of sand with
such marvellous agility and precision of aim, that it
rarely fails to bring the battered game once more
within the reach of its formidable pincers.

The leptis ultimately turns into a sort of fly, with
a long and thin body.

CHAPTER XIV.

THE SPIDER.

*Its Spinning Apparatus—The Web—The Hawk-Spider—The Garden
Spider—The Water-Spider—The Hunting-Spider—Gossamer-Spider
—Fen-Spider—Attachment of the Spider to its Young*

AMONG the insect tribes, few seem to be more
generally regarded with horror and disgust than
the whole family of spiders, and such wingless
insects as resemble them. Notwithstanding this,
there are savages who eat them: Sparrman says,
that the Bashie men consider them as dainties; and
Labillardière asserts, that the inhabitants of New-
Caledonia seek for and devour large quantities of a

spider nearly an inch long, which they roast over a
fire. Reaumur relates, on the authority of M. de
la Hire, that a young French lady could never resist
the temptation of eating a spider, whenever she met
with one in her walks. They are said to taste like
nuts, at least this was the opinion of the celebrated
Maria Schurrman, who not only ate them, but justi-
fied her taste by saying, that she was born under
Scorpio. Latreille informs us, that the astronomer
Lalande was equally fond of this offensive morsel.
Man is truly an omnivorous animal; for there is
nothing which is disgusting to one nation, that is
not the choice food of another. Flesh, fish, fowl,
insects, even the gigantic centipedes of Brazil,
many of them a foot and a half long and half an
inch broad, were seen by Humboldt to be dragged
out of their holes, and crunched alive by the children. Serpents of all sorts have been consumed as
food; and the host of the celebrated inn at Terra-
cina frequently accosts his guests, by politely re-
questing to know, whether they prefer the "eel of
the hedge or the eel of the ditch." To evince their
attachment to their favourite pursuit, most naturalists seem to consider it indispensable to taste and
recommend some insect or other. Darwin assures
us, that the caterpillar of the hawk-moth is delicious;
Kirby and Spence think the ant good eating, and
push their entomological zeal so far as to distinguish
between the flavour of the abdomen and the thorax;
and Reaumur recommends the caterpillar of the
plusia gamma as a delicate dish.

And if the evidence of a poet may be taken in this
matter, the fairies are as fond of these dainties as
the most enthusiastic entomologists: as will appear
from the following quaint and fanciful quotation:—

> "A little mushroom table spread,
> After short prayers they set on bread,
> A moon-parched grain of purest wheat,
> With some small glittering grit, to eat

I.—U

His choicest bits with; then in a trice
They make a feast less great than nice,
But all this while his eye is served,
We must not think his ear was starved:
But that there was in place to stir
His spleen the chirring grasshopper,
The merry cricket, puling fly,
The piping gnat, for minstrelsy.
And now we must imagine first
The elves present to quench his thirst
A pure seed pearl of infant dew,
Brought and besweetened in a blue
And pregnant violet. Then forthwith
He ventures boldly on the pith
Of sugared rush, and eats the sag
And well bestrutted bee's sweet bag.
Gladding his palate with a store
Of emmets' eggs—what could he more?
But beards of mice, a newt's stew'd thigh,
A bloated earwig and a fly:
With the red-capped worm that's shut
Within the concave of a nut,
Brown as his tooth; a little moth,
Late fattened in a piece of cloth;
The unctuous dewlaps of a snail;
The broke heart of a nightingale
O'ercome in music."*

Spiders have been divided into various classes,
and although they have something in common, yet
each has likewise something which distinguishes it
from the rest. The above wood-cut represents the

* Herrick's Hesperides.

monstrous bird-spider (*mygale avicularia*) of South
America; it is at least two inches long, and reputed
(although on authority which has been denied) to
hunt for and devour birds. In general outline and
shape they all present a strong family likeness.
The body is divided into two parts: the fore-part,
containing the head and breast, is separated from
the hind-part by a ligature, or very slender thread.
The fore-part, together with the feet, which are inserted into the breast, is covered with very strong
scales. The hind-part is clothed in a very fine and
supple skin, which is covered with hair. In different
parts of the head, they have several fine eyes—generally eight, and sometimes no more than six; two
in the fore-part, two in the hind-part, and the rest
in the sides. They are all without eyelids, and are
covered with a hard, polished, and transparent crust.
As these eyes are immoveable, they have been multiplied, to convey to them, on all sides, intimations
of whatever it concerns them to know. The fore-
part of the head is furnished with two stings, or
rather branches, shagged or indented with strong
points like a couple of saws, and ending in a nail .
formed like the claw of a cat. Near the point of
the nail is a small aperture through which their
poison is ejected. These arms or branches are extremely formidable to their enemies : they open and
extend at pleasure. When no longer wanted for
use, the nails are each of them bent down upon its
branch, like a pruning-knife clasped upon its handle.
They are all likewise furnished with eight legs, like
those of a crab; and at the extremity of each are
fixed three crooked and moveable claws: that is to
say, a small one placed in the side, like a spur, by
the assistance of which they fasten themselves to
their thread—and two others of a larger size. The
internal curve of these is indented, and they enable
the insects to fix themselves wherever they please,
and to slide either obliquely or downwards, by
grasping whatever comes in their way.

But, besides these eight legs, spiders have two
others inserted in the fore-part of their body, and
which may be called their arms, since they do not
use them for transferring themselves from one place
to another, but only for holding and turning their
prey.   But although thus formidably equipped with
weapons of attack, the spider would still be unsuccessful in providing for its wants, if not furnished
with the means of constructing an ambuscade to
surprise its victim.   The spider has no wings to
assist in the pursuit, while its prey is furnished with
those organs as the means of escape.   This would
prove a fatal disadvantage, if the insect had not been
furnished with a stock of material, which it can
spin into a thread, and employ in constructing a web
or snare, which it spreads in the open air to inter-
cept the prey which is continually passing.   Instinct
informs the spider when the proper season has arrived for weaving this snare: which is invariably
begun when its prey first receives its birth.   When
the web has been completed, the insect retires into
obscurity behind its net, where it patiently awaits
for a victim, to which it has rendered itself invisible.
   The manner of constructing this web is extremely
artful and ingenious.   All spiders are furnished, at
the extremity of their belly, with four or six teat-
like protuberances or spinners.   Each of these protuberances is furnished with a multitude of tubes, so
numerous and so exquisitely fine, that, according to
Reaumur, a space not much bigger than the pointed
end of a pin is furnished with a thousand of them.
Hence, from each spinner proceeds a compound
thread.   At the distance of about one-tenth of an
inch from the point of the spinners these threads
again unite, and form the thread which we see, and
which the spider makes use of in forming its web.
Thus, a spider's thread, even when so fine as almost
to elude our senses, is not a single line, but a rope
composed of at least four thousand strands.   Of

such tenuity, although placed beyond all doubt by
Leuwenhoek's microscopical observations, our imagination is too faint to form even a conception: our
faculties are overwhelmed by a consciousness of
the imperfection of our senses, when used for the
purpose of scrutinizing the works of nature. An
experiment may be easily made with one of our
large field-spiders, which will convince the observer
that this calculation, although very wonderful, is
still accurate. If the abdomen of one of these
spiders be pressed against a leaf, the same preliminary step which the spider adopts in spinning, and
drawn gradually to a small distance, it will be instantly perceived that the proper thread of the insect is formed of four smaller threads, and these
again of threads so fine and numerous, that the number issuing from each spinner cannot be estimated
under a thousand. The Author of nature has also
conferred upon the spider the power of closing the
orifices of the spinners at its pleasure. This enables the insect, when dropping from a height by its
line, to arrest its descent at any point of its downward progress, and remain suspended in mid-air.

The situations which spiders select for the construction of their nets are extremely various. Some
prefer the open air, and place them in a horizontal,
a vertical. or oblique direction, among shrubs or
plants much resorted to by flies and other small insects; others spread their toils in the corners of
windows and rooms where prey always abounds;
while many construct their nets in stables and deserted dwellings, which, at first sight, hold out no
great promise of plunder.

When a house-spider intends to begin a web, it
selects some recess, as the corner of a chamber or
piece of furniture, into which it may retreat under its
web, and secure to itself, either upwards or downwards, a passage to escape from any danger with
which it may be threatened. It then presses its

U 2

spinners against one of the sides, and glues to it
one end of the thread. The insect proceeds from
one side, as far as the place to which it intends to
extend its web, while the thread lengthens in the rear.
The thread is fastened to one of the spurs or claws
with which the spider's feet are furnished, lest it
should come in contact with the wall while it is intended that it should traverse the air. When the
insect has reached the point on the opposite side to
which it purposes to continue the web, it there
fastens this first thread by means of glue; it then
pulls the thread, and renders it tight. Close by this
thread another is fixed, which the insect carries forward by running along the first, like a tumbler on
his rope. The second thread is glued on one side
of the point where the work was begun. The first
two threads are used like a scaffold to assist in building all the rest. All the threads are stretched and
fastened, one after another, with equal art and industry, and the whole is executed with wonderful
expedition.

Those threads which are destined to form the
outer margin or selvage of the web require additional strength; and for this purpose they are tripled
or quadrupled by a repetition of the operation just
described. From these marginal threads others are
spun in various directions, the interstices are filled
up by threads spun by the spider as it runs from one
to the other, until the whole, when finished, assumes
the gauze-like texture which excites our admiration.

These webs present merely a horizontal surface;
but to those which are formed in out-houses or among
bushes in the open air, a very ingenious appendage
is added. From the edges and surface of the main
web the spider carries up a number of single threads,
often to the height of many feet, meeting and crossing each other in various places. In their arrangement, these lines are not unlike the tackling of a
ship; and in their flight across them, the flies become

inevitably entangled. Their efforts to get away rarely fail to precipitate them into the net spread below for their reception; and whenever this takes place, their doom is fixed.

But the ambuscade is still incomplete. The spider seems to be well aware that its grim visage, if not concealed, would scare away the game for which it lies in wait. It therefore constructs a small silken apartment under the net, where it takes its station, unseen and unsuspected. " In this corner," says Philemon Holland, in his quaint translation of Pliny, " with what subtiltie doth she retire, making semblance as though she meant nothing less than that she doth, and as if she went about some other business! Nay, how close lieth she, that it is impossible to see whether any one be within or no!" But how does the spider, thus removed from the sight of its toils, discover when its prey has been entrapped? For this purpose, the following ingenious contrivance is adopted: it spins and draws several threads from the edge of the net to that of the hole in which it conceals itself. When a fly falls into the net, these threads by their vibrations give the spider intimation of the event: they also serve as a bridge over which it instantly passes to secure the captured prey.

Goldsmith has given so lively an account of some of the habits of the house-spider, that it deserves to be transcribed.

" I perceived, about four years ago, a large spider in one corner of my room making its web; and, though the maid frequently levelled her fatal broom against the labours of the little animal, I had the good fortune then to prevent its destruction; and, I may say, it more than paid me by the entertainment it afforded.

" In three days the web was with incredible diligence completed: nor could I avoid thinking that the insect exulted in its new abode. It frequently traversed it round, examined the strength of every part of it, retired into its hole, and came out very frequently. The first enemy, however, it had to encounter was another and a much larger spider, which, having no web of its own, and having probably exhausted all its stock in former labours of this kind, came to invade the property of its neighbour. Soon then a terrible encounter ensued, in which the invader seemed to have the victory, and the laborious spider was obliged to take refuge in its hole. Upon this I perceived the victor using every art to draw the enemy from its strong-hold. He seemed to go off, but quickly returned; but when he found all arts vain, he began to demolish the new web without mercy. This brought on another battle; and contrary to my expectations, the laborious spider became conqueror, and fairly killed its antagonist.

"Now then in peaceable possession of what justly was its own, it waited three days repairing the breaches of its web, and taking, as I could perceive, no sustenance. At last a large bluebottle fell into the snare, and struggled hard to get loose. The spider gave it leave to entangle itself as much as possible, but it seemed to be too strong for its cobweb. It sallied out, and stopped the motion of the fly's wings by quickly weaving around them a web; and, thus hampered, it seized and dragged it into its hole.

"I once put a wasp into the net; but when the spider came out to seize it, as usual, upon perceiving what kind of an enemy it had to deal with, it instantly broke all the bands that held it fast, and contributed all that lay in its power to disengage so formidable an antagonist. When the wasp was at liberty, I expected that the spider would set about repairing the breaches which were made in its net; but these it seems were irreparable, wherefore the web was now entirely forsaken, and a new one begun, which was completed in the usual time.

"I had now a mind to try how many cobwebs a single spider could furnish, wherefore I destroyed this, and the insect set about another. When I destroyed the other also, its whole stock seemed entirely exhausted, and it could spin no more. The arts it made use of to support itself, now deprived of its great means of subsistence, were indeed surprising; I have seen it roll up its legs like a ball, and lie motionless for hours together, but cautiously watching all the time; when a fly happened to approach sufficiently near, it would dart out all at once, and often seize its prey.

"Of this life, however, it soon began to grow weary, and resolved to invade the possession of some other spider, since it could not make a web of its own. It formed an attack upon a neighbouring fortification with great vigour, and at first was as vigorously repulsed. Not daunted, however, with one defeat, in this manner it continued to lay siege to another's web for three days, and at length having killed the defendant, actually took possession.

"The insect I am now describing lived three years; every year it changed its skin, and got a new set of legs. I have sometimes plucked off a limb, which grew again in two or three days. At first it dreaded my approach to its web, but at last it became so familiar as to take a fly out of my hand, and on my touching any part of the web, would immediately leave its hole, prepared either for defence or attack."

But the ingenuity of the house-spider, although very great, is still inferior to that of the garden-spider. "As the net," says Kirby, in his admirable account of the proceedings of this spider, "is usually fixed in a perpendicular or somewhat oblique direction, in an opening between the leaves of some shrub or plant, it is obvious that round its whole extent will be required lines to which can be attached those ends of the *radii* that are farthest from the centre. Accordingly, the construction of these exterior lines is the spider's first operation. She seems careless about the shape of the area which they enclose, well aware that she can as readily inscribe a circle in a triangle as in a square, and in this respect she is guided by the distance or proximity of the points to which she can attach them. She spares no pains, however, to strengthen and keep them in a proper degree of tension. With the former view she composes each line of five or six or even more threads glued together; and with the latter she fixes to them from different points a numerous and intricate apparatus of smaller threads. Having thus completed the foundations of her snare, she proceeds to fill up the outline. Attaching a thread to one of the main lines, she walks along it, guiding it with one of her hindfeet that it may not touch in any part and be prematurely glued, and crosses over to the opposite side, where, by applying her spinners, she firmly fixes it. To the middle of this diagonal thread, which is to form the centre of her net, she fixes a second, which in like manner she conveys and fastens to another part of the lines encircling the area. Her work now proceeds rapidly. During the preliminary operations she sometimes rests, as though her plan required meditation. But no sooner are the marginal lines of her net firmly stretched, and two or three radii spun from its centre, than she continues her labour so quickly and unremittingly that the eye can scarcely follow her progress. The radii, to the number of about twenty, giving the net the appearance of a wheel, are speedily finished. She then proceeds to the centre, quickly turns herself round, and pulls each thread with her feet to ascertain its strength, breaking any one that seems defective, and replacing it by another. Next, she glues immediately round the centre five or six small concentric circles, distant about half a line from each other, and then four or five larger ones, each separated by a space of half an inch or more. These last serve as a sort of temporary scaffolding to walk over, and to keep the radii properly stretched while she glues to them the concentric circles that are to remain, which she now proceeds to construct. Placing herself at the circumference, and fastening her thread to the end of one of the radii, she walks up that one, towards the centre, to such a distance as to draw the thread from her body of a sufficient length to reach to the next. Then stepping across, and conducting the thread with one of her hind-feet she glues it with her spinners to the point in the adjoining radius to which it is to be fixed. This process she repeats until she has filled up nearly the whole space from the circumference to the centre with concentric circles distant from each other about two lines. She always, however, leaves a vacant interval around the smallest first spun circles that are nearest to the centre, but for what end I am unable to conjecture. Lastly, she runs to the centre, and bites away the small cotton-like tuft that united all the radii, which, being now held together by the circular threads, have thus probably their elasticity increased; and in the circular opening resulting from this procedure she takes her station, and watches for her prey."

The manœuvres of a spider which wants to escape from any object surrounded by water, are extremely interesting. In his treatise on the Apple and Pear, Mr. Knight states, that if a spider be placed upon an upright stick, having its bottom immersed in water, it will, after trying in vain all other modes of escape, dart out numerous fine threads, so light as to float in the air, some one of which, attaching itself to a neighbouring object, furnishes a bridge for its escape. An experiment, made by Kirby, confirms the truth of this statement. " I placed," says he, " the large field-spider upon a stick, about a foot long, set upright in a vessel containing water. After fastening its thread (as all spiders do

before they move) at the top of the stick, it crept
down the side until it felt the water with its fore-
feet, which seem to serve as antennæ; it then immediately swung itself from the stick (which was
slightly bent), and climbed up by the thread to the
top.   This it repeated perhaps a score of times,
sometimes creeping down a different part of the
stick, but more frequently down the very side it had
so often traversed in vain.   At length, it let itself
drop from the top of the stick, not by a single thread,
but by *two*, each distant from the other about the
twelfth of an inch, guided as usual by one of its
hind-feet; one of the threads being apparently
smaller than the other.   When it had suffered itself
to descend nearly to the surface of the water, it
stopped short, and, by some means which I could
not distinctly see, broke off, close to the spinners,
the smallest thread, which, still adhering by the end
to the top of the stick, floated in the air, and was so
light as to be carried about by the slightest breath."
Shortly afterward he found one of these threads
extending from the top of the stick to a cabinet,
seven or eight inches distant; the prisoner had then
made its escape, using this thread doubtless as a
bridge.

The spiders which form nets of concentric circles,
differ from the house-spider with respect to the
situation in which they remain, while watching for
their prey.   Instead of lying concealed under the net,
they place themselves in its centre, with their head
downwards, and retire to a little apartment formed
under some leaf, near one side of the net, only when
they happen to be alarmed by the approach of danger, or driven to seek for shelter by stress of weather.   This apartment is also used as a slaughter-
house; for the moment an ill-starred fly, or other
insect, comes in contact with the net, the spider
springs upon it with the rapidity of lightning; and
if the captured insect be of small size only, the

spider conveys it at once to the place of slaughter;
and, having at its leisure sucked all its juice, throws
out the carcass. If the insect, being somewhat
larger in size, should struggle to escape, the spider,
with surprising address and agility, envelopes its
prey in a mesh of threads passed round its body in
various directions; both its wings and legs being by
these means effectually secured, it is then conveyed
to the den, and devoured. Sometimes a bee, or
large fly, too powerful to be mastered by the spider,
happens to get entangled in its toils; in this case,
the wary animal, conscious of its incapacity to con-
tend against such fearful odds, makes no attempt
either to seize or embarrass the intruder: on the
contrary, it assists the entangled captive in its efforts
to free itself, and often goes so far as to break off
that part of the net from which it may be suspended;
apparently content to get rid of so unwelcome and
unwieldy a customer at any sacrifice.

In the fen ditches of Norfolk, a large spider has
been found, which actually forms a raft for the purpose of obtaining its prey with more facility. It
first constructs a ball of weeds about three inches
in diameter. Taking its station upon this floating
island, it glides along upon the surface of the water;
the moment it sees a drowning insect, it pounces
upon it, not, as it may be well imagined, for the purpose of aiding its escape, but of hastening its
destruction. The body thus obtained is then conveyed upon the floating raft, where it is devoured at
leisure.

The spider has many enemies; and hence its
web is always in danger of being deranged and
damaged; to meet this inconvenience, nature has
furnished the insect with a magazine of materials
for occasional repairs, and which, although frequently exhausted, still continues to be replenished;
this reservoir, however, is drained in time. When
spiders grow old, their supply of gum is dried up;

1.—X

but even when this calamity happens, the cunning creature is not altogether destitute of resources which avail it for some time longer. A crafty old spider, having no longer the means of securing a subsistence, seeks out a young one, to which it communicates its wants and necessities; on which the other, either out of respect for old age, or from a dread of old pincers, resigns its place, and spins a new web in another situation. But if the old spider can find none of its species which will, either from love or fear, resign its net, it must then perish for want of subsistence.

A species of spider (*Mygale cementaria*), inhabiting the south of Europe, constructs a cylindrical cavity more than two feet long, in some sloping bank, calculated to let the water run off; the inside is lined with a web of fine silk. But in addition to the sagacity of choosing a steep bank and the luxury of furnishing its retreat with silk, this spider has the power of constructing a regular door: for this purpose it joins and cements layers of clay or chalk with its glutinous secretions, and thus contrives to make a door exactly circular, and so nicely fitting into the aperture of the cell, as to prevent its being distinguished by the casual observer from the surrounding earth. But the most marvellous circumstance yet remains to be told—the sagacious creature positively fabricates a hinge of silk, which it invariably fixes to the highest side of the aperture, so that it can very easily be pushed open from within by the insect, and shuts by its own weight. Thus barricadoed, the gallery furnishes a secure habitation for the male and female, with twenty or thirty of their young. No noise however loud, no thumping however violent, will bring the cunning inhabitant out of its cell; but if the least attempt be made to force the trap-door, a curious scene takes place—the spider immediately runs to it, and fixing some of its legs to the silk which lines the

door, and the rest to the walls of the gallery, it
pulls with all its might against the intruder. Observers have convinced themselves of the fact by
lifting up the door with a pin, when they have felt
the counter tugs of the spider endeavouring to shut
it. As soon as the creature is convinced that farther efforts are useless, it relinquishes the contest,
and retires to the bottom of the gallery. All
attempts to observe the manners of this creature in
captivity have proved fruitless, as it soon perished.
These spiders prowl about at night, and having
secured their prey, drag it within their den, and consume it at their leisure.

The water-spider (*Aranea aquatica*) is another
which spins no web to catch its prey; but, nevertheless, offers one of the most singular objects of
contemplation. If we possessed no other evidence
that the world had been planned and created by an
Intelligent Being, the habits, proceedings, and instincts of this little creature would be alone sufficient to prove the fact. As soon as it has caught
its prey on the shore, it dives to the bottom of the
waters, and there devours its booty. It is, therefore,
an amphibious animal; although it appears more
fitted to live in contact with the atmosphere than
with the water. The diving-bell is a modern invention; and few facts excite our wonder more than
the possibility of a man's being enabled to live and
move at the bottom of the ocean. This triumph of
reason over the unfriendly element, however, was
anticipated by an insect,—the spider in question.

This creature spins some loose threads which it
attaches to the leaves of aquatic plants; it then
varnishes them with a glutinous secretion, which
resembles liquid glass, and is so elastic as to admit
of considerable distention and contraction; it next
lays a coating of this same substance over its own
body, and underneath this coating introduces a
bubble of air. Naturalists conjecture that it has the

power of drawing this air in at the anus, from the atmosphere at the surface of the pool, but the precise mode in which it is separated from the body of the atmosphere, and introduced under the pellicle covering the insect's body, has not been clearly ascertained.   Thus clothed, and shining like a ball of quicksilver, it darts through the waters, to the spot in which it had fixed its habitation, and disengaging the bubble from under the pellicle, it dexterously introduces it into a web formed at the bottom. After repeatedly moving from the top to the bottom of the water, and at each journey filling its habitation with a fresh bubble of air, at length the lighter completely expels the heavier fluid, and the insect takes possession of an aerial habitation, commodious and dry, finished in the very midst of the waters. It is about the size and shape of half a pigeon's egg. From this curious chamber the spider hunts, searching sometimes the waters, and sometimes the land for its prey, which, when obtained, is transported to this sub-aquatic mansion, and devoured at leisure. The male as well as the female exhibits the same instincts.   Early in the spring, the former seeks the mansion of the latter, and having enlarged it by the introduction of a little more air, takes up its abode with its mate.   About the middle of April, the eggs are laid, and, packed up in a silken cocoon in a corner of their house, are watched with incessant care by the female.

In modern times, much interest has been excited by the elevation of bodies in the air by means of a balloon.   The discovery consisted in finding out a manageable substance which was, bulk for bulk, lighter than air; and the application of the discovery was to make a body composed of this substance bear up, along with its own weight, some heavier body which was attached to it.   This expedient, so new to us, proves to be no other than what the Author of nature has employed in the *gossamer spider.*

We frequently see this spider's thread floating in
the air, and extended from hedge to hedge across a
road or brook of four or five yards' width. The
animal which forms the thread has no wings where-
with to fly from one extremity to the other of this
line, nor muscles to enable it to spring or dart to so
great a distance; yet its Creator hath laid for it a
path in the atmosphere; and after this manner,
though the insect itself be heavier than air, the
thread which it spins from its bowels is specifically
lighter. This is its *balloon*. The spider, left to
itself, would drop to the ground; but being tied to
its thread, both are supported. By this contrivance,
the creatures mount into the air to such immense
heights, that when Dr. Martin Lister ascended York
Minster, he still saw these insects much above him.
In the fine summer days, the air may be seen filled,
and the earth covered with filmy webs —

The fine nets which oft we woven see, of scorched dew.
SPENSER.

Most nations have associated something poetical
with their presence. The Germans, from constantly
observing them in the beginning of the autumn,
have styled the phenomenon "the flitting summer."
The French, unable to account for the existence of
such pure films, in the open and beautiful autumnal
skies, called them the threads of the "Virgin." And
we the gossamer—

Lovers who may bestride the gossamer
That idles in the wanton air.

Mr. White gives a curious account of a shower of
these gossamers. In September, 1741, being intent
on field sports, he found the whole face of the country covered with a coat of web drenched in dew, as
thick as if two or three setting nets had been drawn
one over the other. His dogs were so blinded by
them as to be obliged to lie down and scrape them-

Y 2

selves.   About 9 A. M. these films, some an inch
broad and six long, fell from a height, and continued
to do so the whole day, with a velocity which proved
their weight.   When the most elevated parts of the
country were ascended, the gossamers were seen to
fall from higher regions ; and twinkling and glitter-
ing in the sun, they appeared like a starry shower,
fixing the attention even of the most incurious.

These are now known to be the work of a spider,
for they have been either caught in their balloons, or
been seen to take flight.   To produce such effects,
their numbers of course must be prodigious.   Dr.
Strach says, " that twenty or thirty often are found
on a single stubble ;" and adds, " that he collected
two thousand in half an hour, and could easily have
got twice as many had he wished it."

Dr. Lister has seen them in the air in vast numbers.   The mode in which they mount is strikingly
singular.   It is now generally admitted that several
kinds of spiders have a power of darting out a
thread in any direction, and to a comparatively great
distance.   The mechanism, however, of this extraordinary effort is not at all understood.   I saw a
spider descend from a window-ledge, by means of a
thread, and gathering up its legs, elevating its abdomen, and lying on its back, it shot out another to
the bricks, as straight and direct as an arrow.   The
distance, I am sure, could not have been much less
than eight inches.

This appears to be the mode adopted by the bird-
spider.   It shoots out a thread, which being lighter
than the air, mounts, and buoys up the insect itself,
as the tail of a kite does the body.   Some of them,
it would appear, not only bestride their film, but roll
it up in a mass, and thus sail in a balloon.

"Every day in fine autumnal weather," says
White, "do I see these spiders shooting out their
web and mounting aloft.   They will go off from the
finger if you will take them into your hand; last

summer one alighted on my book, as I was reading in the parlour, and running to the top of the page, and shooting out a web, took its departure from thence. But what I most wondered at was, that it went off with considerable velocity, in a place where no air was stirring; and I am sure I did not assist it with my breath; so that these little crawlers seem to have, while mounting, some locomotive power, without the use of wings, and move faster than the air in the air itself." Their motion in flying is smoother and quicker than when a spider runs along its thread.

There are many questions connected with our aeronauts, which are more readily asked than answered, and the first is, why do they mount at all? Kirby is of opinion, that they are destined to thin the air of those swarms of gnats and other insects, which ascend to considerable height in the summer evenings, and as a corroboration of his conjectures, adds, that their exuviæ are detected in the gossamers which have fallen.

It is doubted also, whether the " sea of gauze silvered with dew," which is found in the summer morning, covering the fallows, is ever carried up into the air. The dew itself is greedily drank by these spiders. The cause of the showers of gossamer is also a matter of dispute among naturalists.

Spiders frequently manifest various modifications of their instinctive craft and cruelty. There are some species that lie concealed in a rolled up leaf, and pounce upon any insect that may be unwarily passing. Others that lurk in the cup of a flower, and murder the fly that comes to seek honey. Others counterfeit death, and thus inveigle their prey within their reach. Others seek the blossoms of umbelliferous plants, which resemble them in colour and in shape, and thus entrap their victims.

There is a tribe of hunting-spiders that leap like tigers on their prey, and what is more extraordinary

have the faculty of doing so sideways. One of
these jumped two feet on an humble bee. They approach the object of their intended attack with the
noiseless and imperceptible motion of the shadow
of a sun-dial. If the fly move, the spider moves
also; backwards, forwards, or sideways, and that
with so much precision as to time and distance, that
the two insects appeared as if bound together by
some invisible chain, or actuated by the same spirit.
If the fly take wing and pitch behind the spider, the
head of the latter is turned round to meet it so
quickly, that the human eye is deceived, and the
spider appears to be motionless. When all these
manœuvres bring the fly within its spring, the leap
is made with fearful rapidity, and the prey struck
down like lightning.

The redeeming trait in the history of these cruel
creatures is, their affection for their young. All
spiders envelope their eggs in a silken cocoon; some
hide them in clefts of walls, or in a cylinder formed
of leaves; some carry them attached to their abdomen, or bear them about as a cat lifts its kitten;
none ever desert their precious charge. A spider,
to be met with under clods of earth, may frequently
be seen to carry a silken globe full of eggs fixed to
its body. The tenacity of affection exhibited
towards this, its sole treasure, is truly touching;
nothing, not even its life, is valued in comparison
with this little globe. If an attempt be made to deprive it of this valued deposite, it strenuously re-
sists: take it away entirely, and the insect remains
motionless and rooted to the spot stupified and me-
lancholy: restore it, and you restore the animal to
life: it eagerly seizes it, and runs off to place it in
a securer spot.

Bonnet threw one of these spiders, to whose abdomen the bag of eggs was attached, into the den
of the ant-lion. The animal, as if aware of its
danger, instantly took to flight, but not quickly

enough to prevent the ant-lion from seizing the bag
of eggs between its formidable pincers; the mother
made every effort to withdraw herself from her
dangerous foe, and in her struggles the bag became
loosened, and was retained by her enemy.   Instead,
however, of saving her own life, which she could
easily have done by running off, she instantly turned
and seized the bag between her jaws, and struggled
to regain her lost treasure; the enormous strength
of the ant-lion was too great for her powers, even
though stimulated by the full force of maternal instinct, and the eggs were consequently drawn under
the sand; still, however, she retained her hold, and
rather than relinquish that, without which life was
a burden, she suffered herself to be buried alive with
her progeny.   It was now that Bonnet compas-
sionated her fate and rescued her from the jaws of
death, but he could not restore to her the bag of
eggs so tenaciously held by the ant-lion.   She lingered at the spot where the eggs were buried, regardless alike of her own danger, and of the efforts
of Bonnet to remove her from her enemy, by pushing her off with a piece of twig.

Her cares are not confined to the egg only, but
when the young themselves are evolved, she allows
them to cling to her body, until such time as they
shall become strong enough to hunt for themselves;
and thus laden, she may be seen in her ordinary
haunts.   Much has been said of the venom of spiders, but De Geer and others, who have made the
experiment on themselves, have never found any ill
effects arising from the trial.

Spiders have been domesticated; a Parisian ma-
nufacturer kept and fed eight hundred of these
creatures, in one apartment; they became so tame,
that whenever he came in with his dish of flies, they
descended to take their food.   This story, related
in the French Dictionary of Natural History, if true,
proves, that even these solitary and cruel creatures

may in some degree be tamed, and lose their natural propensities to attack and eat each other.

Another instance is mentioned by Latreille, in which a spider appears to have acquired tame habits. A Frenchman of the name of Pelisson, being imprisoned in the Bastile, was deprived of pen, ink, and paper, and reduced to the society of an ignorant and sullen Basque, whose only occupation was playing on the musette. A spider made its web at the edge of the window which lighted the prison; and to relieve the dreadful ennui of his situation, Pelisson undertook to tame it, by placing flies in its way, while the Basque played upon his instrument. By degrees the spider became accustomed to the sound, and ran from its hole to receive its prey. Thus by being always summoned by the same sound, and having its food placed gradually at a farther distance from the web, the insect in a few months became so well disciplined, that at the first signal, it would leave its hiding place, and come and take its flies at the bottom of the chamber, under Pelisson's eyes.

CHAPTER XV.

CATERPILLARS.

Their singular Habits—The Grub of the Domestic Moth fabricates a Mantle—Habits of the Field Moth—Caddis-worm

THE habits of some insects during their larva or caterpillar state are so singular, and manifest so much ingenuity and design, that a short account of them cannot fail to prove interesting.

Few insects appear more deserving of admiration than those which possess the art of fabricating garments for their own use. Like the human race, they come into the world naked ; and their birth is scarcely completed, when they begin the task of clothing themselves. The reader will easily perceive that the insects here alluded to are the little moths which, in warm weather, are seen to issue from our closets, where furniture, cloth, ermine, feathers, all fall a sacrifice to the depredations, not indeed of the moth itself, but of the worm which is evolved from the egg of the moth. All that the moth does is to deposite its eggs on these different articles ; but it is the grub that proceeds from these eggs that effects all the mischief. The grubs of the different sorts of domestic moths do not make their garments after the same fashion, nor of the same materials. It is probable that the different species of moths vary as much in this respect as the inhabitants of different countries · the shape of their garment is peculiarly convenient; it is a small cylindrical tube open at both ends, and exactly fitted to the body of the grub; the stuff used for this purpose is fabricated by the moth. The tissue is a mixture of hair and silk; but as this would not be sufficiently soft for the tender body of the worm, it is lined internally with pure silk. Articles manufactured of hair, fur, or wool supply the caterpillar of the moth with the raw material which it wants for the fabrication of its stuff; they select those hairs which appear most suitable to their purpose; cut them with their teeth, and with admirable skill incorporate them with their silky tissue.

They never change their garment; that which they put on in infancy continues to shelter them during the whole of their lives. But they are able both to lengthen and widen their vesture whenever they think proper. To lengthen it is a very simple process: it only requires that a few new threads, or new hairs, should be added to each end of their garment; but to widen it is a matter of more difficulty:

to effect this object, the insect adopts the same steps as a human mechanic would pursue under similar circumstances. It splits its garment on the two opposite sides, and in the intervals thus formed, skilfully inserts two pieces of stuff of the necessary width, it does not at once split its coat from one end to the other: this would cause the parts to separate too widely, as well as expose the caterpillar in a state of nakedness to the action of the open air: to avoid these inconveniences, it splits each side only half the length of the whole garment; it then proceeds to the other end, which it enlarges in a similar manner. Thus, instead of two whole

This figure shows the garment split in half the length.

length openings, filled up by two whole length pieces, four half length openings and pieces are used. A reasonable agent could not follow a more ingenious or more efficient plan. A coat made in this fashion is not the work of a day nor yet of a month; different caterpillars labour with different degrees of diligence; and even the same worm, when deprived of its clothing in an advanced stage of its existence, will finish in one week what it had previously taken it perhaps months to execute.

The garment of this caterpillar is always of the same colour as the stuff from which its raw material has been taken; if a worm, enveloped in a blue coat, happen to remove to a piece of red cloth, the additions which may be made to the ends of the tube, or the pieces inserted in the sides to widen it, will be of a red colour; if it happen to travel over cloth of different colours, its garment will exhibit a corresponding variety of hues.

These caterpillars live upon the same materials

which compose their covering. It is singular that these substances should be digested by them; and still more singular that their colour should be so little affected by this digestive process ; for the ex- crements of these caterpillars are invariably found to be of the same colour (though lighter) as the substances which they may have eaten.

These caterpillars make short excursions : when the part in which they first settled has been shaven quite bare, the animals remove to another spot in search of a fresh supply. Those which settle upon garments of fur do not like to walk over long hairs ;

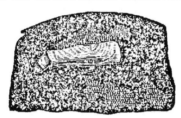

they therefore never proceed except scythe in hand, and cut off every pile which comes in their way. Now and then they are seen in a state of repose; they then fix their case to the body of the cloth with little threads, and thus, as it were, come to an an- chor.   They fix themselves still more firmly to the cloth, when about to fall into a torpid state during the winter, or when about to undergo their meta- morphosis ; they then close exactly both the ends of their case with silken threads, in order that they

Y

may be in a state of greater safety while assuming first the form of chrysalis, and subsequently that of a moth.

The admiration which the ingenuity and proceedings of the domestic moth inspired in the mind of Reaumur did not prevent him from endeavouring to discover the best means of destroying them, and of rescuing our furniture and clothes from their destructive ravages. After various experiments made with different substances, he gives the preference to oil of turpentine, which, as he asserts, proves always fatal to these insects. A few drops of this oil spread upon sheets of paper were invariably found to destroy them. Its smell threw them into convulsions, and covered with livid spots they were seen to expire. It has also been found that the fumes of tobacco will destroy the moth.

But interesting as the proceedings of the domestic moth may justly appear, they are still infinitely surpassed by the ingenuity and industry of the field or rustic moth. This latter tribe construct their garments of materials collected from the leaves of plants; but before these materials can be used, it is indispensable that they should pass through a preparatory process, which may give them the lightness and pliancy necessary to render them fit for their clothing. Their proceedings are so extraordinary, and in appearance so rational and well considered; they are varied in a manner so suitable to the exigency and circumstances of each particular case, that their habits justly deserve to be detailed.

These caterpillars are a species of leaf miners, and are to be found in the greatest numbers in the oak and the elm. The mantle which they fabricate is nearly cylindrical in form, but the ends are not similarly fashioned; the fore end, where the head of the caterpillar shows itself, is rounded, bent, and hemmed; the other end is formed of three triangular pieces, which by their natural spring are brought into a point, and which easily open in order to make way for the extremity of the insect.

When beginning to fabricate this mantle, the caterpillar glides into the pulpy substance of a green leaf, penetrates between the two membranes which form its external coats, and detaches the pulpy substance or parenchyma, which is enclosed in these membranes. This substance constitutes the proper food of the caterpillar; hence, while the animal satisfies the cravings of hunger, it prepares the stuff from which its mantle is to be fabricated; the two membranes of the leaf are the stuff destined for this purpose. Each of these thin substances is to the caterpillar what a piece of cloth is to a tailor; like that useful mechanic, the little animal cuts each piece of the form and proportion which it ought to have, in order to answer the purpose for which it is destined.

Anxious to ascertain how this mantle was made, Reaumur watched his opportunity, and removed one of them, before the insect, which happened to be then busily feeding in the parenchyma of the leaf, had time to retreat: the creature, having discovered its loss, seemed to be in great alarm, and came out tail foremost; it felt about for its mantle, but not finding what it sought, it re-entered between the membranes of the leaf, where it began to feed right and left; having consumed the parenchyma, from a space of adequate dimensions, it proceeded to repair its loss. From the membranes of the leaf it cut two pieces, equal in extent, and similar in shape, each piece being destined to form one-half of the mantle. This part of the process was executed with singular rapidity, as well as with matchless skill and precision. This is far from being a mechanical operation; for the pieces composing the mantle are not regular figures, one end of each being double the size of the other. The materials of the mantle being thus prepared and cut, the next operation was to sew the two pieces together.

The seams are not completed at once: the insect places itself between the two pieces while they are flat; it then brings them together at certain points, with intervals of considerable extent still open, while it twists and turns about its body in all directions; by this means the plane surfaces of the two pieces become gradually moulded into a concave form, suited to the body of the insect. Having thus, like a prudent and judicious tailor, ascertained that the mantle will fit in every part, it brings the edges of the pieces close together throughout their whole length, and sews them so neatly and firmly, that although the place and direction of the seam be well known, it is extremely difficult, even with the aid of a lens, to detect it in the finished mantle.

But the little animal is not content with an outward covering, formed solely of the membranes of a leaf; this would not probably be found either soft enough or warm enough for its purpose: all inequalities which might injure its tender skin are carefully removed from every part of the interior, and the whole is doubled and lined throughout with a coating of silk; the lining being rendered thicker in those parts which, from being prominent, are peculiarly exposed to friction. Reaumur found that the insect whose coat he abstracted completed another in the short space of twelve hours.

The finishing hand having been thus put to the mantle, another operation now remains to be executed. It is necessary that it should be detached altogether from the leaf, in which, as well as from which, it has been fabricated; to effect this requires strength rather than skill: accordingly, the insect crawls partially out of its case, pushes its head forward, as nearly as can be, in a straight line, fastens its fore-legs upon the leaf, and laying hold of the inside of the case with its hind-legs, detaches it instantly from its original place, and drags it forward: it advances thus gradually, and at length fixes the case with silken cords, either to another leaf or another part of the same leaf, containing a fresh supply of provisions. The annexed figure gives a representation of the different operations which have been just described. In the first (*fig.* 1) the worm is seen between the thin membranes of the leaf and destitute of its coat; the second (2) shows the commencement of the cutting process; the third (3) represents the work in a state considerably advanced; the insect being engaged in converting it from a plane into a cylinder; in the fourth (4) it is seen endeavouring to detach its finished mantle from the leaf; the last is a distinct representation of the little animal enveloped in its new coat.

As soon as the insect has fastened its mantle, or, as it may be properly called, its tent, to a fresh portion of a leaf on which it intends to feed, it pierces the outer skin or epidermis, eats only the juicy substance contained between the two membranes of the leaf, and sedulously avoids doing the slightest injury to the upper membrane; it gradually extends its excursions in search of food, considerably beyond the

part to which the mouth of its mantle is attached;
and as it consumes the intervening substance, it
renders the epidermis so transparent, that its own
body and motions became perfectly visible.   As the
pulpy substance nearest to the mouth of the case
becomes exhausted, the insect is of course forced to
advance farther in search of a fresh supply; the
body is, therefore, gradually dragged out of the
case, until at last little remains in it except the tail :
hence the necessity of fastening the mantle to the
leaf, as without this precaution it would drop off,
leaving the insect defenceless.   If the leaf be in the
slightest degree agitated, it immediately retreats
backward into its case, so that whether feeding or
reposing it is always under cover.

The following figures show not only that the case
of the insect is fixed at an angle more or less inclined to the under surface of the leaf, but likewise
give a correct representation of the mantle itself;
the shape, however, frequently varies : in some instances, instead of being indented, it is simply a
cylinder slightly curved.

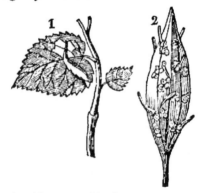

Fig. 1, a mantle with a serrated border.
   2, a mantle which is cylindrical, and fixed at an angle on the leaf.

Other caterpillars, more sagacious than that
already described, mine the leaf near one of its

edges, taking great care not to separate the two membranes where they are joined together by natural indentations.

In this figure, the caterpillar has left his old coat attached to the stalk of the leaf, and has taken the first step in forming a new one, by eating out a portion, which is seen white in the cut.

It will readily be perceived, that by proceeding in this manner, the insect saves much labour; it finds by this means one side cut ready for its purposes, and also joined and sewed at the indentations by the hand of nature, even more neatly and firmly than it could be done by its own labour.

But what is still more extraordinary, these caterpillars are found to vary their proceedings according to circumstances. Reaumur surprised one of them while engaged in the act of making its mantle. To form one side of it, the creature had selected the ready joined edge of a leaf, mining only for the other side; with a pair of scissors, Reaumur cut off the indentations at their roots: by this means, the membranes were of course loosened at their point of junction. Without the slightest hesitation or delay, the worm adopted the only expedient which could remedy the mischief; it instantly set about sewing artificially the two edges, which were previously joined by the hand of nature, and then proceeded in its subsequent operations, just as if it had experienced no interruption. It will be easily perceived that the proceedings of a caterpillar, which makes its coat on the edge of a leaf, must differ in many points from those of another worm, which fabricates it in the centre: the latter may cut away as boldly as it pleases; there is no danger of a fall, since the inequalities of the edges are found to retain the pieces in their original position: if the former, however, were to proceed in the same manner, and separate the side of its coat nearest the centre of the leaf, before it had been thoroughly finished, the whole would necessarily fall to the ground for want of support. Accordingly, as soon as the cunning tailor had repaired the damage which its coat

had sustained from the scissors of the naturalist, it mined a space sufficiently large for the purpose; this part was then rounded, made hollow, and carefully lined with silk; and it was not until all this had been completed, that the insect began to cut its mantle on the side which was nearest the centre of the leaf. In the execution of this part of the operation much caution was evinced. The caterpillar did not cut continuously from one end to the other; it only cut the intervals which lay between the large nervures of the leaf; so that although a considerable proportion of the whole length of the coat was separated from the body of the leaf, it was still retained in its original position by these natural cords or stays. Nor does the silken lining cover every part of the inside towards the centre of the leaf; in order that the coat might be. detached from the leaf, it was necessary that the nervures, or cables, which held it in its place, should be at length cut away. The cunning creature had therefore left loopholes, through which it might thrust its head and cut these natural cables, one after another. As each nervure was cut away, the loophole which enabled the insect to reach it was closed up, and the space nicely lined with silk. All the others having been cut away, the coat became at last suspended by one only of these nervures; at the proper time, this last nervure was cut off, when the insect taking up its finished mantle walked away.

The caterpillars of the moth which feed on woollen stuffs and household furniture do not change their dress, but simply enlarge it as the size increases; but the caterpillars of the field moth fabricate an entirely new suit, whenever they have outgrown their old covering. It is within these mantles that they undergo the usual metamorphosis, and reach their perfect state, when they appear in the shape of moths, in size considerably inferior to those which infest closets and clothes-presses.

Each tribe of the moths fabricates its vestments after a fashion peculiar to itself, and different from that adopted by others.

A moth which feeds on a species of astragalus adorns its robe, as ladies used to do in other times, with furbelows. The body of the habit is a cylindrical tube lined with silk, and ornamented with furbelows puffed out; each flounce seems to mark the growth of the worm; for Reaumur conjectures, that when it has outgrown the first, it adds a second division to its tube, and to that a third: they are rarely found to have more than three flounces; each fur-

below is composed of two semicircles joined together.

Fig. 1, the furbelow-mantle seen stuck to the leaf.
2, the mantle separated.

Another moth (*psyche graminella*) covers its silken
coat with bits of grass, and seems as if it were protected by a coat of mail or a covering of tiles.   This
appears to be done in order to give strength and consistence to the silken tube, and enable it to sustain

Mantle of Psyche Graminella.

the friction to which it is unavoidably exposed from the movements of the insect.

Although the vestments of each tribe are generally formed in a uniform manner, still there are some exceptions to this; for instance, the caddis-worm, so well known to old Isaak Walton, and to all the brothers of the angle, is not at all choice in the selection of the ornaments with which it decorates its coat: shells, stems, leaves, straws, and bits of wood, in short, almost any manageable substance, will serve its purpose. The only thing which is common to all the figures is, the cylindrical tube opens at each extremity.

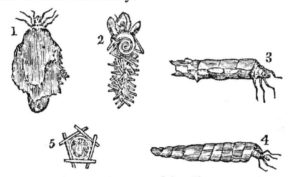

1. In figure 1, the worm has covered its silken case with leaves, so arranged as to present the appearance of a Spanish mantle.
2. In fig. 2, it is bristled all over with stalks of plants, surmounted by a huge shell, and two pieces of wood, looking very much like horns.
3. In fig. 3, the worm is seen cased in two semi-cylindrical pieces of hollow bark; having accidentally lighted upon these materials, it has joined them together, and has thus formed a complete covering with little or no sewing.
4. Fig. 4 represents the worm enveloped in a symmetrical and spiral case of riband beautifully rolled; the parts are so nicely fitted, that it has the appearance of being one continuous piece; a careful examination will, however, show, that it is composed of several detached bits joined together.
5. The last, fig. 5, exhibits a section of one of those cases, with the bits of wood arranged around it.

Sometimes these coats are covered exclusively with shells, which occasionally envelope living snails, fixed in such a way as to prevent them from changing their place

It is not, however, to be imagined, that the worm loads its case with these singular materials without a valid reason. This worm is an aquatic insect; the annexed figure will show that its form is but little

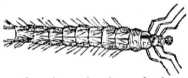

adapted for swimming; its long body, encumbered with six legs, is specifically heavier than water, the element in which it has to seek its food. As a compensation, the Author of nature seems to have endowed it with an instinctive faculty, which enables it to know what substances are lighter than water: these it attaches to its coat, in order to counterpoise its own excess of gravity, and enable it to swim on the surface, in the centre, or at the bottom of the element in which it has to seek its food. This seems to account for the variety and singularity observable in the coats of those insects. When they want to ascend, the quantity of hollow and buoyant substances attached to them is increased: in order to descend, the light and hollow substances are either diminished or counterpoised by an addition of heavy materials, such as shells or gravel.

Another tribe of moths (*the Galeria of Fabricius*),

instead of clothing themselves in the manner above described, shelter themselves in hollow tubes, which they lengthen as they advance. One species (*the Galeria Cerea*) establishes its residence among the warlike and well-armed inhabitants of the bee-hive; where it subsists at the expense of this industrious race, cutting and destroying works which have required the greatest industry and art to execute. It is natural to imagine that the bees do not willingly allow this destruction to be effected by an insect which, when it has reached perfection, is but a contemptible and effeminate moth, and which in its imperfect state is merely a worm easily pierced by their sting; and there can be no doubt that many fall a sacrifice to their just anger. Reaumur has seen several bees chasing a moth all over the hive: the creature, however, ran faster than its pursuers, and after much twisting and turning, got between the interstices and the corners of the cells, where it remained entirely beyond the reach of its enemies. In this situation of perfect security the moth lays its eggs: from these eggs, in the proper season, worms proceed, which instantly attack the wax for the purpose of constructing a gallery. Each caterpillar has its own distinct gallery, which is a winding tube, sometimes eighteen inches long: no part of the comb is safe, and the devastation committed is sometimes so great, that its legitimate inhabitants are often compelled to quit the hive. The interior of these tubes is lined with silk. It constitutes one of the curious anomalies which are to be met with in the works of nature, that bees, which in other respects perform wonders, should never attempt to destroy these tubes—they will eat away paper and cut wood; yet they have never been known to touch these long galleries, which perforate and destroy their combs in every direction.

Z

CHAPTER XVI.

SOCIAL CATERPILLARS.

Move in regular Files—Form Nests lined with Silk—" The Procession-ary"—The Leaf-rolling—The Leaf-bending—The Leaf-mining Ca-terpillar.

The caterpillars described in the last chapter are hermits, which lead a solitary life: there are, however, other tribes which spend either a part or the whole of their vermicular life in society. The perfect insect deposites all its eggs on the same leaf or plant, and the caterpillars proceeding from these eggs are disclosed about the same time, and frequently live together until they assume a different form. The gold-tailed moth (*Arctia Chrysorrhœa*) is one of those insects which lay eggs productive of social caterpillars. They deposite their eggs in a cover, formed of hair plucked from their own body. The moment one of these caterpillars is evolved, it seeks its food on the leaf on which the Author of nature had taught the parent insect to deposite it: a second soon joins the first-born: and a third speedily follows the second: thus a row of caterpillars parallel to each other may be seen reaching nearly across the leaf: a second row then begins to form itself; which, when it has extended across the leaf, is succeeded by a third. The whole of the upper surface of the leaf becomes thus entirely covered, except a small space left open for the first rank to feed upon. The heads of each rank being generally in the same line, they all advance simultaneously; and their progress has very much the appearance of a regular military movement; as may be seen by the annexed figure.

They eat only the upper membrane of the leaf; leaving the larger nervures and the under skin untouched. The parts which they do not consume, are wanted in order to construct a habitation to protect them against the inclemencies of the weather, and conceal them from their natural enemies. As soon as they have satisfied the calls of appetite, some of the young caterpillars set about tying the leaf, which, having been already rendered thin and supple, is easily made to assume a concave shape. The threads used in joining the edges of the leaf, so as to give it a cup-like shape, are so many, that they form a little silken roof, under which the caterpillars feed. The exposure, however, to the light and heat does not seem to be agreeable to them; they therefore add to the thin silken roof threads in such quantities, that a perfectly white and impervious web is made. These, after all, are but temporary sheds hastily formed, until the insects have had time to construct a more complete and durable fabric. After the lapse of a few days they commence the erection of their new abode, which is a silken tent, sufficiently capacious to contain the whole community, and so closely woven, as to afford them, during the whole of the winter, a complete shelter both from wind and rain. They lay the foundation of their new edifice, by covering a shoot with silk, and carefully nibbling away all the leaf-buds, so as

to prevent them from growing in the spring: they
thus secure their abode from the destruction which
would ensue from the sprouting of the branches.
They then enclose, in a double covering of silk, one
or two leaves at the end of the shoot; these leaves
being thus brought together are worked into the
form of a vault: the nest of these caterpillars may
very commonly be observed attached to our fruit-
trees in the autumn, when the fall of the leaves dis-
closes them to view.   By an inexperienced eye one
of these nests might be mistaken for the web of a
spider: indeed, when deserted by the caterpillars,
they not unfrequently become the abode of this insect.   These nests vary in shape; some being round,
others flat.

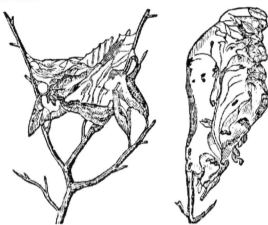

They differ also in extent: in proportion also as
they become enlarged, either in length, breadth, or
capacity, a greater number of leaves, little shoots,
and even branches, are comprised within the limits
of the tent.   The irregularity of their shape arises
from the additional webs which, from time to time,
it becomes necessary to form.   These additional webs
divide the interior of the nest into regular compartments; each of them capable of containing a number

of caterpillars. If a section of these nests be examined with a microscope, the cells may be distinctly perceived; some of them containing caterpillars, others excrements, and others both. The

difficulty, is to comprehend how these insects find
ingress and egress, in such an apparent labyrinth.
But in each web doors or holes may be perceived,
which, in adding new webs to old ones, they carefully avoid obliterating.

Into these nests, which they have been taught to
spin of a texture sufficiently strong to protect them
during the space of eight months, from the sun, the
rain, and the storms, they retire during a part of the
night, as well as during that perilous period in which
they undergo their metamorphosis. So tender are
they, that they find it necessary not only to line their
tent with the softest silk, but also to carpet with the
same material all the roads and approaches which
lead to this habitation. Having lived together till
the beginning of summer, they then separate, and
undergo their usual metamorphosis.

There is a very singular species of caterpillar
which fixes its residence on the oak. It is a stranger
to this country, although well known in France.
From six hundred to eight hundred individuals frequently dwell together in the same nest: the external form of these habitations presents nothing very
striking; it resembles the large knots formed on the
tree itself. In order to accommodate this great

Z 2

number of caterpillars, its dimensions must of course
be considerable.   Some of them measure eighteen
or twenty inches in length, five or six in breadth,
and four in depth.   Each is a simple pocket without
partitions; the sides being composed of several
layers of a grayish coloured silk, which assimilates
so well with the natural hue of the oak, as completely to deceive the eyes.

When the glow of day begins to soften, and the
sun is about to set, these insects quit their habitation in order to proceed in search of food—the twi-
light and the night constituting the period of their
activity.   Their movements are conducted with
wonderful regularity.—A single caterpillar first goes
out of the nest, and is immediately followed by
others which form a sort of procession : the leader
is succeeded by two moving abreast; that rank by
a third, composed of three abreast; and so on till
sometimes the last row contains twenty ranged side
by side; the ranks are so compact, that the tail of
one row is touched by the heads of those which succeed; and in each row the caterpillars also touch
throughout the whole length of the body.   They

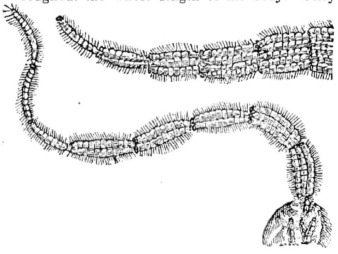

sometimes form single files for some length; then double and triple ones; each being equal in number to the single one, as represented in the figure. The leader of these "processionaries" does not seem to differ from the body of its companions either in size, shape, or colour; nor does there seem to be a natural leader. The first that happens to quit the nest appears, from that circumstance alone, to be considered as the chief; the rest follow in his train. Where the mass is so compact, it seems indispensable that the movement should be regulated with the greatest precision; otherwise a degree of confusion would ensue which would greatly impede, if not entirely stop, their progress. Accordingly, nothing can surpass the uniformity and regularity observable in their march: whatever be the route of the leader, the others follow precisely the same steps. If this leader should ascend to a certain height and then descend, each rank goes to the identical spot before it begins to descend; if it should halt, the progress of the rest is immediately arrested: their march presents an instance of uniformity so complete as to render it difficult at first sight to conceive that the waving line of living creatures which is seen to wind in a thousand figures, can possibly be composed of so many separate individuals.

Another tribe of caterpillars, called by Reaumur

1   2   3   4

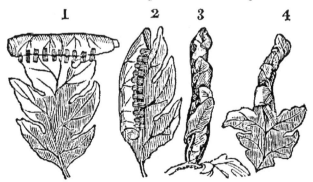

leaf-rollers, settle upon the oak : some of its leaves may be observed rolled from the apex half-way down towards the stalk (*fig.* 1); others from one side towards another (*fig.* 2). Some of these tubes are composed of two leaves rolled together (*fig.* 3), while others are constructed by bringing each of the edges of the leaf towards the principle nervure (*fig.* 4). The fingers of the most dexterous seamstress could not effect with greater precision, and in a more artful manner, that which these caterpillars execute without fingers, needles, or scissors. Their ingenious proceedings are well worth our attention.

However flat the surface of a leaf may at first sight appear, still on nearer inspection some portion of it will be found more or less approaching to a curve ; as soon as this is discovered by the caterpillar it hastens to avail itself of this advantage, and, with great art and dexterity, proceeds to increase the natural curvature. Its head may be seen vibrating like a pendulum, from the edge towards the principal nervure of the leaf. After two or three hundred of these movements, the part on which the insect has been operating may be observed to be rolled up. The mechanical means by which this effect has been produced appears in the shape of a silken cord (*fig.* 5). Two or three of these cords, fixed at a mode-

5

rate distance from one another, will bend the leaf considerably beyond the points to which they are attached. Although Reaumur watched a caterpillar while at work, and saw the leaf roll up under his eyes, still he was unable to satisfy himself as to the cause which brought about this effect. It can scarcely be attributed to the degree of contraction produced in these little threads by the process of drying; for when fresh spun and moist they are so extremely short, that such an effect could scarcely arise from this cause.

If one of these cords be attentively examined, instead of being made up of parallel rows of threads, it will be found to be composed of two sets which cross each other, or decussate. Various reasons

have been assigned for this method of proceeding; the following appears the most satisfactory. The second set of threads can only be carried across the first by the head of the insect: to effect this its body must rest upon the first fasciculus; and consequently the leaf will be drawn forward by its whole weight. By this means the second set of threads alone act upon the leaf, the first set being visibly relaxed. Each of these sets of threads is singly equal to resist the elasticity of the curved leaf, being indeed strong enough to bear the whole weight of the caterpillar. De Geer, attending to the operations of a species of this kind of caterpillar, observed, that at each new thread it spun, the edges of the leaf gradually approached each other, and were bent more and more as the caterpillar spun new threads: when the last spun thread became tight, that which preceded it appeared loose and floating in the air. To effect this, the caterpillar, after it has fixed a thread to the two edges of the leaf, and before it spins another, draws it towards itself by the hooks of its feet, and by these means bends the leaf: it then spins another thread, to main-

tain the leaf in this position, which it again pulls
towards itself; and repeats the operation till it has
bent the leaf in its whole direction. It now begins
again, placing the threads farther back upon the
bent part of the leaf, and by proceeding in this
manner, rolls it up: when it has finished this business, it strengthens the whole by fastening the ends
of the leaf together. The habitation thus formed,
is a kind of hollow cylinder, open to the light at
both ends, the sides of it affording the insect both
food and protection : for within it the creature feeds
in safety. In the same case it also undergoes its
transformation · at the approach of this change the
creature lines the rolled leaf with silk, that the
rough parts of it may not injure the tender chrysalis.
    Sometimes the leaf which is to be rolled up hap-
pens to be thick and its nervures strong; in this
case the insect eats down the prominent part of the
nervures and levels them with the surface of the
leaf; not, however, throughout the whole of their
length, but a bit here and a bit there, leaving the
intervals entire. The parts thus attacked and consumed appeared to Reaumur to correspond both in
number and situation with the points in which the
leaf was to be curved in order to begin a new turn.
The leaf of the oak being deeply notched, its inequalities occasionally project so much, that it is
difficult to bring them within the curve of the rest
of the leaf. A thread tied to one of these projecting points merely bends the edge a little, leaving the
rest nearly flat. A human mechanic would cut off
this inconvenient superfluity; the caterpillar effects
that which amounts to the same thing; it fixes it
with a thousand threads to the side of the leaf; and
then works it with its head into a round form.
    The insect proceeds in this manner to roll the leaf,
until it has encased itself in four or five folds. And
in addition to the silken bands used to secure these
folds longitudinally, a couple are tied to one or both

of the extremities of the cylinder; but so arranged
as to furnish the insect with ready means both of ingress and egress. While this singularly constructed
mansion protects the insect from its numerous enemies, it furnishes it also with food. It nibbles and
consumes successively the layers which compose
its case; so that when the cylinder is examined,
after the lapse of a certain space of time, it will be
found at last to consist only of the outermost roll.
Having eaten itself out of house and hold, it then
sets about constructing another dwelling.

The last of the habitations formed by the caterpillar differs somewhat from the first; it is larger in
size, to accommodate the insect, now grown more
bulky. The leaf is not bent so much, and consequently it does not offer the same resistance: the
insect appears aware of this fact, and contents itself
with making its cordage less strong. Instead of
bending the leaf by little cables placed at intervals,
it spins a continuous web, which extends the whole
length of the leaf. This web, like the cords already

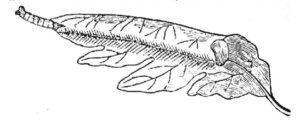

described, is composed of two decussating sets of
fibres: the first set acted on by the weight of the
insect's body draws the leaf downwards; the second
set secures in its proper place the additional curve
which has been thus gained.

Within this cylinder the caterpillar undergoes its
metamorphosis into a chrysalis and imago. In its
former state the skin is at first so soft that it requires
protection; and to ensure it, the inside of the cell
is lined with a slight layer of silk. When about to

assume the form of a perfect insect, it gets rid of its
chrysalid envelope by the efforts which it makes to
pass through the end of the cylinder: this being
narrower than the body of the insect, scrapes off,
and retains the skin.

The habitation of a small leaf-rolling caterpillar
is curious, from the pains taken to place it in a perpendicular position on the leaf itself.   For this purpose a portion of the leaf is cut off in the manner
represented in the annexed figure.   Before it cuts in

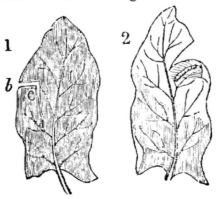

the direction of *c d* the leaf is bent as seen in *fig.* 2.
In effecting this object, the caterpillar employs the
means already described: it mounts the threads,
and contracts them by the weight of its own body.
The leaf having been thus bent is then cut in the
direction *c b*, and rolled up as near the perpendicular as possible.

There is another caterpillar whose proceedings are
somewhat similar; it rolls up into a trumpet-shaped

tube the portion of the leaf contained between two indentations.   The bottom of the tube is then closed by another piece of leaf attached to it by means of silken cords.

Another tribe of caterpillars, equally numerous with the leaf-rollers, may be termed leaf-benders. Some of these give the leaf but a slight bend, while others bend it almost thoroughly.   And so admirable is the instinct with which they are endowed, that in feeding they consume only a portion of the leaf; the upper membrane and the nervures are left untouched, which secures to them both a place of shelter and a magazine of provisions.

These caterpillars do not require to be accommodated with a narrow case composed of many folds ; they are content with one large curve, which is produced by a very curious process.   The insect takes advantage of that part of the edge of a leaf which happens to be naturally somewhat bent : to this some threads are attached ; the other end of these threads is fixed near the great nervure in the centre of the leaf; owing to the natural bend of the leaf some vacant space is interposed between these threads and the surface.   The insect mounts upon the threads ; its weight increases the bend ; the edge of the leaf is brought nearer the central nervure ; and to keep it in this position, the animal spins and applies a new set of shorter cords.   As the insect does not want a narrow case, but merely a curve which describes the segment of a large circle, it begins

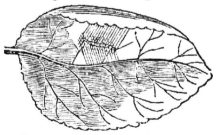

A a

now to spin a new set of threads; one end of these
is glued to the old web, and the other end near to or
beyond the centre of the leaf, as it may seem necessary.

These two webs incline towards each other at a
certain angle. The effect upon the leaf is the same
as if the curve had been produced by threads nearly
double the length of those which compose either
web. The leaf having thus acquired a greater bend,
the insect mounts at the angular junction of the two
webs, and begins to spin a third set of threads,
which, like the first, has one end attached to the indentations of the leaf, while the other is fastened
near the central nervure. This is then crossed with
a fourth web formed in the manner already described. These parts of cross webs may be seen
rising one above another, until the requisite curve
has been given to the leaf. It may be asked why
the insect does not at once spin one long thread
instead of two shorter ones crossing each other?
Simply because it cannot: the length of the thread
is determined by the length of the animal's reach.
While engaged in fabricating these successive layers
of webs, the insect may frequently be seen descending to cut the inferior threads, which, from the
greater tension of the superior one, have become
slack, and consequently useless. This operation it
performs by means of its fore-legs, using them as
we do our hands. When the insect feeds upon the
parenchyma and one membrane of the leaf, it is
extremely cautious not to touch the other membrane or the nervures. By this means not only are
the materials of its covering provided, but the process of fabricating it is greatly facilitated; and the
tent, though considerably diminished in weight, is
not less firm, since the natural cordage (the nervures)
is left entire. The more minutely we examine the
works of nature, the more clearly shall we trace
evidence of design. Whether we contemplate the

measured movements of revolving worlds, or the humble labours of a puny insect, we shall be forced to recognise in them the arrangements and contrivances of an Omniscient mind.

Some species of caterpillars simply tie several leaves together with silken threads, and thus form a hollow tube in which they lodge and feed. They carefully destroy the bud at the extremity of the shoot, lest its sprouting should tear asunder their silken bands.

The number of caterpillars which enclose themselves by the process of rolling, bending, or tying leaves together is very great; nor is this habit confined to one class. Spiders, beetles, and various other insects, proceed under the impulse of the same instinct. The description which has been already given of the habits of one class will equally apply to the proceedings of all the other tribes.

Some caterpillars, not possessing the art of those which have been already noticed, content themselves with the shelter which they procure by eating away the pulpy substance contained between the upper and under surfaces of the leaf. They are so small, that even the thinnest leaf is capable of furnishing them with an ample lodging. If several leaves be

1. The habitation of miners of galleries.
2. ——————————————— areas.
3 The habitation of those which mine first a gallery then an area.

examined, whitish spots or streaks may be observed
on their green surface : these mark the paths and
progress of the insects which mine them. Some
caterpillars form galleries only, some only areas ;
while a third tribe, after having made a gallery, mine
an area at the end of it.

Each of these galleries or areas is generally occupied by a single insect; and when there happens
to be more than one tenant, no inconvenience arises
from the circumstance ; for the comparative size of
the leaf is so great as to furnish an ample territory
for the accommodation of a number of these diminutive inhabitants. In some cases, many of these insects, having arrived at a certain size, may be seen
under the same tent, and associating together in the
most peaceable and harmonious manner; while
others, to the number of twenty or thirty, herd together from the moment in which they are first
evolved from the egg, and unite their efforts in excavating a common covering for the whole community. That beneficent Power which has given existence and life to this minute atom, has at the same
time made an ample provision for all its wants by
conferring upon it an instinct which operates as
surely and as unerringly as the most obvious of
nature's laws. This instinct teaches the perfect
insect that one leaf is incapable of furnishing nourishment to all her young: hence the provident
mother never deposites upon the same leaf a greater
number of eggs than the number of caterpillars
which its pulpy substance will be found capable of
sustaining. Having thus placed an adequate number
of eggs on one leaf, the insect proceeds to another,
and then to a third, until her whole stock has been
laid.

The larva, having been evolved from the egg, immediately begins to mine ; and the spot at which it
commenced its operations may readily be known;
and by holding up the leaf between the eye and the

light, the exact situation of the insect may also be discovered. The narrowest part of the gallery is that through which it has been entered; the insect as it proceeds grows in size; it requires more food as well as more space: hence its mine becomes gradually wider; the head of the creature will therefore be found towards the widest part, and the tail towards the narrowest end of the streak. The instruments which these insects use in mining are their

The commencement of the gallery is under the stalk of the leaf; the gallery is seen gradually to widen, and at the farthest and widest part the insect is lodged.

teeth; some of them are provided with a beak which they employ like a pickaxe. The central hook is fixed in the leaf as a fulcrum, and is bent and moved about in various directions.

Many of these miners are incapable of conducting their operations, except in their native gallery; when removed to another leaf their instinct seems to forsake them: they appear unable to begin another mine, and consequently perish. Others, however, endowed with different instincts, have been known to change the leaf on which they feed whenever the

supply of nourishment originally provided for them
begins to fail.

When about to undergo their metamorphosis, some
of these insects quit their habitations, while others
continue in them. The latter class adopt a precaution which well deserves attention; the range of the
gallery which they have mined is not equidistant
from the upper and lower membranes of the leaf,
being much nearer the former; hence, the caterpillar
cannot be seen through the under surface of the leaf,
because a considerable portion of the parenchyma,
or pulpy matter, remains unconsumed between the
floor of the gallery and the inferior membrane of
the leaf. On the upper surface, however, the caterpillar eats away all the parenchyma; so that on that
side the epidermis alone forms a thin and vaulted
roof, through which the insect may be readily seen.
But when about to assume the defenceless state of
a chrysalis, its instinct impels it to seek a place of
greater security: with this view it dives from its
gallery, making its way directly downwards until it
reaches the lower surface of the leaf, where it dis-
tends a portion of the parenchyma, which was left
uneaten and interposed between the lower epidermis
and the gallery of the insect: at this period it would,
therefore, be vain to look for the insect in its usual
gallery, near the upper skin of the leaf, and it might
be concluded that the little inhabitant had entirely
forsaken its original abode; but on turning up the
leaf, a small and rounded protuberance may be perceived, under which the creature has been instinct-
ively taught to shelter itself, during its torpid state,
from its natural enemies

Many of these mining caterpillars turn into moths,
which, had they been as large as they are beautiful,
would have presented an appearance marvellously
brilliant. Assisted by a magnifier, the eye may perceive the little creature radiant with shining gold,
its wings streaked here and there with silver of daz-

zling white, and dotted with jetty spots so placed as to heighten the whole effect.

There is a tribe of caterpillars which, from their regular and measured method of moving, have been called "Surveyors." They first fix the head and bring the tail close to it, the intervening body being bent into an arch; the head is then stretched out again and fixed in another place. By this means each progressive movement is rendered of equal length, and hence the name which has been bestowed upon them. Many of these possess the curious faculty of remaining stiffly in the same position, and jutting out into the air, so that not only their natural enemies, the birds, but even man, have mistaken them for twigs of the shrubs on which they happen to be placed.

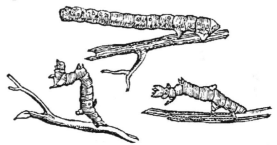

Rosel's gardener, having taken up what he thought a piece of wood, dropped it with horror, when he perceived that it began to writhe between his fingers.

Other caterpillars place themselves in attitudes which present a very formidable appearance, and although perfectly harmless, make a very disgreeable impression upon the mind. The caterpillar of a hawk-moth, when in a state of repose, assumes the position of the sculptured sphinx.

Most of the surveyors possess a contrivance for transporting themselves from one place to another, which must not be overlooked : wherever they advance, they fix a silken cord; hence their track is constantly marked by a line of silk. The use of this provision becomes immediately apparent whenever the leaf or twig on which they are found happens to be shaken. The creature drops from its place, and would fall quite to the ground, if it did not possess the means of suspending itself; but it is furnished with spinners, which secrete silken matter, and it possesses also the faculty of giving out as much of this substance as may be required for its purposes; it seems to have a sphincter for this especial object. By means of a silken apparatus thus prepared, it is enabled at any time to descend from the top of a high tree, and mount again, without undergoing the fatigue of climbing up the twisted branches; the descent is regulated by the wishes and purposes of the insect, rapid or slow as may be required; and if necessary, its descent may be instantly arrested, and the animal may remain for any length of time suspended in mid-air. The two annexed figures will explain the mechanism of these proceedings. In the first, the creature is seen suspended by its thread; in the second, it is represented in the act of mounting: for the latter purpose, it seizes the silken cord between its two teeth, and curving up that portion of its body, in which its six true legs are situated, it lays hold of the cord with the last two pair; this secures to it another fixed point; it then lifts up its head a second time, lays hold of an additional piece of the silk; and by a repetition of its former action it gradually ascends to the point which it wishes to reach; when safely landed, it disembarrasses itself of the silk which nad been collected between its legs.

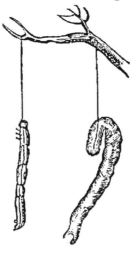

CHAPTER XVII.

CHRYSALIS, OR AURELIA.

Caterpillar when about to change into a Chrysalis fastens itself to a Leaf or Stem—Spins a little Web—Gets rid of its old Cage—Suspends itself by a Girth or Band formed of Silk.

THE insect, having lived its appointed time in the caterpillar state, and incapable of perpetuating its species, prepares for those wonderful changes of form and functions which are destined to end in the production of a creature perfect in its kind. If a human being, surrounded by enemies eager to injure or destroy him, felt that he should fall into a state which would incapacitate him either to flee or defend himself from his foes, he would naturally endeavour to find some secluded spot into which he might retire in the hour of peril. The larvæ of insects when preparing for their first metamorphosis seem to act upon a similar principle: they appear to be aware of their defenceless condition; and that Being who gave them life has instructed them in the best means of preserving this precious gift. Some have been taught to weave for themselves a silken case; others, ignorant of this art, secrete themselves under ground, and in the kindly shelter of their earthy tomb find that security and rest which are denied them elsewhere. Others seek some solitary spot far removed from their ordinary haunts, and there suspend themselves beyond the reach of their natural enemies.

The positions in which they place themselves are extremely various: in one species the suspension is vertical; in another the head is higher than the tail; in a third the body is placed in a horizontal position. Some fix themselves by the tail only, with the head hanging down; others pass a girdle of silk around their bodies, and are thus suspended in a sort of hammock: while others appear simply glued to the wood or stone to which they are attached.

When the moment of change approaches, the caterpillar fixes upon some part of a leaf or stem, where it spins a little web; it first lines a small space to which it attaches additional threads, so as to make a little cone, or rather button, projecting downwards: this being finished, it fixes itself to the end of the cone by means of hooks with which its two last feet are furnished; and in order that its hold may be made firm, a part of the body, impelled by alternate elongations and contractions, is well driven into the meshes of the cone. This being effected, the head of the insect is then permitted to hang downwards. Shortly afterward, however, it is seen to quit this vertical posture, and to curve its

back by elevating the head; and in this position it
will remain for more than half an hour.' This
movement is frequently repeated; and at each succeeding repetition of it, the body of the caterpillar
acquires a greater degree of convexity. A strain is
thus occasioned in the skin of the back, which soon
produces a rent in that part. This process—a work
of at least twenty-four hours and great labour—

causes the skin to break at last, and a portion of the
chrysalis becomes visible through the rent. While
confined by the skin of the caterpillar, the chrysalis
is long and narrow; but as soon as a fissure has
been made in this outward covering, it begins to
contract, and its anterior portion swells out so much,
that the rent is thereby rapidly enlarged. As soon
as the fissure has been rendered sufficiently large to
permit a portion of the chrysalis to protrude, the
mode of action is changed. By various contortions
and movements of the body, the skin is thrust towards the tail, much in the same manner as we push
down a stocking towards the foot. The length of
the skin becomes thus compressed into a multitude
of folds.

But the most singular part of the operation remains to be described. The caterpillar was suspended to the silken cone by legs and hooks attached to its own skin; that skin, however, with its append-

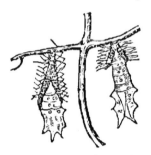

ant legs and hooks, the chrysalis must cast off; but, although destitute of limbs or hooks, it yet contrives to fix itself on the same cone to which the caterpillar was attached. When the skin has been well thrust down, the insect seizes some part of it in one of the indentations between two of the rings of its body: this secures a resting-place, which enables it to withdraw its tail altogether from the old skin.

Wholly freed from its former covering, the chrysalis is now attached to a frail and withered slough, and suspended in mid-air in a situation of great peril. It becomes now indispensable that it should fix itself to the silken cone. But to a creature hanging with its head downwards, and destitute of limbs, this would seem a hopeless undertaking. Destitute and helpless, however, as its condition appears, nature has not left it without adequate resources. It elongates that part of the body which is above the rings, by which it holds on, and seizes by the interval between two rings still higher than those, another part of its caterpillar skin. Having in this manner advanced by three or four steps to the required height, it feels about with its tail for the silken cone. Having at last found this cone, it fixes itself to it

by means of hooks with which that part of its body
is furnished.

To withdraw the tail from the withered case; to
climb up that case, and hook its body to the silken
cone, is an operation so delicate and hazardous as
to excite the greatest wonder, that an insect which
executes it only once during the whole term of its
existence, should be found capable of executing it
so well. " Assuredly," says Reaumur, " it must
have been taught to perform its task by some great
master."

But the chrysalis does not seem to be content with
merely withdrawing itself from its ancient hide · it
will not suffer it to remain suspended in its own
neighbourhood.   In order to rid itself of the annoyance of the offensive slough, it bends a section of
the lower part of its body into the form of the letter
S, and then gives the whole a jerk, which causes

both its own body and the attached slough to spin
round eighteen or twenty times on their axis.   As
the slough and chrysalis must necessarily go round
together, and as the slough is farther than the chrysalis from the centre of gyration, it is evident that
the attaching hooks and threads of the slough must
suffer a greater strain than those of the chrysalis:
consequently the former give way first.   This is no
sooner perceived by the chrysalis, than it resumes
                     B b

its vertical position, and allows the skin to drop. If the first series of pirouettes prove unsuccessful, the chrysalis tries another in the contrary direction; and if after repeated efforts it fails to get rid of the nuisance, it calmly and patiently submits to an evil which it cannot remove.

This vertical position does not however suit all caterpillars; there are some which fix themselves in an inclined or even horizontal position. To effect this, a set of threads is passed round their bodies, and then attached to the wall or a part of some plant from which they remain suspended.

These girths or supporting belts are formed in various ways, but always of the same material,—silk spun for that purpose by the caterpillars. The following figures will explain some of those processes by which the suspension is effected. In the first

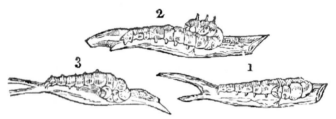

figure (*fig.* 1), the caterpillar is seen to bend its body to the point where the end of the thread is to be fixed: in the second (*fig.* 2), it presents itself in the act of carrying over the body, by doubling itself on its back: while in the third (*fig.* 3), it appears to turn round for the purpose of fixing it on the farther side. When a sufficient number of threads have been thus spun to form its web, the insect gently withdraws its head, assumes a straight position, and quietly awaits the hour of its transformation.

The girth which is passed round the body of the caterpillar in order to suspend it when it shall have assumed the chrysalid form, is fabricated sometimes

in the mode represented in the annexed figures.   On
one side of a stalk or leaf, it glues some of the viscid

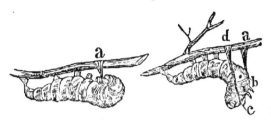

matter secreted by its spinner; it then gradually
brings its head into a position which enables it to
pass the silken cord from *a* to *b* where it is supported by one of its legs; introducing the two other
legs of that side under the rest; the insect then
carries it from *b* to *c*: it is then continued from *c* to
d, which completes the loop, or half circle.   When
a sufficient number of threads has been thus passed
from *a* to *d*, the loop has acquired a requisite strength:
—the insect then holds it up with its two fore legs:
bending its head between these legs, it passes the
loop over its back; and by the action of the rings,
it gradually brings it to that part of the body which
is best calculated to balance the chrysalis.

In spite, however, of all the care which the insect
takes to sustain the loop, it occasionally happens
that the threads slip off its legs and fall.   This is a
woful calamity to the unhappy caterpillar.   It does
its best to repair the damage; with marvellous patience it endeavours to collect the scattered filaments, and secure them once more between its legs.
One unlucky insect was seen by Reaumur, trying
every contortion of limb to effect this purpose, but
all in vain.   After all its exertion, it only succeeded
in gathering about half the number of threads which
had formed the cord, the rest having become hope-
lessly entangled; and being either unwilling or unable to spin an additional supply, it suspended itself,
by this imperfect girdle.   As it might have been an-

ticipated, the suspending girdle proving too weak to
sustain the motions of the chrysalis, gave way, and
the miserable insect consequently fell to the ground
and perished.

If we open one of these chrysalis or aurelias,
from which a brilliant butterfly will emerge at the
proper season, all we shall be able to discover, especially at first, is a mass of pap or soft substance
apparently putrefied, in which every thing seems
confounded; but this soft mass, however confused
it may appear to the eye, contains the elements of
the future insect. Under the action of heat, the
superfluous portion of the nutrimental substances
gradually transpires through the film which encloses
them; the external film itself becomes by degrees
tinctured by a most beautiful vermilion, and the limbs
and features, which at first lay concealed in the
mass, begin to disengage themselves from the case
which contained them, and which now bursts open:
then it is that the head unfolds itself to our view,
the horns and legs lengthen, the wings expand; and
at last the butterfly, retaining no trace or resemblance of its former condition, wings its flight
through the air. The caterpillar, which is changed
into a nymph or chrysalis, and the butterfly that
proceeds from it, are two animals essentially different in form, as well as in manners and habits. The
first being altogether terrestrial, crawled slowly and
heavily along the ground; the second is agility itself, and so far from limiting its motions to the earth,
it appears to disdain reposing on its lap. The first,
all shaggy, frequently presented a hideous aspect;
the other is arrayed in colours glowing with the
most brilliant and beautiful tints The first fed
upon the coarsest and grossest food; the latter
ranges from flower to flower, regales itself with
honey and dew, and perpetually varies its enjoy-
ments.

END OF THE FIRST SERIES.

Printed in Great Britain
by Amazon.co.uk, Ltd.,
Marston Gate.